52 Weekends in the Pacific Northwest

52 WEEKENDS
in the

PACIFIC *NORTHWEST*

A Local's Curated Guide to Year-Round Getaways

Kara Patajo

SASQUATCH BOOKS | SEATTLE

To Kyle, my adventure partner,
and to Lilo, my soul dog

INTRODUCTION

Hey bestie,

The Pacific Northwest has a way of surprising you. One morning, you're sipping coffee while driving through a mountain town you've never heard of, as the road winds through evergreens older than living memory. The next morning, you're wandering an island where every beach feels like a discovery and ferry horns echo across the water, almost as if they're calling you home. This is the Pacific Northwest I know and love—and the one I want to share with you.

The book you're holding isn't your average travel guide. It's something more personal: a collection of adventures from someone who's spent years uncovering the region's best-kept secrets. I'm Kara—that's care-uh—and I've been your Northwestie Bestie on Instagram and my blog for years, sharing the coffee shops, trails, and hidden gems that make this corner of the world so magical.

I wrote this book because it's the resource I always wished I'd had: something that tells you when a destination quietly shines, why the offseason is often peak magic, and where to find that perfect latte to accompany your next adventure. As a true PNW girl (anything over 75 degrees F and I'm basically melting), I live for those slower moments where you encounter fewer crowds and enjoy a much more authentic experience, with the bonus that you'll likely get better value for money.

Here's what I discovered after years of exploring: our seasons aren't just different weather—they provide completely different experiences. Spring brings waterfalls roaring with snowmelt and meadows carpeted in wildflowers. Summer offers endless daylight for island-hopping and mountain adventures. Fall transforms forests into golden cathedrals that feel straight out of *Stars Hollow*. And winter? That's when you discover the soul of this place—cozy cabins, storm watching from dramatic coastlines, and that unique peaceful tranquility you can only experience when wandering a snow-covered trail.

That's why I organized this book by seasons. When you flip to any section, you'll find destinations at their absolute peak—when the light is perfect, the activities are ideal, and the magic is undeniable.

Here's how to make this book work for you:

Stuck in the winter blues? Flip to that section for a fresh dose of inspiration. Maybe you'll find a weekend trip that will help you fall in love with the rain and mist all over again.

Planning a group getaway? Share one of these itineraries in your group chat. Sometimes all it takes is a solid plan to get everyone on board. (And if they still won't go? Take yourself on the trip anyway—you deserve it.)

Returning to a favorite destination? Use these pages to discover what you've been missing—the bookstore tucked down a side street, the viewpoint locals keep to themselves, or the perfect coffee shop for watching ferries come and go.

Every itinerary follows a Friday-to-Sunday format, but here's my secret: leave room for serendipity. Some of my best memories came from going off script, especially after conversations with locals who pointed me toward something not found in any guidebook.

A little bit about me: I was born and raised in the shadow of Mount Rainier—or Tahoma, as she's traditionally known. She's the most glaciated peak in the contiguous United States and my daily compass. I catch myself looking for her every morning, and when the clouds part to reveal her snow-covered summit, I still feel that spark of awe.

The fifty-two carefully curated itineraries ahead are windows into my own experiences that have shaped my love for this place—and invitations for you to create your own. From misty coastlines to golden valleys, snowy ridgelines to fairy-tale forests, these pages hold a year's worth of Pacific Northwest wonder.

Thank you for being here. Thank you for choosing adventure. And thank you for letting me be your guide to the place I call home. I can't wait for you to fall in love with it too.

With love and wanderlust,

a.k.a. Your Northwestie Bestie

E

WINTER
GETAWAYS

CRATER LAKE NATIONAL PARK

1 CRATER LAKE NATIONAL PARK

Introduction

Picture impossibly blue waters surrounded by a sparkling white blanket of snow, pristine and untouched as far as the eye can see. This is Crater Lake in winter—Oregon's most dramatic natural wonder in its wildest season.

What makes this place so breathtaking is also what makes it a challenge to explore: its high elevation. At 6,450 feet, the Steel Visitor Center sits over one thousand feet higher than Mount Rainier's famous Paradise. With more than five hundred inches of snow falling here annually, many of Crater Lake's roads are closed in winter, including some with iconic lake views. But for those willing to put in a little extra effort, this winter wonderland is yours to discover, particularly on snowshoes—a popular way to explore the trails through the park.

Snowshoeing through an old-growth forest draped in fresh snow? That's my kind of peace. After chatting with a friendly ranger at the visitor center about current trail conditions, Kyle (my partner) and I strapped on our snowshoes and headed for the Raven Trail. This two-mile trail climbs steadily through the woods, gaining 625 feet in elevation before leading to the crater's edge. As we left the treeline behind, the wind picked up to a brisk 20 mph—thank goodness we layered up with our warmest windbreakers and had cameras ready to capture every moment!

Crater Lake is massive—over twenty square miles of the deepest blue I've ever seen. It's so wide that you have to turn your head to take it all in. And, as an island lover, I was thrilled to spot Wizard Island rising from the water like something out of a storybook. On clear days, you can even spot peaks such as Garfield and Watchman in the distance, adding to the panoramic drama.

Friend to friend, this is an important safety note: stay well back from the lake's edge in winter. Snow cornices—overhanging snow that looks stable but isn't—are a hidden hazard you don't want to mess with. Speaking from experience, the views are just as spectacular from a safe distance!

This time of year, the lake is shrouded in clouds about half the time, so catching a clear view of it does take a bit of luck. But instead of discouraging us, that uncertainty added a sense of adventure to our trip. We had one shot to see the lake, and it paid off beautifully.

Our home base for this winter adventure was Grants Pass, a charming small town nestled along the Rogue River. This place takes its holiday spirit seriously. Giant nutcracker statues line the downtown streets, and this is where I spotted the tallest Christmas tree I've ever seen in my life! Beyond the festive decorations, Grants Pass surprised us with hidden gems—from handcrafted glass art, cozy coffee shops, and the kind of small-town warmth that made our chilly mountain adventure feel perfectly balanced.

At a Glance

Location: Southern Oregon
Best Season to Visit: December through March
Suggested Duration: Two nights

Park Information

- **Entrance fee:** $30 per vehicle (seven days) or $55 annual America the Beautiful Pass
- Only the south entrance (Annie Spring) is open in winter
- Steel Visitor Center operates daily from 10 a.m. to 4 p.m. (winter hours)
- **Check current conditions:** nps.gov/crla or call (541) 594-3000

Winter Essentials

- Traction tires or chains required
- Snowshoes (rentals available at the REI in Medford)
- Waterproof layers and warm clothing
- Full gas tank before entering the park
- Offline maps downloaded (no cell service in the park)

HISTORIC DOWNTOWN GRANTS PASS

Getting There

Seattle to Grants Pass: 418 miles, ~7 hours
Portland to Grants Pass: 245 miles, ~4 hours
Grants Pass to Crater Lake: 82 miles, ~2 hours

Where to Stay

The Lodge at Riverside: Conveniently located just a few blocks from downtown, this riverside retreat blends modern comfort with timeless charm. Enjoy picturesque views of the iconic Caveman Bridge, all while being steps away from Grants Pass's vibrant shops and restaurants.

Weasku Inn Historic Resort: For a peaceful nature escape, this rustic gem offers cozy accommodations steeped in history. Dating back over one hundred years, the inn has hosted legends, such as Walt Disney. With fireplaces in abundance and warm, inviting vibes, it's the perfect spot to unwind. We slept soundly here.

Red Lion Inn & Suites: Traveling with your furry friend? This pet-friendly hotel has everything you need for a comfortable stay, including a complimentary breakfast and easy access to I-5, making it an ideal choice for budget-conscious adventurers.

Bestie Packing Tip: Winter at Crater Lake requires thoughtful gear. Pack breathable merino wool base layers, waterproof pants and jacket, insulated boots, and don't forget sunglasses—the snow glare at seven thousand feet is intense! A waterproof backpack cover is essential, as melting snow from tree branches results in constant dripping.

Itinerary Outline

DAY 1

Drinks at Steam Distillery: Step into old-time charm at Steam Distillery, housed in an 1886 building that once held Grants Pass's first brewery. The steampunk-inspired decor and inventive cocktails make this historic gem a must-visit. Yes, there might be a wait, but trust me—it's worth every second.

Bestie Tip: Before settling in for drinks, peek through the windows of the Glass Forge Gallery & Studio, just next door. You'll know it by its whimsical *Alice in Wonderland* mural! This treasure trove showcases art made using traditional Italian glassblowing techniques. You can browse stunning pieces and watch artists at work as they shape molten glass into incredible creations.

Dinner at The Bohemian Bar & Rooftop: With a modern ambiance and rooftop dining, this restaurant shines with New American cuisine. Frequently dubbed the best restaurant in Grants Pass, its menu features hearty salads, pastas, and steaks. Its zero-proof drinks are surprisingly satisfying too!

DAY 2

Coffee and breakfast at Rogue Roasters: Kick off your big adventure day at this organic coffeehouse serving seriously good brews. Whether you use the drive-through or cozy up inside, you'll love its seasonal menu—my pumpkin spice latte was *chef's kiss*! Traveling with a non-coffee drinker? The real fruit smoothies on the menu disappear fast, even the twenty-ounce size!

To-go lunch from Babe's Bakery: Before heading to the mountains, swing by Babe's Bakery to grab a sandwich for the road. The made-from-scratch bread and generously sized Bigfoot sandwiches are ideal for sharing after a day of snowshoeing.

Explore Crater Lake National Park: Before departing, ensure that your car has a full tank of gas. Also check that it's equipped with traction tires or chains and that you know how to use them. Download offline maps since there's no cell service in the park. The scenic two-hour drive to Steel Visitor Center via Annie Spring Entrance Station builds anticipation for what's ahead.

At the visitor center, you can watch a short documentary about Crater Lake's natural and cultural history, chat with a ranger for up-to-date conditions, shop for souvenirs, and take advantage of the water fill-up stations and restrooms.

Once you're ready, strap on your snowshoes and follow the Raven Trail. The route winds through a peaceful forest and steadily climbs 625 feet over four miles (round trip) to Rim Village, where the jaw-dropping views of Crater Lake begin.

> **Bestie Tip:** Wear waterproof layers, even on sunny days! Melting snow from tree branches creates a constant drip, so a waterproof backpack or cover is essential.

Weather backup plan: If Crater Lake isn't cooperating (road closures, whiteouts, or clouds hiding the lake), don't despair! The Cathedral Hills Trail System in Grants Pass offers year-round forest paths and valley views at a much lower elevation. Or explore historic downtown, as The Glass Forge Gallery & Studio is mesmerizing, and those holiday decorations make perfect photo ops.

Dinner at The Vine: After a snowy adventure, nothing beats a warm, filling meal, and The Vine delivers. This farm-to-table gem has laid-back vibes and delicious comfort food. I couldn't get enough of its spaghetti and meatballs—pure coziness on a plate!

House of Glory Artisanal Desserts & Café: For the perfect end to your day, indulge your sweet tooth at House of Glory. This spot is a dessert lover's dream, with treats such as gelato, bubble waffles, and decadent cakes. I couldn't resist its homemade peppermint bark gelato in a sweet waffle cone and topped with OREOs and caramel—an easy 10/10. Bonus: The boho decor is totally Instagram-worthy!

DAY 3

Breakfast at DASSH Bakery: Treat yourself to small-batch pastries that melt in your mouth. The bakery's cinnamon rolls and croissants are perfection, and its rotating soup of the day is an unexpected but delightful breakfast addition.

Leave No Trace

The outdoors are, first and foremost, home to the plants and animals that live there. If you love summertime wildflowers, make sure you don't love them to death—stick to the trail and avoid stepping on fragile meadows. That's just one example of how even well-meaning visitors can unintentionally harm these places. Most people have good intentions but may not realize the full impact of their visit, so it's important to educate yourself *and* everyone in your group before heading out.

Following the seven "Leave No Trace Principles" is the perfect place to start:

1. Plan ahead and prepare.
2. Travel and camp on durable surfaces.
3. Dispose of waste properly.
4. Leave what you find.
5. Minimize campfire impacts.
6. Respect wildlife.
7. Be considerate of others.

You can discover more details at LNT.org.

The Takeaway: This winter adventure represents the boldest kind of Pacific Northwest experience: snowshoeing to over seven thousand feet of elevation to witness one of America's bluest, most awe-inspiring lakes formed by an ancient volcano and accessible only to those willing to work for it. This trip isn't for everyone; winter driving skills and snow safety knowledge are essential. But for those who come prepared, a journey to Crater Lake's winter wonderland offers the kind of once-in-a-lifetime experience that changes how you see the power and beauty of the Pacific Northwest.

Ready to plan your own winter adventure? Check park conditions before you go, pack smart, and prepare to be amazed by Oregon's crown jewel dressed in its winter finest.

2 LEAVENWORTH

Introduction

Picture a Bavarian village nestled in snow-capped mountains, where half a million twinkling lights transform every building into a fairy-tale scene, and the scent of roasted nuts drifts through the crisp winter air. This is Leavenworth in winter—pure magic without the fairy-tale price of a European vacation.

Growing up, my family visited Leavenworth nearly every summer. My brother Alec and I would race to finish our ice cream cones before the sun melted them, hunt for wooden toy puzzles, and dine alfresco with our chocolate lab, Kyia. Our home bookshelves became a museum of handmade wooden animals—dolphins, elephants, and countless others crafted right here in this alpine village. Those were the days when life felt absolutely perfect.

Twenty-seven years later, I finally experienced Leavenworth in winter—arguably its most magical season, when the Bavarian village transforms into a real-life Christmas town.

This trip had been on my family's bucket list for years, and surprisingly, it was my parents' first winter visit despite growing up in Washington! Just like on our fall adventure (see page 242), we stayed at Sleeping Lady Mountain Resort, this time booking the Steller's Jay suite to accommodate our large group.

Here's an insider secret: the best time to visit *is not* during December. I know it's tempting to experience peak Christmas

LEAVENWORTH CITY CENTER

magic, but the village becomes overwhelmingly crowded during December and early January. Instead, we opted for mid-January, and it was perfect. Snow blanketed the hillsides and covered the rooftops (though thankfully not the roads), creating a winter wonderland without the shoulder-to-shoulder crowds. Plus, who doesn't love extending holiday festivities for as long as possible?

The beauty of a January visit is having space to breathe while still enjoying all the winter activities—from riding Washington's only alpine coaster to feeding reindeer at a local farm. You'll experience the full magic of Leavenworth's Village of Lights without feeling like you're fighting through crowds for every photo opportunity.

Want to check current conditions before your trip? The Leavenworth Chamber of Commerce provides multiple live webcams online, so you can see exactly what winter wonderland awaits.

At a Glance

Location: Central Cascades of Washington
Best Season to Visit: January through February
Suggested Duration: Two nights

Winter Activities Available

- Alpine coaster (year-round operation)
- Snow tubing at Leavenworth Ski Hill
- Reindeer farm visits
- Village of Lights display (through February)
- Cross-country skiing and snowshoeing
- Indoor attractions (museums, escape rooms, glassblowing)

Getting There

Seattle to Leavenworth: 117 miles, ~2 hours 10 minutes
Portland to Leavenworth: 288 miles, ~4 hours 30 minutes

Winter Driving Tip: Mountain passes can require traction tires or chains. Check Washington State Department of Transportation conditions before departing.

Where to Stay

Posthotel: If you've browsed social media for places to stay in Leavenworth, chances are you've come across this boutique, wellness-centered hotel. Located steps from the village, it's an adults-only retreat (eighteen-plus), perfect for a grounding winter getaway with spa services and modern amenities.

Sleeping Lady Mountain Resort: For a true nature escape, stay a couple of miles out of town at this historic, environmentally mindful retreat. It's my kind of place—relaxing, eco-conscious, and dedicated to the community, with 100 percent of its net profits supporting local arts, the environment, and the history of North Central Washington. Plus, it's pet friendly!

Howard Johnson by Wyndham: Finding accommodations during the peak winter season can be tough, but this spot offers a fair price and is just a few blocks from the heart of the action.

Bestie Packing Tip: Headed to Leavenworth in the winter? Pack your warmest snow gear—think parkas, puffy jackets, beanies, gloves, and waterproof boots. You never know when a spontaneous sledding session, snow-tubing run, or sleigh ride might pop up, so it's best to be ready for whatever snowy adventure comes your way!

SLEEPING LADY HOT TUB

Itinerary Outline

DAY 1

Leavenworth Adventure Park: Washington's only alpine coaster opened here in 2023, and the Tumwater Twister runs year-round! You can ride solo or with a partner while taking in stunning views of the village below. Control your own speed—up to 27 mph for thrill-seekers or at a more leisurely pace for scenery lovers. My favorite part? The mid-ride photo captures pure excitement, available in digital format for purchase as a priceless memory. If you're planning to visit on a weekend, be sure to book your tickets online a day or two in advance, as spots fill up quickly.

Bestie Tip: Keep things simple and stash anything loose—such as scarves, hats, or bags—before hopping on. This is one ride where minimalism is the move. You won't need your phone (filming isn't allowed anyway), and if you drop it mid-ride, you're not getting it back. So just sit back, hold on tight, and enjoy the ride!

Dinner at the Kingfisher Restaurant & Wine Bar: Even if you're not staying at the Sleeping Lady Mountain Resort (which you really should—it's near and dear to my heart), this hidden gem within the resort is worth a visit for a memorable dining experience. The menu changes with the seasons and depends upon the availability of local ingredients, but if you can, try the roast Alaska salmon. It's perfectly crafted with chardonnay beurre blanc, lemon, potlatch seasoning, and dill. Pair it with butter-whipped potatoes and a seasonal vegetable—you won't be disappointed!

DAY 2

Breakfast at Argonaut Coffee & Biscuits: Some mornings need rescuing, and Argonaut delivers with fresh buttermilk biscuits and expertly crafted espresso. The breakfast sandwich and hipster avocado toast are favorites, and the lattes are so exceptional you'll want one for now and one to go.

Visit the Leavenworth Reindeer Farm: Nothing says winter wonderland quite like reindeer. This family-run farm offers close encounters with domesticated caribou. After a brief educational presentation, you'll get to feed the reindeer treats—a perfect photo op! Like many popular activities in Leavenworth, this one sells out fast, so make sure to book your tickets ahead of time.

Go snow tubing: For those of us who aren't skiers or snowboarders, snow tubing at Leavenworth's one-hundred-foot hill is pure joy. It's fun for all ages, and with a convenient rope tow, you'll be whisked back to the top with ease. Tickets are available in-person only, so plan accordingly for a day of snowy fun.

Indoor alternatives: In the mood to stay warm and cozy indoors? Slow things down with a visit to the Nutcracker Museum, explore local history at the Greater Leavenworth Museum, or put your puzzle-solving skills to the test at Escape Room Leavenworth.

Lunch on the outdoor patio at Rhein Haus: No visit to Leavenworth is complete without dining at a biergarten, and Rhein Haus is my go-to spot. Its second-story patio offers the best view of town, making it a must for outdoor dining. The German food is fantastic—we loved the Hungarian beef goulash (a special), giant pretzels, and bratwurst. And, of course, sampling local beers is a highlight for many!

Stroll around the village: Leavenworth boasts around a hundred charming shops, including Kris Kringl, where the Christmas spirit lives year-round. You'll find everything from local art and outdoor gear to toys. For a sweet treat, head to The Gingerbread Factory, which might just be the most adorable bakery ever. Its gourmet cookies and seasonal lattes are a must-try!

Hidden Gem: Don't miss Boulder Bend Glassworks—it's a bit off the main square but worth the detour. This art gallery isn't just for browsing; you can actually blow your own glass! Saturdays are typically the best days to have these hands-on experiences.

LEAVENWORTH

LEAVENWORTH CITY CENTER

Catch a live performance: Leavenworth's performances vary each year, but past shows have included ice sculpting, fire dancing, and glassblowing. Keep an eye out for the latest schedule to catch live entertainment.

See the Village of Lights: As the sun sets, the village transforms with over half a million twinkling lights. They cover buildings, trees—everywhere you turn. It's a magical experience that makes a winter visit unforgettable. While the lights are visible during the day, they truly shine against the night sky.

Dinner at Bären Haus: This cozy, brick-walled corner spot is a Leavenworth staple. Known for traditional German fare, such as schnitzel, Reuben sandwiches, and bratwurst platters, Bären Haus also serves a hearty specialty lasagna.

DAY 3

Breakfast at 59er Diner: A stone's throw from Highway 2 (and scenic Lake Wenatchee State Park!), the 59er Diner is as nostalgic as it gets—think poodle skirts, jukebox jams, and old-fashioned malts. Breakfast is served all day, so there's no need to rush your morning. My family loved visiting the original 59er Diner, which was tragically lost to fire in 2016, but luckily, the new location keeps the retro charm rockin'. It's the perfect spot to fuel up before hitting the road!

The Takeaway: Here's Leavenworth's best-kept winter secret: January offers the perfect balance of snow, holiday magic, and breathing room. The lights still twinkle, mountains wear their white winter coats, but the crowds have thinned just enough to make this alpine village feel like your own private discovery. Whether you're tubing down a snowy hill, feeding reindeer, or sipping cocoa beneath a canopy of lights, this postholiday pocket of magic is winter wonderland perfection—without the December hustle.

Ready to experience your own winter fairy tale? Book accommodations early (winter is popular!), pack warm layers, and prepare to fall in love with Leavenworth's most magical season.

3 PAINTED HILLS

Introduction

Imagine hills that look like an artist's palette come to life—layers of red, gold, and black striping ancient hillsides in patterns so vivid they seem almost unreal. This isn't a landscape you'd expect to find in the Pacific Northwest, yet here it is: the Painted Hills, a forty-four-million-year-old masterpiece hiding in Eastern Oregon's high desert.

While the Pacific Northwest is celebrated for its waterfalls, rugged coastlines, and dramatic mountains, this hidden gem often escapes even lifelong residents' attention. Part of the John Day Fossil Beds National Monument and one of Oregon's Seven Wonders, these vibrant, fossil-rich hillsides transport you to what feels like another planet. Some say the red rock formations resemble Mars, but for me, it was more than just a visual marvel—I felt chills, not from eeriness, but from the sheer privilege of witnessing such a striking natural phenomenon.

We timed our visit over New Year because why not begin the year with something extraordinary? Tucked away in remote Eastern Oregon, this National Park Service treasure is well worth the trek. I suggest setting up base in Sisters, Oregon—a delightful Western-themed town with cozy lodging options for every budget and award-winning dining, set against the backdrop of towering ponderosa pines.

My first impression of the park brought back memories of the Black Hills of South Dakota, but as we rounded a bend and those first brilliant red hills came into view, we couldn't contain our excitement—we literally shouted with joy! The winter timing proved perfect. We spent over three hours at the park and encountered fewer than five other groups. It almost felt as if we had these ancient wonders to ourselves.

What makes the Painted Hills so special is their accessibility. Even with frequent photo stops (guilty as charged!), you can explore

SUTTLE LODGE

SCOUT COTTAGES

the entire area in a day. The unit features four short trails and one longer trek, and I recommend experiencing them all. Each offers a unique perspective on these geological marvels that have been quietly painting the landscape for millions of years.

At a Glance

Location: Central and Eastern Oregon
Best Season to Visit: January through April
Suggested Duration: Two nights

Park Information

- Free admission to John Day Fossil Beds National Monument
- No services available at Painted Hills unit (bring water and snacks)
- Visitor center located in Kimberly, Oregon (45 minutes away)
- Most colorful after rain, when the hills appear more saturated

Getting There

Seattle to Sisters: 326 miles, ~5 hours 30 minutes
Portland to Sisters: 153 miles, ~2 hours 45 minutes
Sisters to Painted Hills: 100 miles, ~2 hours (scenic high-desert drive)

> **Winter Driving Tip:** Mountain passes may require traction tires or chains. Check the conditions before departing.

Where to Stay

FivePine Lodge and Spa: Nestled less than a mile from downtown Sisters, this romantic retreat beautifully blends nature with elegance. Unwind at the onsite Shibui Spa, featuring a serene thermal soaking tub for the ultimate relaxation experience.

The Suttle Lodge & Boathouse: You might be surprised to find this 4-star gem tucked away in a national forest. Perched on the lakeside, it offers endless outdoor recreation opportunities. Choose to stay in a lodge room or a private cabin, both of which exude the charm of a classic winter hideaway.

The Scout Cottages: Cozy up in a bright and airy cottage that is just steps away from the town. Enjoy luxurious touches such as heated floors, gas fireplaces, and aesthetically pleasing designs. Ideal for solo travelers and couples alike.

> **Bestie Tip:** Planning a family getaway? I know just the place: Black Butte Ranch. This property is all about creating experiences. Picture this: snowshoeing right from your back door, unwinding in a cozy hot tub or soothing sauna, or pampering yourself with a spa day. Bonus? You'll enjoy arguably the most stunning view of the Three Sisters mountains (no hiking required). In total, Black Butte Ranch has over one hundred privately owned vacation rentals.

Itinerary Outline

DAY 1

Winter fun at Hoodoo Ski Resort: Your adventure begins at Hoodoo Ski Resort, a winter playground in the western slopes of Santiam Pass. Whether you're carving down the slopes on skis, snowboarding, or tubing with the family, Hoodoo's appeal lies in its approachable, budget-friendly vibe—especially on Thrifty Thursdays!

Indoor alternatives: Not feeling the ski vibe or just craving some serious R&R? Head to Shibui Spa. Get there early to soak it all in—literally—with a warm soak and sauna before indulging in a massage that will leave you completely relaxed and refreshed.

Dinner at High Camp Taphouse: Arriving in Sisters feels like coming home when you enter High Camp Taphouse. Known for its purpose-driven mission and mouthwatering Himalayan cuisine, this pleasant spot delivers big on flavor. If I could only order one dish, it would be the *momo* (Tibetan dumplings). And here's a fun tidbit—this eatery was featured in Guy Fieri's *Diners, Drive-Ins,*

HOODOO SKI RESORT

and Dives! Chef Nurbu even played the episode for us while we dined, making the experience even more memorable.

DAY 2

Breakfast at Sisters Bakery: If you're asking for local breakfast recommendations, expect to be pointed toward Sisters Bakery. Its seasonal Winter in Paradise menu offers tropical-inspired pastries to brighten the chilly season. The pineapple upside-down donut is my top pick—it's like a little slice of sunshine!

Explore the Painted Hills Unit of the John Day Fossil Beds National Monument: After breakfast, gear up for a two-hour drive through Oregon's high desert. You'll pass through Redmond, Prineville, and the snowy Ochoco National Forest before descending into the mesmerizing Painted Hills. Despite the snowy journey, the Painted Hills's arid climate with only twelve inches of annual precipitation means the odds are in your favor that you'll enjoy their rich, vibrant colors.

Trek all five trails in the Painted Hills (all but one are very short!). Each trail offers its own unique perspective, so why not explore them all? Most are short and easy, making it perfect for a full day of discovery.

- **Painted Hills Overlook Trail:** Start here for a grand panoramic introduction.
- **Painted Cove Trail:** This iconic boardwalk trail becomes even more enchanting after it rains, when the puddles reflect the hills' watercolor-like hues.
- **Red Scar Knoll/Red Hill Trail:** A hidden gem where vibrant reds and yellows seem to dance as you wind around. Don't miss the bench at the end—it's a sweet spot for soaking in the views.
- **Leaf Hill Trail:** Fossil enthusiasts will love this quarter-mile loop circling an ancient research area with leaf and seed impressions, offering both history and stunning mountain views.
- **Carroll Rim Trail:** Save the most "hike-like" trail for last. This moderate trek rewards you with 360-degree views and the fun of spotting landmarks you've already visited.

Important: #DontHurtTheDirt: This landscape is extremely fragile. Keep your feet on marked trails only (not wildlife paths) to protect fossils and the beauty of the park for generations to come.

Photography Tip: If you have a telephoto lens, be sure to pack it. While we didn't spot much wildlife during our visit (aside from one curious cow), zooming in on the hills through my viewfinder made the landscape feel even more magical. The fragile beauty of these hills can only be admired from a distance, which makes a telephoto lens—or even binoculars—a must for capturing their full marvel!

Discover Western Charm in Sisters

- **Paulina Springs Books:** Grab a novel by a local author or find a book at this local bookstore to learn about the area's rich history.
- **Rescued Living:** Pick up unique home decor, such as the adorable Oregon-shaped coasters I couldn't resist.
- **Stitchin' Post:** Dive into Sisters's strong quilting culture and admire the craftsmanship.

Dinner at The Barn: Central Oregon's thriving food truck scene shines at The Barn. Cap off the day with wood-burning fires, local brews, and an array of food truck options. Don't leave without trying Boone Dog Pizza—it's a crowd favorite. Indoor seating makes this the spot to unwind.

DAY 3

Breakfast at Sisters Coffee Company: This flagship coffee shop is a dream for caffeine lovers and foodies alike. Its spacious, log-cabin-like interior welcomes you with the aroma of fresh coffee and a menu filled with breakfast bowls, sandwiches, and pastries.

Snap a photo with the Sisters Mural: Before heading out, capture a photo at the vibrant Sisters Mural (351 West Hood Avenue). It's the perfect backdrop to commemorate your trip.

SISTERS MURAL BY KATIE DAISY AND KAREN ELAND

The Takeaway: Seeking an otherworldly landscape that defies Pacific Northwest expectations? The Painted Hills, streaked with fossil-rich soil layers spanning millions of years, feel more like Mars than Oregon. This bucket-list adventure, with Sisters as your charming base camp, combines geological wonder with mountain town magic. Along the way, you'll savor Tibetan momo dumplings, sip lattes in log-cabin-style cafés, and potentially squeeze in snowy fun at Hoodoo Ski Area.

Ready to witness forty-four million years of Earth's artistry? Pack your telephoto lens, respect the fragile landscape, and prepare to experience one of Oregon's most unexpected wonders. The Painted Hills await—a masterpiece hiding in plain sight, just waiting to paint your weekend with colors you never imagined possible.

4 BELLEVUE

Introduction

Artificial snow begins to fall as enchanting characters parade along tree-lined streets, upbeat holiday music echoes off downtown buildings, and children squeal with delight. This is Snowflake Lane—one of the Pacific Northwest's most beloved holiday traditions and the amazing heart of winter in Bellevue.

Bellevue means "beautiful view" in French, and it truly lives up to its name. Nestled along the shores of Lake Washington with the Cascade Mountains as a dramatic backdrop, this sophisticated city transforms into a winter wonderland each December. I didn't discover this magical event until my first year at the University of Washington in 2015, when I figured out the bus routes from campus and was able to experience it firsthand.

Since that first visit, I've made Snowflake Lane an annual tradition, sharing the joy with family, bringing my parents and brother one year and my partner's sister and brother-in-law another. It's one of those experiences I love so much that I can't help but share it with others.

As a Visit Bellevue Outdoor Recreation Ambassador for over four years, I had the incredible honor of pressing the button to make it snow once! Can you believe it? The moment I watched the artificial snow begin to fall, knowing I'd triggered that magic for hundreds of families below, remains one of my most treasured holiday memories.

While Snowflake Lane steals the spotlight, Bellevue offers plenty more seasonal delights. There's a botanical garden adorned with nature-inspired lights, a reindeer festival, and an ice-skating rink. Having experienced numerous light displays across Western Washington, I can confidently say that for nature lovers like me, none compares to Bellevue's thoughtful blend of urban sophistication and natural beauty.

If you're ready for a festive urban adventure—with the bonus of getting ahead on holiday shopping in one of the region's premier destinations—Bellevue delivers magic at every turn.

At a Glance

Location: King County, Washington
Best Season to Visit: December
Suggested Duration: Two nights

SNOWFLAKE LANE

Holiday Events & Timing

- Snowflake Lane: Nightly parades at 7 p.m. (lasts ~25 minutes)
- Garden d'Lights: Late November through early January
- Reindeer Festival: December
- Bellevue Downtown Ice Rink: Mid-November through mid-January

Getting There

Seattle to Bellevue: 10 miles, ~20 minutes
Portland to Bellevue: 176 miles, ~3 hours 15 minutes

> **Parking Tip:** Free parking is available at Bellevue Square, Bellevue Place, and Lincoln Square garages during Snowflake Lane (but arrive early!).

Where to Stay

The Westin Bellevue: Looking for a spot close to all the action? This 4-star hotel connects to major shopping areas via a sky-bridge, making it super convenient. Plus, if you book a suite on one of the higher floors, you might just get a stunning view of Lake Washington!

Residence Inn Seattle Bellevue/Downtown: The best of both worlds—nature views and close to I-405. When I stayed here, I was amazed when I opened the curtains to reveal lush greenery—a rare sight in the city! The kitchenettes are a bonus too, so you can save a little on meals by cooking in instead of dining out.

Hilton Bellevue: You don't have to sacrifice location for affordability, as this hotel is just a short distance from downtown. Plus, its got an onsite restaurant and bar that serve up delicious craft cocktails, perfect for unwinding after a busy day.

Itinerary Outline

DAY 1

Dinner at 520 Bar & Grill: If you're in the mood for American classics, check out this inviting space that has an indoor bar and outdoor patio. Its drink menu is top-notch, so it's worth popping in early for happy hour

COUGAR MOUNTAIN REGIONAL PARK

wine or treating yourself to a signature cocktail. And don't forget to save room for dessert!

Garden D'Lights at the Bellevue Botanical Garden: Bundle up (and grab your rain-coat, just in case) to wander through the Bellevue Botanical Garden's enchanting light display. Surrounded by butterflies, great blue herons, and cascading water-falls, you'll truly feel like you've wandered into a dreamscape. Warm up with a hot drink from Copper Kettle Coffee Bar, located in the Shorts House. Tickets are available online only.

DAY 2

Breakfast at Matcha Magic: Even dedicated coffee lovers will dream about matcha for weeks after visiting this woman- and minority-owned café. With a planet-forward menu featuring acai bowls, toasts, and delicious lattes made with house-made ube syrup, pineapple puree, and strawberry puree, it's tough to choose just one drink!

Hike Coal Creek Falls: Of the greenery-filled areas surrounding Bellevue, Cougar Mountain Regional Park stands out. With over thirty-eight miles of trails, it's the perfect quick escape that somehow feels far from the city. My favorite is the Coal Creek Falls trail, a scenic three-mile hike with about 550 feet of elevation gain.

Enjoy the Issaquah Reindeer Festival at the Cougar Mountain Zoo: If you're not from the Eastside, you might not have heard of this conservation-focused zoo, which is dedicated to educating the public and protecting endangered species, such as the Bengal tiger. In December, the Siberian reindeer take on the role of Santa's reindeer, and you can visit with both the animals and the man in the red suit himself.

BELLEVUE BOTANICAL GARDENS

MATCHA MAGIC

Lunch at Fern Thai on Main: Bellevue has amazing Asian cuisine, and Fern Thai is a must-try for delicious Thai food. Offering both well-loved classics and lesser-known dishes, this spot also boasts a refreshing, upbeat interior that's as inviting as the menu.

Ice-skating at the Bellevue Downtown Ice Rink: Feel like a kid again at this pop-up rink in Bellevue Downtown Park. Fun for all ages, there are even skate guides (a.k.a. walkers) to help beginners. If you visit during a busy time, it can get warm, so you won't need heavy winter layers. Plus, lockers are available for rent.

Grab a spot for the Snowflake Lane Parade: This annual tradition attracts a big crowd, so arrive early (between forty-five minutes and an hour) to claim your spot. Ample free parking is available at the Bellevue Square garages.

Shop and dine at The Bellevue Collection: Looking to check some holiday gifts off your list? The Bellevue Collection, where the parade occurs, is one of Washington's premier shopping destinations. With stores such as Made In Washington, Lolli and Pops, and Barnes & Noble, there's something for everyone. Dining options range from fine experiences at Ascend Prime Steak & Sushi or Water Grille to casual favorites such as The Cheesecake Factory or Shake Shack.

DAY 3

Breakfast at Bellden Café: This philanthropic café offers food and drinks you can feel good about, with 25 percent of sales supporting charity partners. Dubbed the "Nicest place in Washington," it boasts an all-woman team crafting Instagram-worthy dishes—such as some of the best avocado toast I've ever had. Plus, its special community drink menu donates 10 percent of proceeds back to local causes.

Reality Break Escapes: Make your weekend getaway even more memorable by taking on the challenge of an escape room. This was where I first experienced one, and I had a ton of fun going on a space mission with my partner and brother. It offers many engaging and creative themed rooms, such as a speakeasy, a spaceship, and even the city of Seattle.

The Takeaway: Bellevue's holiday charm truly captivates. From the twinkle of Snowflake Lane's falling snow to cozy strolls through the Botanical Garden's glowing lights, this city has a way of wrapping you in a holiday embrace. With stunning lakeside views framed by the Cascades, vibrant downtown energy, and seasonal treats at every turn, Bellevue proves that a winter getaway can be both magical and effortlessly close to home.

Ready to experience the Pacific Northwest's most enchanting urban holiday destination? Book accommodations early (December is popular!), purchase Garden d'Lights tickets online, and prepare to fall under Bellevue's winter spell. Whether you're pressing imaginary snow buttons or simply soaking in the seasonal magic, this sophisticated city delivers unforgettable holiday memories just minutes from Seattle.

5 BROOKINGS

Introduction

As much as I adore wintry getaways, sometimes my soul craves something entirely different: a sunny coastal retreat where sixty-degree days feel like pure magic in December. That's when I head to Brookings, Oregon, my favorite gem nestled at the very southern tip of the state, practically on the California border.

Growing up in western Washington, I was familiar with towns on the northern coast, such as Cannon Beach and Seaside. But discovering the Southern Oregon Coast was a game changer. Brookings boasts noticeably warmer temperatures than the surrounding areas, earning it the nickname Oregon's Banana Belt, and after just one visit, I was completely hooked.

While the Natural Bridges initially drew me to the area, I quickly discovered that both the Samuel H. Boardman State Scenic Corridor and the vibrant town itself offered so much more.

During our stay, we woke up to oceanfront views, admired some of the most rugged coastline on the West Coast, and stumbled upon the most spectacular holiday light show we've ever seen. Plus, we walked among towering redwood trees—right here in Oregon! So, if you're on the hunt for a December weekend that feels like a warm-weather escape, Brookings delivers sunshine, sea stacks, and 100 percent coastal magic.

At a Glance

Location: Southern Oregon Coast
Best Season to Visit: December
Suggested Duration: Two nights

Getting There

Seattle to Brookings: 514 miles, ~8 hours 25 minutes
Portland to Brookings: 341 miles, ~5 hours 45 minutes

> **Bestie Tip:** This is a long drive—consider breaking it up with an overnight stop between Wilsonville and Eugene if coming from Seattle.

Where to Stay

Vacation rentals: For a cozy spot all to yourself, consider renting a house or condo. Some of them even come with hot tubs and ocean views.

Beachfront Inn: For unbeatable ocean views from your room and a complimentary breakfast, this hotel is a solid choice. It's the most popular in town—and it's dog friendly! Lilo loved it here.

Harris Beach State Park: With yurts, tent spaces, and RV sites perched above the beach, this option puts you in a fantastic location without stretching your budget.

BEACHFRONT INN

Itinerary Outline

DAY 1

Dinner at the Fat Irish Kitchen & Pub: This warm, family-friendly spot serves the ultimate comfort food, such as Irish stew. It's brimming with hearty beef pot roast and all the good veggies. We loved it with garlic toast, and you can also go for a bread bowl. Pair it with a specialty beer or cocktail for the full experience.

Nature's Coastal Holiday Festival of Lights: Featuring over three million lights, this volunteer-run holiday event is a hidden gem. Located in Azalea Park, this festival will leave you in awe at every turn, as you'll be greeted by whimsical sea creatures, such as whales, octopuses, and sea lions. With numerous paths to wander, there's plenty to see, making the $4 ticket well worth it. I am already dreaming of visiting again!

DAY 2

Breakfast at Bell & Whistle Coffee House: Start your morning along the Chetco River. With fair-trade coffee, grilled sandwiches, and pastries, this café will ease you gently into your day.

Drive the Samuel H. Boardman State Scenic Corridor: This twelve-mile drive along Highway 101 is a must. It showcases some of the most breathtaking stretches of the Oregon Coast. Here are my favorite spots:

- **Lone Ranch Beach Picnic Area:** A large, easily accessible beach with a mix of sandy shores, rocky sections, and tide pools. It's a great spot for some peace and quiet.
- **Cape Ferrelo Viewpoint:** No hiking required to take in this dramatic view of wind-battered sea stacks. You might even spot a whale!

NATURE'S COASTAL HOLIDAY FESTIVAL OF LIGHTS

- **Natural Bridges:** Often considered the most Instagrammable spot on the corridor. The viewpoint is easily accessible, though the trail beyond can be tricky and isn't recommended for casual visitors.

- **Secret Beach:** Accessible via a steep trail from the Natural Bridges parking lot or an unmarked pull-off. Be sure to visit during low tide to explore the beach.

- **Arch Rock State Park:** I can't tell you exactly why, but this viewpoint absolutely stole my heart. A short walk through old-growth trees leads you to a stunning view of Arch Rock.

> **Driving Tip:** Pull completely off the highway at viewpoints—this scenic route has narrow shoulders and steady traffic.

Lunch at Khun Thai: After your scenic drive, head to this great cozy place to grab some pineapple fried rice. Enjoy your meal by dining in or grabbing it to go.

Hike the Oregon Redwoods Trail: Brookings is one of the few places in the PNW where you can find coast redwoods outside of California. These fast-growing giants reach up to about 350 feet into the sky. Choose between a 0.5-mile and 1.2-mile trail to walk among them. One highlight of our hike was stepping inside the hollowed-out shell of a redwood and looking up to the bright sky. Eerie? A little. Exciting? Absolutely.

> **Bestie Tip:** If the weather turns stubborn, skip the trail and go thrift shopping instead! Brookings may be small, but it's packed with charming antique and thrift stores. We scored some seriously good finds at Goodwill—definitely worth a visit!

Dinner at the Wild River Pizza: If you've never had pizza cut into squares, you'll get to try it here! This place is generous with toppings and offers its own microbrews. We loved the Wild Side! If you're traveling with kids in tow, they'll be endlessly entertained in the arcade.

SAMUAL H. BOARDMAN SCENIC CORRIDOR

DAY 3

Breakfast at Compass Rose Café: For a quick and casual breakfast on your last day, stop by for giant breakfast burritos, biscuits and gravy, or delicious toasts, such as avocado or Nutella-stuffed. It also offers vegan options.

Explore Chetco Point Park: Walk along the dramatic trail out to the point, which reveals an expansive view of the Brookings coastline—a bittersweet goodbye you won't soon forget. You can also bring your pups to the popular dog park. Oh, and don't be discouraged by the sometimes smelly parking lot (which is next to a wastewater treatment plant).

The Takeaway: When the rest of the coast is blanketed in gray, Brookings basks in its well-earned reputation as Oregon's Banana Belt, regularly serving up winter sunshine and sixty-degree days. This southernmost coastal town feels like nature's warm-weather loophole—where wild sea stacks, golden light, and towering redwoods come together in a landscape that feels nothing short of cinematic. If your soul's craving blue skies, salty air, and a bit of festive spirit, Brookings proves that sometimes the best winter getaway isn't about embracing the cold—it's about finding your own pocket of sunshine.

PALOUSE FALLS

6

WALLA WALLA

Introduction

There's something magical about driving over the crest of the Cascade mountain range and watching the gray clouds give way to brilliant blue skies. But I never expected that our first stop at Washington's official state waterfall would greet us with a perfect rainbow arcing over Palouse Falls. Since we visited in February, we had the entire place to ourselves—just us, the birds, and that incredible natural light show. It was an epic start to what became one of my favorite winter getaways.

Like most of our winter weekend getaways, this destination is offseason during winter. That means you'll be hanging out with the locals. One reason to visit in February is Restaurant Month, when many fine-dining spots offer special three-course meals at a reduced price. If you're a foodie or celebrating a special occasion, this is a fantastic time to visit. Plus, hotels often offer discounted rates as part of this event. And trust me, the food is flawless. I feel full just thinking about all the amazing meals we enjoyed in the historic downtown, which has earned a spot on the National Register of Historic Places!

What surprised me most was discovering Walla Walla's rich historical significance. On our tour of the Fort Walla Walla Museum, I heard it called the Cradle of Northwest History—hard to believe for such a small town as it is today, but it was once the largest town in the Oregon Territory. Traditionally home to the Cayuse, Walla Walla, and Umatilla tribes, the area evolved with fur trading, Christian missionaries, and gold rushes. There's so much to learn, including the evolution of farming practices, at the Fort Walla Walla Museum.

Beyond the fascinating history and incredible food, Walla Walla offers something unexpectedly peaceful: wide-open landscapes, a walkable downtown listed on the National Register of Historic Places, and that rare winter sunshine that makes the whole valley glow. If you're ready for a getaway that feeds both your curiosity and your appetite, Walla Walla delivers in the most delightful ways.

At a Glance

Location: Southeastern Washington
Best Season to Visit: February
Suggested Duration: Two nights

Getting There

Seattle to Walla Walla: 272 miles, ~4 hours
Portland to Walla Walla: 242 miles, ~3 hours 45 minutes

> **Winter Driving Tip:** Roads are generally clear, but check conditions for the mountain passes if you're coming from Seattle during storm periods.

Where to Stay

Cameo Heights Mansion: For a romantic bed-and-breakfast escape, swap the hustle and bustle of town for serene vineyard views at Cameo Heights Mansion. Each of its seven suites is inspired by a different country, with the English Tudor suite exuding a regal, pink-hued charm that feels straight out of a fairy tale.

The FINCH: This is my personal favorite hotel in Walla Walla, blending energetic design with vintage flair. Its prime location makes it easy to explore downtown's attractions. Even in the heart of winter, you can cozy up around the outdoor firepit for s'mores or sip on local herbal tea in the lobby.

Comfort Inn & Suites: Conveniently located just off the highway, this hotel offers an affordable stay with a complimentary breakfast to start your day. Close to both the colleges and Fort Walla Walla Museum, it's an ideal base for exploring the area.

Itinerary Outline

DAY 1

Discover Washington's official waterfall Palouse Falls: Just fifty-five miles north of Walla Walla lies our state's official waterfall, and if waterfalls make your heart skip a beat, this detour is essential. Palouse Falls State Park offers scenic picnic areas and walking paths with picture-perfect views of the 198-foot waterfall, winding river, and rugged basalt canyons. While summer weekends bring crowds, winter transforms this place into a tranquil retreat where you might be the only visitors. After a cold snap, you might be lucky enough to witness the rare sight of the partially frozen falls—pure magic.

Dinner at Yamas Greek Eatery: This was my first authentic Greek dining experience, and it exceeded every expectation. This warm, inviting spot serves up five varieties of homemade hummus—a must-try in its appetizer platter. The garlic fries with tzatziki sauce were calling my name, and they were possibly the best fries I've ever had. Paired with a savory wrap, our meal was convincing evidence that Greek food is the best! Plus, every dish is crafted for sharing, making it an ideal spot to indulge and savor together.

DAY 2

Breakfast at the Maple Counter Café: They say humans are creatures of habit, and I'm living proof. Drawn to the homey charm of this spot, it felt like stepping into grandma's kitchen, only to realize it's part of the same

PALOUSE FALLS

WINGMAN BIRDZ + BREWZ

family as the Oak Table Café (see page 167), a cherished brunch spot we've been to many times on the Olympic Peninsula. The star of the show? Its signature apple pancake. But don't let the name fool you; this isn't your typical pancake. It's more like a soufflé—a fluffy, pastry-like delight that's as hearty as it is heavenly. If you're craving something savory, the café's eggs Benedict are a delight.

Fort Walla Walla Museum: Dive into history at Fort Walla Walla Museum, where five engaging exhibit halls unravel tales of the Oregon Trail, horse-powered farming, and the Washington State Penitentiary. It's the perfect spot to warm up on a crisp winter morning. And don't miss the gift shop (no admission required), where you can snag locally made ceramics, soap, and its famous sweet onion mustard.

> **Bestie Tip:** Bring headphones to tap into the new immersive multimedia tour, accessible by scanning a QR code with your phone. It's like getting a private tour, at your own pace.

Visit Walla Walla's Oldest Park: For a breath of fresh air, head to Pioneer Park, where you may be surprised by ducks using crosswalks, majestic old-growth trees, and the occasional peacock strutting about. It's a serene slice of nature where locals stroll with their pups. As a first-time visitor, I was awed by the diverse bird species residing in the free Pioneer Park Aviary. Just remember, feeding the birds is discouraged.

Lunch at Wingman Birdz + Brewz: I initially stopped by this family-friendly pub to sample cider from Freewater Cider Company, crafted just across the Oregon border. But what keeps me coming back are its inventive signature sauces, such as the peanut butter and jelly—imagine Thai peanut sauce with a delightful raspberry drizzle. Oh, and don't skip the sweet potato waffle fries; they're a must-try!

Stroll downtown Walla Walla shops

- Sip an afternoon latte at Carte Coffee or Colville Street Patisserie.
- Bring home world-renowned truffles from Bright's Candies.
- Decorate your home, discover new recipes, or find that perfect personalized gift from Sweetwater Paper & Home (a.k.a. "the little shop with a lot").
- Find your next read at Book & Game Co.

Dinner at Saffron Mediterranean Kitchen: Indulging in fine dining is a must in Walla Walla, and Saffron is a fine choice. At the chef's suggestion, we tried the citrus tabbouleh salad, brimming with grapefruit, blood and Cara Cara oranges, and feta. A salad that doesn't taste like a salad? Yes, please. For a fusion of fresh Spanish and Italian flavors, this is the place to be.

Catch a movie at the Gesa Power House Theatre: There's something special about watching a performance or film in a 120-year-old converted power plant. Gesa Power House Theatre is more than just a venue; it's become a community cornerstone. Whether it's Shakespeare, stand-up comedy, or a musical act, you'll feel like you're part of something truly special here.

DAY 3

Breakfast at Bacon & Eggs: When a café has a wall dedicated to hot sauce, you know flavor is the name of the game. The out-of-the-box menu delivers options such as breakfast tacos, tofu stir-fry with kimchi, and stuffed brioche French toast with Nutella and bananas. The upbeat urban vibe combined with mouthwatering dishes makes for a morning that's anything but ordinary.

Explore the Whitman Mission National Historic Site: Between the quiet walking trails and the educational Whitman Mission Museum, this is definitely worth a stop before you leave Walla Walla. Although it shares a somber story, it's one that's central to our American history.

The Takeaway: Framed by Washington State's official waterfall, Walla Walla is well worth a winter visit. With golden hills rolling out like a painting and Restaurant Month serving up three-course perfection, this town blends unexpected elegance with frontier charm. It's a place where history lingers in the architecture, flavor takes center stage, and the quiet magic of the offseason leaves you wondering why you didn't come sooner.

BACON & EGGS

IVERSON TRAIL PRESERVE

7 CAMANO ISLAND

Introduction

After many rejuvenating trips to Whidbey Island, I found myself wondering, *Why haven't I explored its neighbor to the east?* Enter Camano Island—an easily accessible gem connected by a bridge to Stanwood, so no need to worry about ferry schedules or reservations. With fewer than eighteen thousand residents (compared to Whidbey's seventy thousand), Camano feels a bit more laid-back and sleepier, but it holds plenty of charm for those willing to seek out adventure, even in the depths of winter.

My timing couldn't have been more perfect. As a glass art enthusiast, I was thrilled to discover Camano's annual Great Northwest Glass Quest. This ten-day treasure hunt takes place in February and transforms the entire island into an adventure playground. Participants scour community sites and businesses for plastic clue balls, which contain instructions on how to redeem handblown glass treasures. Our day was spent exploring forest trails, grocery stores, and picnic areas. While we didn't find a clue ball (though we did stumble upon a geocache!), the thrill of the hunt and attention to all the small details made it a memorable experience. If you're able to stay for a weekend, your chances of finding a treasure will increase!

For me, the true treasure of Camano isn't the glass balls—it's the island's hushed natural spaces that feel worlds away from Seattle's bustle. The beach parks and forest preserves offer peaceful trails perfect for a quiet escape, especially along the stunning Saratoga. The Pacific madrone trees, with their red peeling bark, create a gorgeous contrast against the gray winter waters, particularly at Camano Island State Park. On nearly every visit, we've spotted whales gliding through the water. Though they're sometimes on the Whidbey side of the channel, look out for dorsal fins and the misty sprays from their blowholes.

CAMANO ISLAND STATE PARK

Camano Island is just an hour from the city, but it feels like a different world entirely, proving that sometimes the best getaways are hiding in plain sight.

At a Glance

Location: Northwest of Everett, Washington
Best Season to Visit: February
Suggested Duration: Two nights

Getting There

Seattle to Camano Island: 64 miles, ~1 hour
Portland to Camano Island: 237 miles, ~4 hours

> **Travel Tip:** No ferry required! The bridge connection makes timing predictable and stress-free.

Where to Stay

Vacation rentals: Camano offers a variety of picturesque beach homes and forest cabins on Airbnb. These hidden gems often feature stunning sunset views, and some come equipped with fun extras such as bikes and kayaks.

Home2 Suites by Hilton Marysville: Located just off I-5, south of Camano, this modern 3-star hotel boasts an indoor pool and contemporary rooms, perfect for a comfortable stay near the Tulalip Resort.

Camping at Camano Island State Park: Open year-round, the lower loop of the campground offers a bluff-side spot with breathtaking views of the water. For a cozier option, reserve one of the rustic cabins online.

Bestie Tip: If you're camping, skip the campground bathrooms and head to the recently renovated restrooms at North Beach. These single-room facilities are the nicest park bathrooms I've ever seen, and they make getting ready in the morning feel like a hotel experience. After freshening up, take a leisurely walk along the beach—you're already there, after all!

Itinerary Outline

DAY 1

Shipwreck Coffee: Every trip to Camano Island starts here—it's become our tradition. This nautical-themed coffee shop feels like a cozy retreat. And its caramel sauce latte? Perfection. If I could, I'd drink it every day! As a delightful touch, the baristas top your drink with chocolate-covered espresso beans that add a satisfying crunch. Not a coffee drinker? The premium fruit smoothies are equally amazing.

Dinner at Tapped Public House: No visit to Camano is complete without dining at Tapped Public House. It's our favorite spot for good reason. With a great selection of drinks on tap, a mouthwatering entrée menu, and a dog-friendly outdoor patio, it checks all the boxes for a casual meal out.

SHIPWRECK COFFEE

CAMANO ISLAND STATE PARK

DAY 2

Breakfast at Cama Beach Café: Start your day at Cama Beach Café, where you'll enjoy breakfast overlooking the water. The eggs Benedict and Swedish pancakes are divine, especially when paired with small-batch coffee. The café's charming ambiance matches the island vibe.

Explore Cama Beach Historical State Park: After breakfast, spend some time exploring the fifteen miles of trails in Cama Beach Historic State Park. From the serene beaver marsh at Cranberry Lake to the rocky shores teeming with marine life, there's plenty to discover. Don't miss the historic beachfront cabins—they offer a fascinating glimpse into the island's past.

Weather backup plan: Need a break from the rain? Head to Matzke Fine Art Gallery and Sculpture Park for a dose of indoor inspiration. It's worth calling ahead—they sometimes offer classes you can join while you're in town!

Walk at the Iverson Trail Preserve: To see many habitats all in one place, head to Iverson Trail Preserve. This peaceful spot offers a mix of forests, meadows, and stunning views of Mount Baker. The trails are mostly flat but can get muddy, so come prepared. Bird-watchers, this place is for you!

Shop locally at the Camano Commons Marketplace: Camano Commons Marketplace is the heart of the island, bustling with dining options, shopping opportunities, and even a library. With plenty of outdoor seating, it's a welcoming space for everyone.

- Eat lunch at the Baked Café.
- Discover local art at the Loft.
- Add a plant to your collection at the Instagrammable Cactus + Co.
- Grab organic coffee from Camano Island Coffee Roasters.
- Enjoy an ice cream cone at Camano Scoopz.

Dinner at the Blue Heron Kitchen & Bar: First seafood, then dessert. For a comfortably upscale dining experience, visit this bright space, which serves fish, pasta, and sweets such as chocolate raspberry tart and apple crumble.

Catch the sunset at Camano Island State Park: End your day watching the sun set behind Whidbey Island. Whether you choose to sit where the waves meet the shore or on a peaceful bluff bench, it's the perfect way to wind down. With 6,700 feet of shoreline, you're sure to find your ideal spot.

DAY 3

Breakfast at Mustard Seed Baking Co.: Get an early start at Mustard Seed Baking Co. and snag one of its mouthwatering cinnamon rolls. If you have a long journey ahead, its customizable sandwiches make for a perfect on-the-go lunch. You can't go wrong with the signature panini!

The Takeaway: Camano Island may be quieter than its famous neighbor across the channel, but that's precisely what makes it so special. With peaceful trails that showcase Pacific Northwest beauty, community-driven treasures—such as the Great Northwest Glass Quest—that welcome visitors to experience island life, and easy access by bridge that eliminates ferry stress, it's the kind of place that invites you to explore with intention. The real magic happens when you slow down enough to notice the madrone bark, listen for whale spouts, and savor that perfect caramel latte at Shipwreck Coffee. Before long, you'll be asking yourself how this place is only an hour away from Seattle!

BREMERTON MARINA

8 BREMERTON

Introduction

There's a reason the Kitsap Peninsula is called the natural side of Puget Sound, and it wasn't until I spent a weekend in Bremerton that I truly understood why. As someone who's fallen hard for islands, I discovered that peninsulas can be just as captivating—after all, they're surrounded by water on three sides. Sometimes all it takes is a little salty air, warm hospitality, and a thriving local scene to remind you why exploring your own Pacific Northwest backyard never gets old.

Bremerton, the largest town on the peninsula, is a maritime community steeped in naval history that feels both storied and vibrantly current. Part of its appeal is its accessibility—it's just a pleasant one-hour ferry ride from Seattle. But once you arrive, you'll discover a downtown packed with diverse cuisine, including Filipino, Thai, and ramen spots, as well as charming local shops to wander through. I've never been as obsessed with a soap store as I am with F.R.O.G. Soap.

The community's deep appreciation for nature is displayed everywhere you look, with nearly fifty parks scattered throughout the area. With sweeping views of the Olympic Mountains, peaceful forests where ravens call overhead, and tranquil shorelines, there's no shortage of ways to reconnect with the great outdoors. Whether you arrive by ferry or freeway, Bremerton offers that perfect combination of maritime charm and natural beauty that makes you wonder why it took so long to discover this gem.

For an easy, breezy weekend getaway where everything feels within reach and getting there is half the fun, Bremerton has become one of my favorite hidden gems.

At a Glance

Location: Kitsap Peninsula, Washington
Best Season to Visit: December through March
Suggested Duration: Two nights

Getting There

By Ferry: Seattle to Bremerton: ~1 hour
By Car: Portland to Bremerton: 172 miles, ~2 hours 40 minutes

Where to Stay

Marina Square Suites: Ever had the urge to move into a place while on vacation? That was exactly what I thought as I stepped into my suite at Marina Square. Sunlight streamed through the expansive windows, framing a breathtaking waterfront view. These suites feel more like stylish apartments than hotel rooms, offering extra space and the convenience of a full kitchen in some units. The central location makes it easy to enjoy leisurely morning and evening walks along the water, adding to the charm of this stunning retreat.

MARINA SQUARE SUITES

Vacation rentals: With limited hotel options in Bremerton proper, a vacation rental can be a fantastic alternative. Whether you're looking for an entire home or a compact condo, these rentals offer the opportunity to find a place that matches your style.

Camping at Illahee State Park: For an option that doesn't skimp on natural beauty, camping at Illahee State Park is a great choice. Open year-round, this forested park lets you wander through one of the peninsula's last remaining old-growth forests while staying just steps from the water. It's a serene escape that brings you closer to nature.

Itinerary Outline

DAY 1

Shop at Life in Mauve: While wandering through the charming Manette neighborhood, stop by this boho-chic jewelry and lifestyle boutique. Packed with pretty pink vibes and carefully curated treasures, it's perfect for unique finds and memorable gifts that capture the local artistic spirit.

Dinner at The Boat Shed: When you're on a peninsula, waterfront dining is a must, and The Boat Shed consistently delivers. This beloved community staple has been serving the area for over forty years, offering a cozy spot to savor fresh seafood with calming water views. Whether you're enjoying a warm bowl of New England clam chowder or diving into flavorful fish tacos, the combination of delicious food and a relaxing outlook makes for a dazzling dining experience.

Catch the sunset from the Manette Bridge: Winter sunsets have a way of painting the sky in saturated hues, and one of the most memorable I've seen was from the Manette Bridge. With the silhouette of the marina, the USS *Turner Joy* in the foreground, and rippling waves below, it was a scene straight out of a postcard. It's a beautiful way to wrap up the day.

VISTA GARDENS

DAY 2

Breakfast at American Donut Makers: Kick off the day with a box of happiness from a bright pink gem, where the donuts are as cheerful as the decor. My personal favorite? The old-fashioned maple. But don't miss its flagship 7th Inning Stretch donut, loaded with peanut and caramel, or creative offerings such as the Cinnamon Toast Crunch donut. Arrive early—these treats tend to disappear fast!

Explore the Puget Sound Navy Museum: Even if history isn't usually your thing, this museum might surprise you. Dive into the fascinating world of nuclear aircraft carriers, explore rotating exhibit—such as the influence of military fashion on mainstream trends—and learn about the Navy's critical role in the Puget Sound. With free admission, it's a must-visit for anyone curious about the region's rich maritime history.

Create glass art at Eastern Wind Glass: Let your inner artist out to play. This colorful gathering space offers classes where you can learn to fuse glass into pieces of art that you'll cherish for a lifetime. We made sea-themed holiday ornaments with zero experience, and now they're some of our most-loved decorations. Be sure to book a class online! Note: Finished glasswork can be picked up at a later date.

Lunch at Evergreen Pizza Co.: Warm up by the wood-fired oven at Evergreen Pizza Co. Its pizzas are the perfect comfort food after a morning of exploration. During our visit, a thoughtfully crafted mule menu was featured—the cranberry mule was our top pick. Pair it with a delicious slice, and you've got a lunch to remember.

Explore Vista Gardens: For an enchanting escape, head to Vista Gardens, a hidden four-acre oasis that's a true local treasure. Overlooking the Port Washington Narrows, this urban garden showcases sustainable gardening practices perfected by the Albers family. It's a mellow spot to ground yourself in the natural world. Since it's on private property, be sure to contact the gardens before visiting. Donations are appreciated.

LIONS PARK

Beach walk at Illahee State Park: Illahee State Park offers a beautiful blend of nature and history. With its sandy beach, wooden pier, massive naval guns, and towering old-growth trees, it's a park worth exploring. Whether you're strolling along the beach or taking in the sights, it's a refreshing way to spend an afternoon.

Dinner at Mezcalitos Mexican Restaurant: End your full day with a cozy, flavorful Mexican experience. My first time trying table-side guacamole was here, and it did not disappoint. Watching it being prepared fresh at the table was just as much fun as eating it. Pair that with handcrafted margaritas and delicious Mexican egg rolls, and I bet you'll have found a new favorite spot.

DAY 3

Breakfast at Cups Espresso & Café: Imagine curling up in the sunshine-soaked window benches at Cups Espresso & Café—pure bliss! Its breakfast sandwiches, burritos, and coffees are a perfect start to the day. If I lived in Bremerton, this might be my daily go-to for breakfast.

Walk at Lions Park: Cap off your trip with a visit to Lions Park, where you come face-to-face with breathtaking views of the Olympic Mountains. This surprise stop quickly became a highlight, with the scenic backdrop, splashing birds, and friendly dogs creating a playful atmosphere.

The Takeaway: Not quite an island, but every bit as enchanting, Bremerton proves that peninsulas deserve just as much love. With salty sea breezes, welcoming locals, and a ferry ride that feels like a mini adventure before you even arrive, this maritime town offers an easy escape from the city without ever feeling far from nature. Whether you're browsing indie shops downtown, exploring naval history, or walking along a quiet shoreline under a pastel sky, Bremerton is proof that some of the Pacific Northwest's best gems are hiding in plain sight. Sometimes the most memorable getaways happen when you step off that ferry and discover a place that feels both comfortably familiar and delightfully new.

TOLMIE STATE PARK

9

OLYMPIA

Introduction

My first memory of Olympia takes me back to a fifth-grade field trip to the Capitol Building, where I wandered those gleaming marble floors with my Nikon digital camera hanging from my neck, completely awe-struck. The intricate architectural details and stately walnut and mahogany desks, with the blend of governmental gravitas and rich tradition, left a lasting impression.

Returning as an adult, I've discovered that Olympia offers so much more than its iconic landmark. This artsy capital city invites exploration with seventy murals scattered across downtown, thriving small businesses, and serene parks that become more enchanting with each season. One of my personal favorites is an underrated park I've visited countless times, each season unveiling a new side of its charm. It's a haven for wildlife where a mighty river and the Puget Sound converge, offering a retreat that feels miles away from the everyday.

Beyond its natural beauty, Olympia is underrated as a foodie paradise. The abundance of locally sourced ingredients, the commitment to sustainability, and the availability of exceptional craft beverages shine through every dish and drink.

While most of the itinerary below focuses on Olympia and Tumwater, those with a sense of adventure will find that the greater Thurston County region has its own treasures waiting to be discovered, offering even more off-the-beaten-path experiences.

At a Glance

Location: Thurston County, Washington
Best Season to Visit: December through March
Suggested Duration: Two nights

Getting There

Seattle to Olympia: 60 miles, ~1 hour
Portland to Olympia: 114 miles, ~1 hour 45 minutes

> **Travel Tip:** Easy access via I-5 makes Olympia perfect for a spontaneous getaway or multicity Pacific Northwest tour.

Where to Stay

The Marie Bed & Breakfast: If you find yourself squealing with delight every time you pass a charming Victorian home (guilty!), then the Marie is your dream stay. Built in 1892, this historic gem showcases elegant Queen Anne architecture, lush gardens, and thoughtful details that transport you back in time. The homemade organic breakfast is the cherry on top of an already enchanting experience.

Courtyard Olympia: For those preferring to be in the heart of town, this modern Marriott Bonvoy property offers spacious rooms and the handy perk of Starbucks coffee onsite.

La Quinta Inn & Suites by Wyndham Tumwater: Conveniently located just off I-5, this budget-friendly option provides all the essentials for a comfortable stay, plus it has a pool and hot tub for unwinding after outdoor adventures.

Itinerary Outline

DAY 1

Walk the Tumwater Falls Trail: This popular half-mile trail offers a fantastic return for minimal effort. The scenic, wooded path forms a loop following the Deschutes River, making it perfect for a leisurely stroll. While it's more of an urban park than a traditional hike, it's a dream for photographers with its picturesque bridges, cascading waterfalls, and salmon (seasonally dependent).

Dinner at Pellegrino's Italian Kitchen: One bite reveals why Pellegrino's consistently ranks among the South Sound's top Italian destinations. The specialty pastas are a standout, such as the Mediterranean pesto gnocchi, where each creamy, pillow-like bite is crafted with care and plated to perfection. The food is a feast for both the eyes and the palate, making it a must-visit for any Italian-food lover.

DAY 2

Breakfast at Left Bank Pastry: For an authentic taste of France, make your way to this Instagram-worthy bakery, where you'll find a delightful selection of sweet and savory croissants. My top pick? The cinnamon croissant, which, in my (perhaps controversial) opinion, gives traditional cinnamon rolls a serious run for their money.

LEFT BANK PASTRY

NISQUALLY WILDLIFE REFUGE

Visit the Washington State Capitol Campus: Explore this sprawling 143-acre, garden-like campus that combines history and natural beauty. Take the free fifty-minute guided tour of the iconic Legislative Building, easily spotted thanks to its impressive 287-foot masonry dome—the tallest in North America. Tours are available daily on a first-come-first-served basis.

While you're there, explore the beautiful grounds and trails around Capitol Lake, which is currently being restored to its natural estuary state. Keep your eyes peeled for unique photo angles of the Capitol building—this place is full of possibilities for photographers.

Lunch at Vic's Pizzeria Wildwood: For artisan pizza lovers, it doesn't get much better than Vic's, a beloved local institution that's been serving up delicious pies for over twenty-five years. Enjoy hand-tossed dough, six house-made sauces, and plenty of vegan options. Feeling ravenous? Try the double-crusted pizza for a hearty feed. Pair your pizza with locally brewed cider or beer, and you've got a match made in culinary heaven.

NISQUALLY WILDLIFE REFUGE

Explore the Billy Frank Jr. Nisqually Wildlife Refuge: Nine times out of ten, this park is my reason for visiting Olympia. If you've ever visited the Paradise area of Mount Rainier, you've likely seen the Nisqually Glacier—the source of the glacier-fed Nisqually River. But did you know you can also visit where the river ends? This refuge feels like a hidden gem, almost like the Pacific Northwest's unofficial fourth national park. With a well-established visitor center, numerous trails, and abundant wildlife, it's a nature lover's dream. In winter, it's especially excellent for spotting bald eagles—one time, Kyle and I counted nearly eighty!

Bestie Tip: Bring binoculars and a telephoto lens for the best wildlife viewing experience. Besides eagles, you might spot harbor seals, great blue herons, and deer. And don't forget a windbreaker, like I did the first time I visited! The boardwalk over the tideflats is exposed, and a brisk wind can make it chilly, but bundling up ensures you can enjoy every moment of wildlife watching in comfort.

Dinner at Iron Rabbit Restaurant & Bar: Whether you're craving artichoke heart Alfredo or a gourmet burger with wedge fries, Iron Rabbit elevates comfort food to exceptional levels. This sustainably focused gem offers a welcoming, family-friendly atmosphere, where every thoughtfully crafted dish delivers both satisfaction and memorable flavors.

TOLMIE STATE PARK

DAY 3

Breakfast at Two Sisters Coffee Co.: For a morning pick-me-up, Two Sisters Coffee Co. is a must. I'm always eager to try its ever-changing coffee flight—a fun and flavorful way to discover new favorites. Each month brings a fresh lineup of four 8-oz drinks, and you can always count on them being delicious. Pair your coffee with one of the hearty breakfast sandwiches or flavorful egg bites for a perfect start to your day.

Hike in Tolmie State Park: For your scenic finale, explore this gem that blends serene beaches with lush evergreen forests. Three miles of trails offer various experiences, from shoreline walks to forest exploration. On clear days, Mount Rainier views from the beach are spectacular, providing a breath-taking farewell to your Olympia adventure.

Bestie Tip: Looking for a value-packed indoor activity? Head to the Olympic Flight Museum to learn all about vintage aircraft. It's a fun and fascinating way to spend a rainy morning—and you'll walk away having learned something new!

The Takeaway: Olympia surprises you in the best possible ways. One moment you're wandering marble halls beneath the tallest masonry dome in North America, and the next you're scanning skies for bald eagles at what feels like our unofficial fourth national park: the Nisqually Wildlife Refuge. Add cinnamon croissants, wood-fired pizza, and creative coffee flights, and you discover a destination that seamlessly blends government grandeur, natural wonder, and seriously satisfying cuisine into an unforgettable getaway. Sometimes the most rewarding adventures happen in your own backyard—and Olympia proves that our state capital deserves a spot on every Pacific Northwest explorer's list.

HISTORIC DOWNTOWN POULSBO

10 POULSBO

Introduction

Lovingly known as Little Norway, this one-of-a-kind waterfront town on Puget Sound traces its rich Scandinavian roots back to the 1880s. That heritage weaves through every corner of the town, from the distinctive Nordic-inspired architecture with steep gabled roofs to the genuinely warm atmosphere that greets every visitor. While the cultural heartbeat pulses year-round, it's during events such as the Viking Julefest Bonfire on the winter solstice that the town's spirited history truly comes alive.

I first stumbled upon Poulsbo's holiday magic completely by accident. On a sunny December weekday, I ventured into the town with the simple goal of finding a coffee shop where I could work. As I walked through the streets, I was taken aback by the festive transformation—my previous summer visits hadn't prepared me for this! The holiday spirit was irresistible, and soon I found myself abandoning my laptop to wander decorated streets, soaking in the storybook ambiance.

Visiting during the Christmas season feels like stepping into a Nordic fairy tale. Streets adorned with twinkling lights, store windows filled with intricately crafted gingerbread houses, and air filled with joyful bustle create that cozy alpine village feeling—but with the added charm of salty sea breezes and the convenience of avoiding snowy mountain passes.

From time-honored classic pastries at generations-old bakeries to waterfronts teeming with marine life, every moment here celebrates the perfect blend of tradition and nature. This is where you come to experience the season in true Little Norway style.

At a Glance

Location: Kitsap Peninsula, Washington
Best Season to Visit: December
Suggested Duration: Two nights

Getting There

Seattle to Poulsbo: 80 miles, ~1 hour 25 minutes (without the ferry)
Portland to Poulsbo: 187 miles, ~3 hours

> **Travel Tip:** Take the scenic ferry route through the peninsula to enjoy beautiful water views, or stick to highways to arrive faster.

Where to Stay

Fairfield Inn & Suites: Offering an indoor pool, hot breakfast, and a well-equipped fitness center, this is the ideal choice for those seeking a classic hotel stay. The rooms have a fresh, modern feel, and the hotel is conveniently located just a short drive from downtown.

Hotel Scandi: Nestled in the heart of walkable downtown, this boutique stay occupies the site of Poulsbo's first hotel, which opened in 1892. Steeped in history, the interiors have been beautifully restored and updated. Enjoy private rooms with shared bathrooms and common living spaces that exude charm and comfort.

Camping at Kitsap Memorial State Park: For those who love the outdoors, cabins and campsites set within a tranquil forest are available year-round. With fewer visitors during this season, you'll likely have your pick of spots. Reservations can be made online.

Itinerary Outline

DAY 1

Liberty Bay Waterfront Park: Get your bearings by stretching your legs on a leisurely boardwalk stroll while scanning for harbor seals in the water and bald eagles overhead. The waterfront provides a perfect introduction to Poulsbo's maritime charm, especially during December when holiday decorations frame the water views.

While you're there, pop into the nearby SEA Discovery Center—a small but mighty aquarium that's well worth a visit. Donations are appreciated.

Dinner at the Brass Kraken Pub: Let the good views continue into dinner at a spot where American classics and a buzzing atmosphere await. It's the perfect place to enjoy some pub fare while overlooking the waterfront. The pub fare is tasty, but what you'll remember is sharing the incredible sunset with friends while overlooking Liberty Bay.

Grab drinks at Valhöll Brewing: End your evening at a craft microbrewery, where you can order a flight of house-made creations, such as Golden Warrior, Nordic Sun, and Odin's Raven, or try a refreshing nonalcoholic root beer. Grab a seat by the outdoor fire or settle in at an indoor picnic table to enjoy the laid-back vibe and local flavors.

DAY 2

Breakfast at Sluys Poulsbo Bakery: For over fifty years, this renowned bakery has consistently brought delicious made-from-scratch Danish pastries, bundoughs (signature sweet rolls), and breads to the Kitsap community. The bakers pride themselves on both creativity and tradition when it comes to recipes, some of which originated in the Old World. Trust me, the Viking Cups are worth the wait.

BYRDIE'S COFFEE

Explore Little Norway's historic downtown: Wander through the walkable streets of Poulsbo, where Nordic heritage meets modern charm:

- **Grab a latte at Byrdie's Coffee:** perfect fuel for your exploration.
- **Browse at Liberty Bay Books:** Find your next great read.
- **Get inspired at The Verksted Gallery:** Discover local and regional art.
- **Hunt treasures at the Cats Meow:** You might discover unique secondhand finds.
- **Savor treats at Boehm's Chocolates of Poulsbo:** Its sea salt caramels are legendary.
- **Learn about marine life at the SEA Discovery Center:** Grab the chance if you missed it yesterday.

Lunch at Tizley's EuroPub: Enjoy a comforting lunch of European classics such as Swedish meatballs, shepherd's pie, and schnitzels. Request a table on the outdoor patio for lovely views looking down on the town.

Explore Port Gamble

- Take a scenic ten-mile drive to this quaint National Historic Landmark mill town that feels like stepping back in time. The perfectly preserved Victorian buildings and waterfront setting provide a fascinating contrast to Poulsbo's Nordic charm.
- Shop for beautifully crafted artisanal, fair-trade goods at Tango Zulu Imports. I left with two floral embroidered pot holders that totally brightened up my kitchen!
- Browse Port Gamble General Store & Café for home goods, candies, and the not-to-be-missed seashell museum upstairs. Hungry? The veggie sandwich and pie are perfect for enjoying at waterfront picnic tables.

Dinner at Sogno di Vino: Wind down with a romantic dinner under the canopy of a hundred-year-old magnolia tree. Its Tuscan-inspired menu features wood-fired pizza, flavorful pasta, and fresh fish entrées. Wine lovers will find themselves in heaven here, with carefully curated selections that pair perfectly with the intimate atmosphere.

DAY 3

Breakfast at ChocMo Chocolatier & Café: With decadent drinking chocolate and tempting truffles, this isn't your typical breakfast spot. Alongside morning favorites like crepes, waffles, and pastries, this café handcrafts its own chocolates. Too early for sweets? Grab a box to take home instead. The relaxed pace makes it the perfect place to savor your final morning in Little Norway.

Explore Kitsap Memorial State Park: For one last postcard-worthy view, stop here along the Hood Canal. The rocky shores are fun to explore, but it's those peekaboo views of the water through the forest that create the most memorable final impressions of the peninsula's natural beauty.

Weather Tip: If rain arrives, spend extra time browsing Poulsbo's shops or visit the Poulsbo Historical Society & Museums to dive deeper into the town's Norwegian heritage.

The Takeaway: Strolling along Poulsbo's waterfront, it's impossible not to be charmed by the steep gabled roofs, carved wooden signs, and colorful facades that echo its Nordic roots. This Little Norway creates its own enchanted world with its festive spirit, boutique shops, and gingerbread-trimmed streets that truly feel like a Hallmark movie come to life. Whether you're nibbling on a Viking Cup from Sluys Bakery or ducking into a cozy shop downtown, Poulsbo offers a refreshing blend of heritage, creativity, and small-town magic that's especially heartwarming in winter.

PILOT BUTTE

11

BEND

Introduction

I was twenty-four when I first ventured into Central Oregon's high desert, crossing the Cascades on a snowy February morning to celebrate Kyle's twenty-fifth birthday in Bend. Growing up, I'd been on a few Oregon Coast family trips, but I'd never explored this side of the state, and that drive over Santiam Pass was pure magic. Snow dusted the pines as we crossed into an entirely different world: expansive skies, rugged terrain, and a sense of openness that felt both exhilarating and humbling.

Bend sits at 3,625 feet above sea level, greeting visitors with crisp, invigorating mountain air. We encountered an extreme cold snap during that first visit—temperatures dropped to single digits, and we woke up to find the water bottles frozen solid in our car. Yet, despite the chill, there was something incredibly refreshing about the high desert's intensity. Our entire weekend was bathed in brilliant sunshine with vivid blue skies that made everything seem sharper and more alive.

That trip became the foundation for an annual tradition. We've discovered Bend exclusively in its offseason, when the town slows down but still offers incredible outdoor adventures and cozy indoor retreats. Each winter visit deepens our appreciation for this high-desert gem, where extreme weather, bright sunshine, and endless outdoor possibilities create something truly special.

From hiking snow-covered trails that reward you with panoramic views to watching sunsets that paint the mountains in golden light, Bend in winter offers a perfect blend of adventure and tranquility. It's become our go-to destination for embracing the season rather than enduring it.

At a Glance

Location: Central Oregon
Best Season to Visit: January through March
Suggested Duration: Two or three nights

Getting There

Seattle to Bend: 328 miles,
~5 hours 40 minutes
Portland to Bend: 163 miles,
~3 hours 10 minutes

> **Winter Driving Tip:** Mountain passes can require chains or traction tires. Check road conditions at TripCheck.com before departure, and expect your car to get dusty from the crushed rock traction treatment on roads.

Where to Stay

The Oxford Hotel: This location is designed to spoil you, with gelato, coffee, and the Deschutes River just steps from your posh room. Make your stay unforgettable with vinyl albums and a pillow menu to customize your experience to perfection.

LOGE Bend: If you took the spirit of Bend's outdoorsy culture and turned it into a hotel, it would be this. With hammocks hanging from the ceilings, bike racks by the front door, and its proximity to Mount Bachelor, you will find the perfect blend of comfort and adventure. We stayed here on our first visit to Bend and never felt more at home in a hotel.

Campfire Hotel: In this town of year-round adventure, it's no surprise that this hotel boasts an outdoor saltwater pool you can dive into even in winter—don't worry, it's heated. The central location is a plus, and the Canteen serves up drinks and tapas for a carefree vibe.

Itinerary Outline

DAY 1

Dinner at Bend Brewing Company: Bend is famous for its breweries, and this is one we always return to. It has twelve beers on tap, plus plenty of nonalcoholic beers and mocktails. Pair these with light pub food or a whole meal.

Go for a sunset hike at Pilot Butte: Determined to find the most stunning sunset spot in Bend, we tackled the two-mile hike up Pilot Butte (the road closes in winter, making it hike-only). We didn't quite reach the summit before the sun dipped behind the mountains, but the views were absolutely worth it. Even with snow on the ground, I had an iced coffee in hand—it was worth it for the surreal high-desert experience.

> **Winter Tip:** Bring microspikes or Yaktrax for icy sections, and start early enough to allow extra time for snowy conditions.

DAY 2

Breakfast at McKay Cottage Restaurant: This historic home turned restaurant became a staple from our very first Bend visit. It's impossible not to feel relaxed in this charming setting. I'm obsessed with its McKay Mocha, made with locally crafted chocolate and espresso. Whether iced or hot, it always sets my day off on the right foot.

McKAY COTTAGE

SMITH ROCK STATE PARK

STEELHEAD FALLS

Explore Smith Rock State Park: Smith Rock's dramatic landscape along the Crooked River is a must-see. For those up for a challenge, the Misery Ridge Trail offers a 3.5-mile hike with one thousand feet of elevation gain. Going counterclockwise gives you close encounters with the rock formations and stunning views of the Cascade Range. Watch out for icy patches, especially in shaded areas.

> **Photography Tip:** The contrast between red rock and snow creates incredible photo opportunities reminiscent of the American Southwest. Conditions are especially ideal when the morning light hits the formations.

Hike to Steelhead Falls: This easy half-mile round trip perfectly complements Smith Rock, leading to roaring falls that pour into a wide basin. We hiked it during a light, barely-there snowfall, which added to the magic. Note that the marked trail ends at the falls viewpoint.

Lunch at The Lemon Tree: We stumbled upon this vibrant lunch spot by chance, drawn in by its bright yellow tapestry and lively atmosphere. The beautifully presented brunch dishes are a feast for the eyes and the palate, especially the soul-warming shakshuka on a sunny winter day!

THE LEMON TREE

MT. BACHELOR SKI RESORT

Check out the High Desert Museum: For history enthusiasts, a visit to this museum is essential. Exhibits on nature, culture, and wildlife—including otters and Gert the fox—tell the story of the Plateau Indian Nations and their regional heritage. It's perfect for warming up while learning about the area's rich cultural landscape.

Dinner at the Podski Food Cart Lot: This food cart lot is a culinary adventure, with offerings ranging from Italian street food to authentic Thai dishes. My favorite is Toasty, which serves 100 percent vegan Mexican meals, such as the Bend Bowl, which is packed with smoky tempeh, cilantro, lime crema, and a burst of flavors in every bite.

Shop at The Gear Fix: I joke that I'd drive three hundred miles just to visit this outdoor store, but it's true! Its selection of second-hand outdoor clothing and gear, sold on consignment, is exciting for any outdoor enthusiast. It'll make you feel like a kid in a candy shop!

Catch the sunset along the river at Drake Park and Mirror Pond: This beloved city park is the ideal spot to unwind, bird-watch, or take a peaceful stroll. The towering ponderosa pines and the serene reflections on Mirror Pond make it a glorious end to the day.

DAY 3

Breakfast at Thump Coffee—Roastery & Bakery: This was actually our first stop when we arrived in Bend on that initial visit, and I've never looked back. I simply can't resist its lattes with house-made caramel—absolute perfection. Be sure to grab a bag of beans to take home! With a rotating food menu, you can indulge in delicious toasts, breakfast sandwiches, and fresh pastries. Plus, the mountain views from here are just the cherry on top.

Mt. Bachelor Ski Resort: Hit the slopes at the Pacific Northwest's biggest ski resort. Mount Bachelor is a grand mountain with boundless options. If you're a beginner, you can take lessons. Otherwise, explore 101 runs of fun!

Bestie Tip: For a classic winter activity right in the heart of town, head to The Pavilion for a covered, open-air public ice-skating session. Be sure to check the

GRAND FOREST PARK

schedule online ahead of time, since the rink is also used for curling and hockey throughout the week.

The Takeaway: For adventurers, there's something about winter in Bend that lingers long after you've left the high desert. The call of the outdoors remains strong—whether you're hiking to Steelhead Falls, carving turns through powder at Mount Bachelor, or watching sunset paint the Cascades from a snowy butte.

And in between the bigger adventures, it's those distinctly Bend rituals that make it feel special: sipping a McKay Mocha while planning your day, browsing secondhand treasures at The Gear Fix, or grabbing a soul-warming bite from a food truck at The Podski.

Winter in Bend isn't about enduring the season—it's about embracing the crisp air, brilliant sunshine, and that uniquely high-desert combination of adventure and tranquility that keeps calling you back year after year.

12 BAINBRIDGE ISLAND

Introduction

There's a reason so many people choose to live on Bainbridge Island and commute to Seattle: it offers a laid-back island escape with a close-knit community, all just a quick ferry ride away. I'll never forget my first visit during my freshman year at the University of Washington. It was one of those perfect late winter days—the sky clear and blue, the air crisp. We walked onto the ferry, and as the city skyline unfolded in front of me, I couldn't help but snap something like a hundred photos. For that view alone, riding the Seattle–Bainbridge ferry is absolutely worth it.

At the time, Bainbridge was a complete mystery to me. I hadn't yet explored Washington's other islands, and this was one of the last trips I took without a planned itinerary (this was before my travel-writing days!). That freedom to wander and let the island unfold, block by block, was magical. We stumbled upon satisfying sandwiches to enjoy alfresco, a bookstore where I lost track of time, and a quiet waterfront trail that offered glimpses into Bainbridge's history and natural beauty. It was a reminder to leave space for serendipity.

Since then, I've made it a point to introduce my friends and family to Bainbridge's special magic. Whether cheering on my brother Alec and my partner Kyle during the annual Chilly Hilly bike ride or strolling through the lush Grand Forest with my best friend Megan, each visit feels like a new adventure. The moment you step off the ferry, you're greeted by a charming blend of local shops, welcoming pedestrian-friendly streets, and that peaceful island vibe that's both timeless and refreshing.

There's just something about this place that sticks with you—a little slice of island life that feels both timeless and refreshing.

At a Glance

Location: Kitsap County, Washington
Best Season to Visit: January through April
Suggested Duration: Two nights

Getting There

By Ferry: Seattle to Bainbridge Island: ~35 minutes (Washington State Ferries)
By Car: Portland to Bainbridge Island: 199 miles, ~3 hours 15 minutes

Ferry Tip: Check current schedules at WSDOT (wsdot.wa.gov). Walk-on passengers don't need reservations, but be sure to arrive early during peak times. The ferry ride itself is half the experience—it's *seriously* perfect for Seattle skyline photography!

Where to Stay

The Inn at Pleasant Beach: This upscale boutique hotel boasts private balconies, cozy fireplaces, and even a multi-bedroom townhouse suite. The elegant beachy decor creates a serene and inviting atmosphere, making it a place you'll never want to leave.

Quality Inn & Suites Bainbridge Island: A pet-friendly option providing all the essentials at reasonable rates, including a hot breakfast to fuel your island explorations.

Fay Bainbridge Park & Campground: Surprisingly, you can camp right on the island! This is an ideal spot to ease into the camping experience, as the town is nearby for any forgotten necessities.

Itinerary Outline

DAY 1

Grand Forest Park: Don't make my initial mistake and overlook this hidden gem just minutes from downtown. This second-growth forest offers eight miles of serene trails, where you'll encounter towering trees, tranquil ponds, and an array of small wildlife. It's the perfect place to embrace the outdoors and enjoy a peaceful walk.

Dinner at Doc's Marina Grill: When you're on an island, waterfront dining is a must. For your first meal, head to this laid-back spot where you can savor classics such as clam chowder or fish and chips. Feel like trying something new? Try the blackened wild salmon sandwich or the Korean fried chicken sandwich for a delicious twist on the usual fare.

DAY 2

Breakfast at Pegasus Coffee House: If I had to count my favorite coffee shops in the Pacific Northwest on one hand, this one would definitely make the cut. Located in an ivy-covered old brick hardware building, this is the type of coffee shop you usually only see in movies. It has small-town warmth and big-time delivery. The care that goes into crafting each drink is undeniable, and the menu, which includes avocado toast, pastries, and panini, will have you coming back for more.

> **Bestie Tip:** A thoughtful activity offered here is sending a free postcard to family and friends from Pegasus—all you need to do is write a message and include where you want it to go!

Stroll downtown: After fueling up, explore the heart of Bainbridge. The town is small enough to explore on foot, with outdoorsy shops, art galleries, and inspired corners waiting to be discovered.

- **Gear up at Wildernest Outdoor Store:** It's perfect for island adventure supplies.
- **Browse art at Millstream Bainbridge:** Discover Pacific Northwest artistic talent.
- **Get creative at little island crafts:** Gather materials for your next project.
- **Cozy up at Eagle Harbor Book Co.:** Lose yourself in a good read.

Bloedel Reserve: No trip to Bainbridge is complete without a visit to this nature reserve. I first learned about it in a college architectural history class at the University of Washington. With 140 acres of carefully cared-for gardens, you can't miss this. Deer, frogs, and birds all call the reserve home.

PEGASUS COFFEE

Sure, the scenery's stunning, but what really stuck with me was the sense of calm and clarity I felt from just being here.

Lunch at Café Hitchcock: With a nod to seasonality and local ingredients, this little café seems to do it all: kombucha on tap, loaded sandwiches, and daily soups. Dishes are colorful, veggie-rich, and packed with flavor.

Go tide pooling at Rockaway Beach: Since Bainbridge sits directly across the water from downtown Seattle, it offers marvelous skyline views. My favorite is from Rockaway Beach, which is tucked into a residential area with limited parking. True to its name, this rocky beach reveals tide pools during low tide and provides excellent ferry-watching opportunities.

Sip wine at Bainbridge Vineyards: End your day with a relaxing wine tasting at this sustainably crafted vineyard. Bainbridge Vineyards is known for its organic, B Corp–certified wines, and it's the perfect place to unwind with a glass in hand.

BLOEDEL RESERVE

SEATTLE SKYLINE

Dinner at Bruciato: If you're in the mood for pizza, Bruciato offers Neapolitan-inspired pies with both classic and creative toppings. Don't be surprised if your server hands you scissors to cut your pizza! And save room for the mouthwatering tiramisu—it's the ultimate end to your day.

DAY 3

Breakfast at Madison Diner: On your final day, dine in a retro train car from the East Coast. The inside is just as cool as the outside, with a nostalgic vibe that'll take you back in time. For something a little different, try the WaffleWich—a breakfast sandwich served between two golden waffles. It's a fun twist on a classic!

Visit the Bainbridge Island Japanese American Exclusion Memorial: Before leaving Bainbridge, take a moment to learn about the heartbreaking history of the Japanese Americans who lived here during World War II. In 1942, 227 residents were forcibly removed from their homes and sent by ferry to an incarceration camp. This moving memorial, managed by the National Park Service, honors their resilience and ensures their stories will never be forgotten.

The Takeaway: Just a stone's throw from Seattle, Bainbridge Island offers that perfect breath of fresh air when city life feels overwhelming. From sipping expertly crafted lattes in the storybook setting of Pegasus Coffee House to wandering beneath towering old-growth trees in Grand Forest, it's a place that naturally invites you to slow down and savor the moment.

Whether you're tide pooling at Rockaway Beach with the Seattle skyline as your backdrop or browsing downtown's cozy shops, Bainbridge delivers that magical mix of wonder, warmth, and whimsy. Sometimes the most refreshing adventures are hiding just across the water, waiting to remind you that island time isn't just a vacation mindset—it's a way of life worth embracing, even if just for a weekend.

SUNCADIA RESORT

13

CLE ELUM & ROSLYN

Introduction

The Snoqualmie Pass area, extending into Cle Elum, has long been a cherished getaway for western Washington residents. Its easy access via I-90 and its status as one of the most popular mountain passes make it a common stop for travelers moving between eastern and western Washington. Growing up, my family would pass through Cle Elum every summer on camping trips in Wenatchee and Leavenworth, but it wasn't until I started spending more time here that I discovered this mountain town offers so much more than a convenient pit stop.

During the winter, Cle Elum transforms into an outdoor recreation hub that welcomes everyone, not just seasoned skiers and snowboarders. My first experience at Summit Tubing Park had me grinning from ear to ear while racing my best friend Megan down the hill. While the covered lift is convenient, we found that walking back up the hill gave us more runs and definitely more laughs.

Cle Elum was also where I faced my apprehension about snowmobiling. As someone initially nervous about the experience, I can assure you it's as thrilling or as leisurely as you want it to be, as you are in total control of the speed. I wasn't winning any races, but I thoroughly enjoyed the peaceful ride through snow-covered forest service roads. Reaching viewpoints that overlook Lake Cle Elum, with its tranquil winter beauty, was a highlight. And if you keep your eyes peeled, you might spot rabbit tracks or other signs of wildlife in the snow—little reminders of nature's quiet presence made visible for a short season.

What makes Cle Elum special is its perfect winter balance: exhilarating outdoor adventures that embrace the season, complemented by cozy moments unwinding in hot tubs, browsing through local bookstores,

LAST RESORT SNOWMOBILE RENTAL

or savoring a warm cup of coffee at a charming café. It's a destination that invites you to slow down, explore, and create lasting memories.

At a Glance

Location: Kittitas County, Washington
Best Season to Visit: January through March
Suggested Duration: Two nights

Getting There

Seattle to Cle Elum: 82 miles, ~1 hour 15 minutes
Portland to Cle Elum: 236 miles, ~3 hours 45 minutes

> **Winter Driving Tip:** Snoqualmie Pass may require traction tires or chains during winter months. Check WSDOT (wsdot.wa.gov) conditions before departure and allow extra travel time for mountain weather.

Where to Stay

Suncadia Resort: This sophisticated mountain retreat offers accommodations from lodge rooms and condos to entire houses perfect for family getaways. With activities such as golfing, spa days, bike rides, and even glice skating, there's always something to enjoy. Some folks love it so much that they make it their permanent home!

SUNCADIA RESORT

TIMBER STILTS

Vacation rentals: Cle Elum has some incredible vacation rentals, and they're perfect for a cozy stay. Think A-frames, cabins with massive windows that let in all the natural light, and even a treehouse cabin called Timber Stilts, which I adore! There's a rental for every budget and taste.

Best Western Snowcap Lodge: While it might not be the cheapest option, Best Western Snowcap Lodge earns its spot for consistently excellent reviews. Plus, its location is super convenient, as it's right next to Gravity Coffee, a Safeway, and a fuel station, making it a practical choice.

Itinerary Outline

DAY 1

Snow tubing at The Summit: Kick off your adventure at Snoqualmie Pass with a thrilling ride down a five-hundred-foot hill! Make sure to book your spot in advance, as this popular activity fills up fast. With eighteen lanes to choose from and a covered lift to whisk you back to the top, all you need is your snow gear and a big smile. Each session lasts one hour and forty-five minutes, providing plenty of time for multiple runs and photo opportunities.

Dinner at The Brick Saloon: Step into history at Washington's oldest continuously operating bar. The Brick Saloon offers a unique ambiance complete with a century-old running water spittoon along the bartop, brought over from England. Savor classic American dishes, and don't miss out on the cocktails and mocktails to wind down your first adventurous day.

DAY 2

Breakfast at Basecamp Books and Bites: Books, coffee, and delicious food—what more could you ask for? Start your day with the large Basecamp Burrito—perfect for sharing. Or, if you're visiting later in the day, check out the speakeasy downstairs for a cozy, hidden gem vibe.

> **Bestie Tip:** Don't be surprised if you end up lingering longer than planned—this is the kind of place where the coffee flows and the books practically find you. No

need to bring your own read, as chances are, you'll stumble upon one (or a few) that you won't want to put down.

Explore our national forests on snowmobiles: Feel the thrill of the open trail with snowmobile rentals from The Last Resort. They offer top-notch machines (heated throttles, anyone?) and all the gear you'll need, so just show up ready for adventure. With electric snowmobiles now available, you can experience this adventure with modern comfort and environmental consciousness.

Check Out Speelyi Beach: Before heading back to town, stop at Lake Cle Elum for a winter surprise. If you've only visited in the summer, prepare to be amazed—winter's significantly lower water levels reveal a vast, unexpected beach. This eight-mile-long lake offers stunning views, especially on a crisp day when the surrounding snowcapped mountains create a breathtaking backdrop. It's a sight that will leave you in awe!

Lunch at Dru Bru: Sample local German-style brews, such as the Cle Elum Classic or Pacific Crest Pale, paired perfectly with a pizza. My favorite is the Sweet Heat—hot honey and chili flakes give it an awesome kick!

Stroll downtown Cle Elum: Spend a relaxing afternoon exploring East First Street's small businesses.

- Grab an expertly roasted coffee at **Pioneer Coffee Roasting Co.**
- Pick out a perfect plant companion at **Bright & Day**.
- Enjoy sweet treats and local favorites at **Cle Elum Bakery**.
- Hunt for unique mountain treasures at **Attic Treasures Thrift Store.**

Dinner at Swiftwater Cellars: For an upscale dining experience, head to Suncadia's Swiftwater Cellars. The ambiance nods to nearby Roslyn's coal mining history, with

BASECAMP BOOKS AND BITES

touches such as pickaxes at the entrance. It's an ideal spot for a celebratory dinner, paired with fine wine and rich history.

DAY 3

Breakfast at Stella's: Wrap up your trip with a visit to this cozy café, where warm vibes and hearty breakfasts await. Whether you're in the mood for a smoothie, a sandwich, or a colorful wrap, there's something for everyone.

Go fat biking: Have you ever ridden a bike in the snow? If not, this is an ideal place to start. Roslyn, about eight miles from Cle Elum, is home to a community of fat biking aficionados and groomed trails, which means the snow is packed down so that you can ride on it without sinking in. Pick up a rental from the Ride Roslyn bike shop, where you can start your ride. Choose from the easy, flat Coal Mines Trail or head up to the hills of Roslyn Urban Forest for more of a challenge. Whenever Kyle rides these trails, let's just say he's not in a hurry to head home.

> **The Takeaway:** For the ultimate winter recharge, the Snoqualmie Pass and Cle Elum areas deliver a snow-filled playground that welcomes every adventure level. Whether you're racing down the hill at the Summit Tubing Park, exploring frosty trails on a fat bike, or cruising forest roads on a snowmobile, the outdoors here invites you to play hard and breathe deep. When you're ready to slow down, cozy up at Basecamp Books and Bites—where great coffee, hearty food, and the just-right book come together. It's a destination that proves winter can be embraced, explored, and thoroughly enjoyed just eighty-two miles from Seattle.

14 LINCOLN CITY

Introduction

I know the sun doesn't actually shine all winter long on the Oregon Coast, but it sure feels like it does when you're surrounded by the vibrant hues of handblown glass floats and the warmth of a heartfelt welcome in Lincoln City. While the jury's still out on my absolute favorite coastal town, Lincoln City's name is definitely in the running—and for good reason.

What sets this place apart is its incredible Finders Keepers program, the first coastal tradition to gather public excitement around local artistry in such a hands-on way. Each year, over three thousand handcrafted glass floats are hidden along the shore for lucky beachcombers to discover and keep. Lincoln City pioneered this magical tradition over twenty-five years ago, and there's no better time to participate than in winter, when crowds thin and floats are most plentiful. Every beach walk with Lilo becomes a treasure hunt filled with possibility.

Beyond the thrill of float hunting, Lincoln City offers seven miles of public shoreline—the longest stretch in the area—plus cozy coffee shops, eclectic boutiques, and local art galleries that provide perfect indoor retreats on rainy days. It's a town filled with genuine character where retirees swap stories with visitors, artisans showcase their work with pride, and friendly dogs trot beside their owners along the endless sandy beach.

The magic of this place isn't just in finding that perfect glass float or catching a rare sunny winter day by the sea. It's how leaving always feels difficult, with me standing on the shore, lingering just a little longer, and already planning my return. No matter how many times you visit Lincoln City, it always pulls you back for more coastal treasures and warm community connections.

At a Glance

Location: Central Oregon Coast
Best Season to Visit: January through March
Suggested Duration: Two nights

Getting There

Seattle to Lincoln City: 270 miles, ~5 hours 25 minutes
Portland to Lincoln City: 97 miles, ~2 hours

Coastal Driving Tip: Weather can change quickly on the coast—check conditions and pack layers for both sunny and stormy possibilities.

Where to Stay

Salishan Coastal Lodge: This 4-star retreat is more than just a place to stay—it's a complete experience. With a golf course, bike skills park, aerial adventure park, zip lines, and an indoor tennis center, the adventure opportunities are endless. Whether you're swinging a club or soaring through the treetops, you'll find it hard to run out of things to do here!

The Coho Oceanfront Lodge: Picture cozying up by a firepit with your toes in the sand, perched on a bluff with the soothing sound of waves crashing below. The Coho offers beach bonfire magic without the hassle, perfect for winter stargazing. The mid-century modern rooms add a touch of chic to your coastal escape.

Inn at Wecoma: Centrally located and top-rated, this hotel balances comfort and value. If you want to be close to shops and restaurants, this is a great option right off Highway 101.

Itinerary Outline

DAY 1

Go float hunting—Finder's Keepers: Walk Lincoln City's seven miles of public shoreline during daylight (above the high tide line) to find colorful treasures placed by Float Ferries. They hide over three thousand every year between Roads End and Siletz Bay! To my surprise, they hide more during the winter than in the summer, so this is the perfect time for float hunting.

Bestie Tip: If you're as obsessed with glass art as I am, don't worry if beach hunting doesn't yield treasures! Head over to the Lincoln City Glass Center or Volta Glass Gallery, where you'll find an impressive selection of glass orbs and art. Bonus—they're located just across

ROADS END TIDEPOOLS

the street from each other and share the same owner, making it a breeze to explore both.

Dinner at Pelican Brewing Company: After an afternoon of float hunting, there's no better way to wind down than with a tasty meal at Pelican Brewing Company. Nestled on the scenic Siletz Bay, this craft brewery offers a warm, modern ambiance that's perfect for soaking in the views. I couldn't get enough of its tower of onion rings paired with a spicy dipping sauce, while Kyle devoured the Tsunami Burger.

PACIFIC GRIND CAFÉ

DAY 2

Breakfast at Pacific Grind Café: Start your day at my go-to Lincoln City spot! This eclectic coffee shop has all the charm you'd expect from a coastal town, and they serve up some of the best locally roasted coffee from nearby Depoe Bay. My latte arrived with the prettiest latte art in a quaint ceramic mug, and I couldn't help but smile as I sipped it. In a hurry? They also offer a convenient drive-through service.

Go on a beachcombing tour with a local expert: One of the most popular of Explore Lincoln City's Exploriences—free learning events led by locals—is the beachcombing tour with rock hound Laura Joki. Laura is a treasure trove of knowledge about the area's geology. For example, did you know that the Oregon Coast is geologically connected to Yellowstone? On this tour, you'll learn how to identify gemstones, fossils, and agates, and then you'll head out to find your own! This awesome experience is offered only in the winter, and during our tour, it was clear how much the community admires Laura. Residents would stop her to share their latest rock finds, highlighting just how infectious the curiosity for rockhounding can be. Check the Explore Lincoln City website for the tour schedule.

ROCKHOUNDING WITH LAURA JOKI

Bestie Tip: With Lincoln City boasting the most public beaches on the Oregon Coast, choosing which one to explore can be a bit overwhelming (trust me, I've been there). A favorite for its wonderfully sandy shores is D River State Recreation Site. Known for being the spot where the world's shortest river meets the ocean and for hosting annual kite festivals, it's a must-visit. Keep an eye out for playful seagulls—they love riding the river's current out to the ocean and then flying back just to do it again. It's so amusing to see!

Lunch at Pub Fish & Chips: A trip to the coast wouldn't be complete without indulging in a crispy basket of fish and chips, and this is hands down our favorite spot! We've been coming here for years, and it never disappoints. The casual, welcoming atmosphere, paired with the friendly service, makes every visit feel like home. Its traditional English-style cod fish and chips come in sharing-size portions—three to four pieces are just right for two adults. It's a classic that always hits the spot!

Shop small businesses and explore Lincoln City's unique local artisan scene

- **Summer Gap:** For more than thirty years, artist Connie Shoemaker's boutique has featured nautical, wildlife, and seasonal glass art pieces, and she also creates custom orders. I completely lose track of time here!
- **Searenity Boutique:** This boho gem in the Salishan Marketplace specializes in locally made items crafted by women in the community. It's perfect for finding something special while supporting local artisans.
- **Rock Your World:** Visit rock hound Laura Joki's unique shop, which features handmade jewelry, crystals, and gemstones with stories behind each of them.

Lincoln City Outlets: Beyond typical shopping options, these outlets feature beloved outdoor brands such as Pendleton, Columbia, and Eddie Bauer. And for a fun twist, Scout Northwest Trading Co., a PNW lifestyle store, offers axe throwing—a unique and exciting way to cap off your shopping adventure!

Tide pooling at Roads End State Recreation Site: A local recommended Roads End as their top beach, and it's easy to understand why. Located at the northernmost end of town, this was the first Lincoln City beach we ever visited—we couldn't wait to feel the sand beneath our feet! Time your visit during low tide to spot starfish, sea anemones, and crabs.

> **Bestie Tip:** While I haven't had the chance to try it myself, I've heard the bluff next to the parking lot is an epic spot for winter storm watching. It's not for the faint of heart—you'll need to bundle up and be ready for whipping winds and sideways rain. If cozy is more your vibe, consider finding a restaurant or a stay with a view, such as The Coho Oceanfront Lodge, and enjoy the wild weather from the warmth of indoors.

Indoor alternative: Oregon Coast Aquarium: If you've had your fill of salty air, drive thirty minutes south to this incredible aquarium. The Passages of the Deep exhibit's tunnel design transports you underwater, and you find yourself immersed among fish and sharks!

Dinner at Thai Bay Restaurant: Some evenings, nothing beats enjoying takeout in your hotel room as the sun sets over the coast. On nights like these, we turn to Thai Bay Restaurant for authentic, fresh Thai cuisine. My go-to hot basil stir-fry features vibrant chili basil sauce draped over bell peppers, onions, and mushrooms—a sensory delight that never fails to awaken my taste buds. It's the perfect way to end a day of adventure, wrapped up in the cozy flavors of a delicious meal.

DAY 3

Breakfast at The Wildflower Grill: For a sit-down breakfast in a charming garden-like setting, there's hardly a lovelier spot than The Wildflower Grill. Nestled in a converted cottage, this cozy café is famous for its unique take on French toast: dipped in orange juice for an extra burst of flavor! Adding blueberries takes this dish to the next level.

OREGON COAST AQUARIUM

The Takeaway: Winter in Lincoln City reveals a treasure trove of coastal delights just a short drive from Portland. From searching the shore for vibrant, handblown glass floats that splash color across the rugged beach, to connecting with passionate local experts such as rock hound Laura, this town offers endless ways to engage with both the coast's natural wonders and welcoming community. Whether you're discovering your first glass float, learning to identify agates, or simply savoring that perfect latte while storm watching, Lincoln City proves that the best coastal experiences happen when you slow down enough to truly treasure hunt—both on the beach and within yourself.

SPRING GETAWAYS

OLD TOWN PORTLAND

15 PORTLAND

Introduction

Spring in Portland is pure magic—with birds chirping and nature bursting back into life after the winter, the Rose City shows off its most vibrant colors. My first visit here was a girls' trip with my close friend Megan, whom I've known since seventh grade. It was just the two of us, and it marked our first adventure as adults. We decided to fly from Seattle to Portland on what the flight attendant jokingly called the "I-5 Express," and she wasn't wrong—the flight took less than an hour, and we'd barely settled in before we were already descending.

We stayed downtown at the Woodlark Hotel, and our loft suite instantly won us over. The black spiral staircase, tall ceilings, and gorgeous bathroom (because a luxurious bathroom totally elevates the getting-ready process!) made such an impression on Megan, who'd had no idea what to expect. We ended up spending a lot of time just enjoying the room, indulging in brunch at the Bullard Tavern, and winding down our evenings at Abigail Hall, where we savored moon pies in a chic, feminine setting—all without leaving the hotel!

Our café-hopping adventure completely blew me away. Between ube lattes, coconut cream cold brews, and *hojicha* lattes, I found myself seriously considering whether I should move to Portland! We lucked out with warm sunshine that felt like summer arriving early, allowing us to explore in dresses instead of winter layers—always a win in the Pacific Northwest spring.

What draws me to cities such as Portland is how effortlessly they blend urban energy with outdoor access. Spring rain means Portland's natural beauty is at its peak—lush, vibrant, and impossibly green. You can explore the tranquil Chinese and Japanese gardens, hike through an urban redwood forest, and marvel at the Willamette River. We did all this and more in just two days, proving that Portland delivers maximum adventure in minimal time.

At a Glance

Location: Northwestern Oregon
Best Season to Visit: March through April
Suggested Duration: Two or three nights

Getting There

Drive: Seattle to Portland: 174 miles, ~2 hours 45 minutes
Fly: ~55 minutes by plane
Train: Amtrak Cascades, ~3 hours 30 minutes

Where to Stay

CASCADA Thermal Springs + Hotel: It's safe to say the Pacific Northwest doesn't have another luxury wellness hotel quite like this. Tucked into Portland's Alberta neighborhood, CASCADA feels like a hidden oasis with serene soaking pools and modern, minimalist rooms where you can instantly relax. If you're seeking something equal parts restorative and unforgettable, this is it.

Woodlark Hotel: A perfect option if you're visiting without a car, like we did. Right in the heart of the city, it offers easy walkability to shops, restaurants, and parks, with Ubers always just around the corner for convenience. The design is beautiful, with contrasting tones and thoughtful green touches throughout. It offers the kind of comfort and style that feels luxurious, but at a price that's surprisingly reasonable.

Kimpton RiverPlace: Exuding a lodge-like ambiance, this hotel offers a higher-end experience with riverside cottages or suites that feature unforgettable touches such as soaking tubs, cozy fireplaces, and serene river views. It's pet friendly too!

LESS AND MORE COFFEE

Itinerary Outline

DAY 1

Get drinks from Less and More Coffee: After settling into your accommodations, head over to this cozy coffee kiosk, set in a vintage bus stop, for a Korean-style pick-me-up. My favorite is the ube latte—it reminds me of the drinks I get in Hawaii. And there's also a coffee-free version! The most popular drink, iced tiramisu latte, is a must-try.

Enter book heaven at Powell's City of Books: Ready to get lost in a sea of books? As the world's largest independent bookstore, Powell's has something for everyone. I was anchored in the romance and local-interest sections and left with a few treasures to take home.

Shop Portland-made goods at MadeHere: This all-in-one shop is perfect for a leisurely browse. We loved the ceramics, gourmet popcorn, and candles. If you're a fan of the PNW, you'll adore this gallery-style store filled with locally crafted goods.

DOLLY OLIVE

Dinner at Dolly Olive: Just a short walk away, this southern Mediterranean kitchen offers a welcoming, delicious dining experience. The bucatini pasta pomodoro and tagliatelle al burro were delicious Italian comfort foods. Bonus: it's located across from a beautiful stone church that I admired through the window as we dined.

DAY 2

Breakfast at Ken's Artisan Bakery: I'm obsessed with the Oregon Croissant filled with blackberries, blueberries, and hazelnuts—it tastes like spring in pastry form. We loved this neighborhood gem so much that we returned the morning of our departure, and waited in line with our luggage in tow!

> **Bestie Tip:** Order an extra pastry to enjoy later, especially since the morning's activities are in the same area. Megan and I savored ours on a bench on the Pittock Mansion grounds while soaking up the view.

Explore the Portland Japanese Garden: More than just a peaceful stroll, this garden offers a traditional Japanese teahouse, a Cultural Village, and educational demonstrations such as tea ceremonies and bonsai art. I completely lost track of time watching koi fish swim beneath waterfalls—it's meditative in the best way.

Hike in the Hoyt Arboretum: You might not expect to be able to access twelve miles of hiking trails so close to downtown—I certainly didn't! Discover redwood trees, living fossils, and a bamboo forest that feel worlds away from the urban energy below.

Tour the Pittock Mansion: Dating back to 1914, this historic hilltop home showcases stunning French Renaissance architecture complete with grand staircases and early twentieth-century furnishings. Don't miss the panoramic views of Portland with Mount Hood in the backdrop—absolutely breathtaking on clear spring days.

Eat lunch at Deschutes Brewery Portland Public House: Portland's upbeat brewery scene is worth exploring, and Deschutes Brewery in the stylish Pearl District is a favorite. I'm obsessed with its spiked lemonade (hard seltzer) and Anytime Lemonade Shandy. For your entrée, check out the specials.

Enjoy shaved ice at Wailua Shave Ice Portland: Would you believe me if I told you the best shaved ice I've ever had wasn't in Hawaii but right here in Portland? Wailua Shave Ice completely blew me away. My go-to order is the ube shaved ice, topped with dreamy ube foam, a sprinkle of coconut shavings, and rainbow mochi. It was love at first bite—and just as pretty as it was delicious.

WAILUA SHAVE ICE

PORTLAND JAPANESE GARDEN

WILLAMETTE RIVER CRUISE

Visit McCall Waterfront Park: Known for its gorgeous cherry blossoms, this popular spot features a hundred pink trees planted in 1990. Spring timing is crucial here—peak bloom typically happens in early April, creating Instagram-worthy scenes along the waterfront.

> **Photography Tip:** Visit during golden hour for the most stunning blossom shots, and bring a wide-angle lens to capture the full tree canopies.

Take a sunset river cruise on the Willamette: One of Portland's most memorable activities is taking a sunset cruise aboard the *Portland Spirit*. Bring warm layers (a blanket is a great idea) and relax on the upper deck with patio-style furniture. You'll learn local history while spotting wildlife along the way. While there's an indoor dinner option, we chose the sightseeing tour for a more laid-back experience.

Bestie Tip: As you board your sunset river cruise, the *Portland Spirit* crew will snap a photo of your group. At the end of the night, you'll have the option to purchase a printed keepsake copy. It was an immediate yes from me that went straight onto my fridge!

Dinner at Luc Lac Vietnamese Kitchen: Warm up after your boat ride with fresh bowls of pho, which has been made from family recipes passed down through generations. Delicious bowls and fun cocktails are also on offer.

DAY 3

Breakfast at Bernstein's Bagels: For a quick bite that packs a punch, try New York–style bagels, baked fresh daily. Pair with a homemade schmear or go all out and get it with a sandwich. My favorite is the popper—with sweet onion, avocado, and egg.

Coffee from Kalesa Coffee: If I had to choose just one coffee shop in Portland, it would be this Filipino-inspired gem. Its coconut cold brew with ube whip is as heavenly as it looks. Every time I'm in Portland, even if I'm just passing through, I make a point to stop here for this perfect purple drink.

Explore the Lan Su Chinese Garden (weather backup): If spring rain arrives, the Lan Su Chinese Garden offers covered walkways and pavilions perfect for experiencing traditional Chinese architecture and design. The authentic Ming Dynasty–style garden, rotating cultural exhibits, and teahouse provide a peaceful respite while keeping you dry.

KALESA COFFEE

Final neighborhood stroll: Spend your remaining time exploring neighborhoods such as the Alberta Arts District or Hawthorne Boulevard, discovering more local coffee shops, vintage stores, and street art that capture Portland's creative spirit.

The Takeaway: If you're planning a girls' getaway, I can't think of a better destination than Portland. Whether it's café hopping through the city's experimental coffee culture, river cruising at golden hour, or getting lost in Powell's literary wonderland, you'll never run out of discoveries in the Rose City. All those delicious ube delights are just the cherry on top of a destination that perfectly balances urban sophistication with Pacific Northwest charm. Spring in Portland proves that some cities are simply meant to be experienced with your best friend, one perfect latte at a time.

WENATCHEE RIVER

16

WENATCHEE

Introduction

Do you have special places your family returns to year after year? For me, that place is Wenatchee, which is nestled in a lush river valley and lovingly known as the "Apple Capital of the World." Every summer, my grandparents would pack up their motor home, my parents would load our trailer, and we'd spend two unforgettable weeks together. Those trips were always summer break highlights and the stories I'd eagerly share when teachers asked about our vacations.

I could probably write a whole book about Wenatchee, but some of my fondest memories include swimming the full length of the designated area at Wenatchee Confluence State Park (a huge accomplishment for a kid!), cooling off in the Columbia River between bike rides with my dad and brother, and matching tie-dye shirts with my grandpa that we made ourselves. With around two hundred days of sunshine a year, it's the perfect place to soak up the outdoors.

While those memories are rooted in summer, spring has quickly become my favorite season to visit here as an adult. The surrounding hills burst into life with yellow arrowleaf balsamroot and purple lupine, painting the landscape in golden and lavender hues. Trails such as Horse Lake Reserve and Sage Hills feel straight out of a set of *The Sound of Music* when the wildflowers are in bloom, and they are just minutes from town.

In recent years, I've discovered hiking trails I return to again and again, and I've learned that paddleboarding on a river is a lot trickier than it looks! Visiting Wenatchee in the spring means quieter trails, fewer crowds, and the chance to experience the valley's beauty in full bloom. If you've ever longed for a weekend getaway filled with sunshine, flowers, and riverside memories, this might just be your new favorite underrated spot.

At a Glance

Location: Chelan County, Washington
Best Season to Visit: April through May
Suggested Duration: Two nights

Getting There

Seattle to Wenatchee: 148 miles, ~2 hours 30 minutes
Portland to Wenatchee: 298 miles, ~5 hours

Where to Stay

Hilton Garden Inn Wenatchee: For nature lovers, this chic hotel just steps from the Columbia River is paradise. I remember riding my bike along the Apple Capital Loop Trail and seeing this hotel as it was being built and thinking, *If I needed a hotel in Wenatchee, I would want it to be that one.*

Best Western Plus Wenatchee Downtown: Find everything you need for a comfortable stay here, in a space brightened by funky hues of yellow.

Camping at Washington State Park: Wenatchee is home to two state parks: Lincoln Rock and Wenatchee Confluence. Both offer camping with scenery that is tough to top.

Itinerary Outline

DAY 1

Bike the Apple Capital Recreation Loop Trail: Every Wenatchee trip with my family includes a ride on this iconic ten-mile loop trail. This scenic route winds through town, crossing both sides of the river via two bridges. I've been biking here since I was six, and it's a place that always surprises me when I spot something new, such as osprey, marmots, or deer. Whether you bike, walk, or run, this trail is essential. Bring plenty of water and sunscreen as it's mostly sun-exposed!

Dinner at McGlinn's Public House: While I've enjoyed McGlinn's delicious Southwestern salad many times as takeout (we usually find a shady spot by the river to savor meals), the indoor ambiance strikes a perfect balance between cozy and lively. The patio seating also provides lovely river views during warmer spring evenings.

DAY 2

Breakfast at The Wild Huckleberry: Is there anything better than breakfast in a charming craftsman cottage? I think not! Start your day with the giant cinnamon roll—it's ideal for sharing as an appetizer. If you're feeling adventurous, try the strawberry waffle, but request light whipped cream if you prefer less sweetness.

Explore a spring wildflower wonderland: Springtime in Wenatchee is magical, especially on the trails at Horse Lake Reserve and Sage Hills. The purple and yellow wildflowers blanket the hills, creating a dreamy landscape. Whether you take a short stroll or venture higher for the best blooms, you'll be in awe.

> **Bestie Tip:** Wear light-colored long sleeves and pants to help spot and protect against ticks. Always do a quick check after your hike and pack a pair of fine-tipped tweezers (different from bathroom tweezers).
>
> **Photo Tip:** Try shooting from a lower angle and play with your camera's depth of field—focus on a single bloom with a wide aperture to blur the surrounding sea of flowers for that dreamy, soft look. Just remember to stay on the trail—your boots belong on dirt, not petals!

SAGE HILLS

Take a cold plunge at Wenatchee Confluence State Park: Nothing beats the chill of glacier-fed waters after a hike! Head to the swim area at Wenatchee Confluence State Park for a refreshing dip. Facilities are available, so you can easily change into dry clothes afterward.

Lunch at Union Hill Cider Co.: For a midday treat, this cidery offers breathtaking views and tasty handmade ciders. Enjoy a flight of its best blends and feel free to bring your furry friends along because adventures are always better with them!

Walk through Ohme Gardens: For years, I admired the towering evergreens on the hillside from Highway 97, only to discover the enchanting Ohme Gardens. This ninety-year-old oasis features waterfalls, pools, and winding stone paths that feel like something out of a storybook.

Sunset hike to Saddle Rock: Easily recognizable from afar, Saddle Rock offers one of the best sunset views in Wenatchee. The hike is short but rewarding, totaling just over three miles with a nine-hundred-foot elevation gain. The dusty trail adds to the adventure, so wear shoes that can handle a bit of dirt!

PYBUS PUBLIC MARKET

Dinner at the Saddle Rock Pub & Brewery: After your hike, unwind at this family-friendly brewery. Its menu is packed with comforting dishes such as grilled cheese with tomato bisque, or try the Wenatchee calzone complete with local apples—a perfect regional touch!

DAY 3

Breakfast at Café Columbia: This is my absolute favorite coffee spot in Wenatchee. Its artisan coffee drinks and fresh-from-scratch pastries are irresistible. While it offers a full kitchen menu, I'm always drawn to the display of baked goods—it never disappoints.

Walk in Horan Natural Area: For a final breath of Wenatchee's natural beauty, take a peaceful walk through these wetlands, where the Columbia and Wenatchee Rivers converge. It is home to giant cottonwoods, songbirds, and deer. If you're lucky, you might even see a spotted fawn!

Optional: Downtown exploration: If time allows, explore Wenatchee's charming downtown area with local shops, art galleries, and the weekly farmers' market (seasonal). Don't miss Firehouse Pet Shop—they have the cutest cat and dog finds that go beyond your typical pet store. It's a sure way to step into the community culture beyond outdoor adventures.

Bestie Tip: If your pup has a little too much fun on the trails, head to the self-wash pet spa at Firehouse Pet Shop. First come, first served.

The Takeaway: It's easy to overlook Wenatchee with its more famous neighbor Leavenworth drawing the crowds, but this wildflower wonderland more than holds its own. With easy access to outdoor adventure right from downtown, plus more than two hundred days of annual sunshine, it's a hidden gem that nature lovers discover and return to, year after year. One spring visit among the blooming balsamroot and lupine, and you'll understand why the Apple Capital Valley has captured hearts for generations. Sometimes the most treasured destinations are the ones that grow with you, offering different gifts in every season of life.

ORCAS ISLAND FERRY

17 ORCAS ISLAND

Introduction

If an adventure includes a ferry ride, count me in! The journey to Orcas Island, the largest of the San Juan Islands, offers one of the longest ferry rides in western Washington. That means plenty of time to soak in the stunning views of Mount Baker, tiny forested islands, and the occasional sea lion or seal. I can't think of a single ferry ride that hasn't flown by, and sometimes I wish I could hit pause and savor it a little longer.

Even on the rainiest, windiest days, I find it refreshing to step onto the outer decks. There's often partially enclosed outdoor seating that protects you from the elements—just bundle up and leave your hat in the car!

The San Juan Islands feel refreshingly down-to-earth. With no traffic lights and miles of unspoiled nature, Orcas Island embodies true island vibes—the kind where relaxation comes easier outside peak summer crowds. To me, the island's shape resembles a pair of lungs, which feels fitting because you can truly breathe easy here. It's the perfect place to unplug and free yourself from distractions (you might not have phone service anyway!).

The primary village, Eastsound, sits nestled on a narrow strip of land connecting the west and east sides of the island. This charming hub houses most of the shops and restaurants, offering friendly invitations to connect with the soul of Orcas. Remember that these islands are home to both people and delicate wildlife ecosystems, so take it slow, treat others with kindness, and don't stress too much if the ferry schedule shifts. And do your part to conserve water—while there's plenty of salt water all around, fresh water is a precious resource here.

At a Glance

Location: San Juan Islands, Washington
Best Season to Visit: April through May
Suggested Duration: Two nights

Getting There

Seattle to Orcas Island: 81 miles, ~1 hour 30 minutes + 1 hour ferry ride
Portland to Orcas Island: 255 miles, ~4 hours 15 minutes + 1 hour ferry ride

Bestie Tip: While summer definitely calls for a ferry reservation, spring sits right on the edge. I'd still recommend booking about two months ahead when they open online in late March. If you miss that window, reservations open again two weeks and three days before sailing. Plan to arrive about an hour early—the Anacortes ferry terminal isn't a bad place to soak up views while you wait!

Where to Stay

Outlook Inn: If walkability is your top priority, this charming coastal hotel in the heart of Eastsound is a fantastic choice. And if you're ready to treat yourself, its suites with private water views are unbelievable—seriously, when can I move in?

Vacation rentals: With limited hotels on Orcas, cabins and cottages on Airbnb are a flexible option. Many of these rentals boast incredible views and offer a peaceful retreat, making them perfect for a relaxing getaway.

Camping at Moran State Park: Love camping with a view? The lakeside spots at Moran State Park are hard to beat! While spring is offseason, summer spots fill up fast, so I highly recommend booking your site online ahead of time.

TURTLEBACK MOUNTAIN PRESERVE

Itinerary Outline

DAY 1

Explore the Turtleback Mountain Preserve: As soon as we got off the ferry, we couldn't wait to hit the trails. The Ship Peak loop at Turtleback Mountain Preserve offers stunning views of the surrounding islands and Orcas's interior farmlands hugged by forests. This three-mile hike with an 860-foot elevation gain provides an active, rewarding start to your trip.

Dinner at The Madrona Bar & Grill Orcas Island: Score waterfront views at this airy, quaint seafood restaurant. Kyle loves the coconut shrimp with a sweet Thai chili sauce. Make a reservation ahead of time for the best tables.

DAY 2

Breakfast at Brown Bear Baking: For a sweet taste of France, head to this cheerful yellow bakery with bright orange accents. The small-batch pastries, bread, and quiche are so good you'll want to stock up for later adventures.

Stroll Eastsound: Enjoy a leisurely morning wandering around Orcas's local businesses.

- Step into the island's fascinating past at **Orcas Island Historical Museum**.
- Design custom souvenirs to commemorate your trip at **Print Shop Northwest**.
- Add island-themed reads to your library from **Darvill's Bookstore**.
- Find the perfect piece for your home at **Crow Valley Gallery**.

Eat lunch at The West Side Kitchen: This tiny but mighty spot serves up delicious Asian fusion flavors you won't find anywhere else on the island. With a rotating menu, every visit is a new culinary adventure.

Afternoon at Moran State Park

Cascade Loop Trail (Four Waterfalls Hike): Start with this short 1.2-mile trail that passes four beautiful waterfalls—an island adventure you won't forget. Spring runoff makes the falls particularly impressive.

Mount Constitution: Explore the highest point in the San Juan Islands by foot, car, or bike—the views will leave you speechless.

MOUNT CONSTITUTION

Our first visit was on a rainy day when we were completely clouded in, but our luck changed the next time when the clouds cleared to reveal countless islands in the foreground with mountains leading into Canada beyond.

> **Photography Tip:** The stone tower at the summit provides 360-degree views—try visiting during both midday for clarity and late afternoon for golden light.

Hike around Cascade Lake (optional): If energy and time allow, this favorite trail skirts the lake's perimeter. You can also kayak or paddleboard if you bring your own gear—spring rental availability varies.

Dinner from Ladybug Pizza: Grab a slice or a whole pie and pack it out picnic-style to catch sunset at North Beach. There's something magical about enjoying island pizza while watching the sun dip below the horizon.

DAY 3

Breakfast at Olga Rising: This old island-style café serves up breakfast biscuit sandwiches and the best lattes on Orcas. Try a special seasonal drink such as a Spiced Morning Latte (with brown sugar and cinnamon).

Find treasure at Orcas Island Pottery: Before you catch your ferry home, take a trip to the Pacific Northwest's oldest pottery studio. Often described as a fairyland, this charming spot is tucked into a forest, with handcrafted ceramics scattered throughout the garden-like grounds. It was the first pottery shop I ever visited, and I haven't found another quite like it since.

> **Shopping Tip:** Allow extra time here—the magical setting and unique pieces make it easy to lose track of time, and you don't want to miss your ferry!

MORAN STATE PARK

The Takeaway: How does chasing waterfalls on an island sound? That's the everyday magic of Orcas Island. Between fern-filled forests, peaceful lakes, panoramic overlooks, and creative small businesses that give the island its soul, this place leaves a lasting impression that can call you back again and again. The combination of outdoor adventure and artistic community creates something special—a destination where you can hike to mountain summits in the morning and discover handcrafted treasures in enchanted pottery gardens by afternoon. And yes—bring your pup!

18 SALEM REGION

Introduction

As someone who tracks flower bloom dates in my calendar so that I never miss a festival, the start of a new season fills me with anticipation. I plan trips around these blooms, basically waiting on the edge of my seat for nature's grand reveal. My spring tradition includes the tulip and daffodil fields of the Skagit Valley and South Sound, plus wildflower blooms on the eastern side of the Cascades. But recently, I set out to discover some lesser-known spots, particularly in Oregon, and I was pleasantly surprised by the hidden gems in the Salem region of the Willamette Valley.

While many Portland residents know about the famous Wooden Shoe Tulip Festival, countless other nature spots in the area

DELBERT HUNTER ARBORETUM AND BOTANICAL GARDEN

deserve equal attention. Salem, Oregon's capital city, offers the perfect spring base camp for exploration. Beyond the State Capitol's blooming cherry trees, surrounding communities feature stunning waterfalls, thrilling mountain biking trails, and tranquil gardens that would take more than a weekend to fully experience—but hey, you've got to start somewhere, right?

We made downtown Salem our base camp, which was ideal for exploring the smaller neighboring communities. It was convenient for walking to grab morning coffee or to enjoy dinner after a day of adventure. Plus, the proximity to Minto-Brown Island Park was a huge bonus—can you tell I have a thing for islands? Embrace the warmer temperatures and hopefully sunnier skies by exploring as many hikes and gardens as you can. That said, keep an open mind—about half our trip was cloudy and drizzly. I had packed my woven sun hat expecting sunshine, but it proved equally handy for keeping light rain off my face!

Here's some encouragement if the weather doesn't cooperate: bring waterproof gear and a sense of wonder, and you'll likely have the natural spaces all to yourself. Personally, I count that as a win. Springtime in the Willamette Valley is calling—will you answer?

At a Glance

Location: Mid-Willamette Valley, Oregon
Best Season to Visit: April through May
Suggested Duration: Two or three nights

Getting There

Seattle to Salem: 219 miles, ~3 hours 30 minutes
Portland to Salem: 46 miles, ~50 minutes

> **Travel Tip:** Salem's central location makes it perfect for exploring the wider Willamette Valley, with easy access to both mountain and valley attractions.

Where to Stay

Holman Riverfront Park Hotel Salem: Picture downtown convenience paired with serene riverside access. You're just steps away

WOODEN SHOE TULIP FESTIVAL

from outdoor adventures and the city's vibrant dining scene. For an added touch of comfort, opt for a room with a kitchenette.

Vacation rentals: Immerse yourself in the charm of Salem by staying in a unique, historic home. These vacation rentals offer a glimpse into the city's neighborhoods, giving you a more personalized experience.

Best Western Plus Mill Creek Inn: Conveniently located near I-5, this pet-friendly hotel is known for its warm hospitality. It's an ideal option for travelers looking for a comfortable stay that is close to attractions without breaking the bank.

Itinerary Outline

DAY 1

Explore the Wooden Shoe Tulip Festival: With forty acres of vibrant tulips and over four decades of tradition, this festival is Oregon's largest tulip celebration. It's a dreamy setting, perfect for photos and a leisurely stroll. A unique highlight is Portland Rose Balloons, which offers both traditional hot-air balloon rides and tethered experiences that keep you closer to the ground. Tickets are available online, so book ahead to secure your spot.

Explore The Oregon Garden: Nurture an appreciation for Pacific Northwest ecology at this expansive botanical garden. Take a narrated tram tour around twenty diverse specialty gardens. Afterward, wander the gardens at your own pace and check out the gift shop for some fun finds.

Dinner at Venti's: For those who love vegan-forward menus and craft beer, Venti's is a must-visit. The Hawaiian bowl and spicy penne mac are my favorites, and the flavor profiles are sure to impress. In the evenings, the underground Beer Vault offers a cozy space to enjoy a drink. It's a gem you'll wish were in every city.

DAY 2

Breakfast at Word of Mouth Neighborhood Bistro: For homey vibes and hearty dishes, this is the place to be—and the secret is out, so come early. The cinnamon roll pancakes are one of the best breakfasts I've ever had, exceeding all my expectations. Check the website for current wait times, since reservations aren't available.

Explore the Delbert Hunter Arboretum and Botanical Garden: Even with a light drizzle, our walk along the seven miles of serene trails was magical. The rain enhanced the lushness of the native Oregon plants, particularly the western trilliums that were in full bloom.

Hike at the Baskett Slough National Wildlife Refuge: I had never seen landscapes quite like these rolling green hills, oak groves, and fields of yellow wildflowers. The easy one-mile Rich Guadagno Trail is perfect for a soothing bird-watching session.

Lunch at the Wild Pear: Take a break from your adventures with Vietnamese-inspired dishes in a cheerful, historic setting. Highlights include the pho dip sandwich, pear chicken pizza, and Cecilia's bowl with sesame-ginger dressing.

Explore Silver Falls State Park: Home to ten breathtaking waterfalls, Silver Falls is a must-see. For the ultimate experience, tackle the 7.2-mile Trail of Ten Falls. Or if you're short on time, focus on the South Falls day-use area and the North Falls trailhead. Walking behind a waterfall is an unforgettable experience!

Dinner at Bo & Vine Burger: Handcrafted milkshakes drew us in, but the Parmesan garlic fries made us stay. This spot is known for its creative smash burgers and chicken sandwiches—a perfect end to a day of exploring.

DAY 3

Breakfast at The Governor's Cup: Start your morning at this artsy, laid-back café. Grab a drink and a breakfast sandwich—the Romance in Durango or Wasabi & Avocado are top picks. If the weather's nice, the outdoor seating area is a delightful spot to relax.

BASKETT SLOUGH NATIONAL WILDLIFE REFUGE

Tour the Deepwood Museum & Gardens: Since Salem is known for its museums, it's worth visiting one before you head home. Deepwood is particularly special to me, and it's more a feeling of place and the passion of its caretakers. Enjoy Queen Anne–style Victorian architecture, nature trails, and rotating exhibits of antique period-piece treasures. Call ahead to save your spot on a tour.

Explore Minto-Brown Island Park: If you're visiting Salem for the first time, this park is a great spot to walk, run, or bike. Start at Riverside City Park and explore from there.

SILVER FALLS STATE PARK

BLACK ROCK MOUNTAIN BIKE AREA

DEEPWOOD MUSEUM

Bestie Tip: If you're into mountain biking, check out Black Rock Mountain Bike Area. With awesome jumps, skill-building areas, and nine miles of trails, it's a thrilling alternative.

The Takeaway: Birds chirping, buds bursting, and skies that can't quite decide between sunshine or showers—these are the telltale signs that spring has arrived in the Pacific Northwest. One underrated spot to soak it all in? The Salem region. With blooming gardens, cascading waterfalls, and endless rows of tulips painting fields in impossible colors, this corner of the Willamette Valley feels like a love letter to spring itself. Whether you're tracking flower blooms like I do or simply seeking that perfect balance of outdoor adventure and cultural discovery, Salem proves that sometimes the best spring destinations are hiding right in plain sight, just waiting for curious travelers to answer their call.

MOUNT HOOD

19 HOOD RIVER

Introduction

As the snow melts in the mountains each spring, the Pacific Northwest transforms into a waterfall wonderland, and few places capture this magic like the Columbia River Gorge. This ancient, rugged canyon, carved by the mighty Columbia River, straddles the border between Washington to the north and Oregon to the south. It's a dramatic landscape filled with natural beauty and adventure, making it a must-visit for nature lovers and thrill-seekers alike.

Hood River, affectionately known as the "Windsurfing Capital of the World," has completely captured my heart. Powerful winds funneling through the Gorge create ideal conditions for windsurfing and kite-boarding, offering an exhilarating spectacle that's as captivating to watch as it must be to experience. I'll admit that I sometimes feel a little nervous watching kite surfers ride those white caps, but that high-energy atmosphere is absolutely part of Hood River's irresistible character.

Beyond water sports, Hood River offers so much more. The cheerful downtown is brimming with local shops, cozy cafés, and farm-to-table restaurants. Kyle loves the top-rated mountain-biking trail system that winds through scenic forests with breathtaking Mount Hood views, while I'm drawn to the valley's agricultural bounty—rolling orchards, vineyards, and farm stands bursting with fresh produce, wines, and handmade goods.

Springtime in the Gorge extends an irresistible invitation to explore, with cascading waterfalls, blooming wildflowers, and a landscape coming to life after the winter thaw. Hood River is your gateway to this natural wonderland.

At a Glance

Location: Columbia River Gorge, Oregon
Best Season to Visit: April through May
Suggested Duration: Two nights

HOOD RIVER HOTEL

Getting There

Seattle to Hood River: 228 miles, ~3 hours 30 minutes
Portland to Hood River: 63 miles, ~1 hour 15 minutes

> **Travel Tip:** The drive from Portland follows the scenic Historic Columbia River Highway, offering waterfall views along the way.

Where to Stay

Columbia Cliff Villas: For spacious suites with breathtaking views of the Columbia River, it doesn't get much better than this stunning resort perched right above the water. Upgrade your stay with cozy fireplaces and expansive balconies for the ultimate luxury experience.

Best Western Plus Hood River: If you want to be right on the water with easy access to the shore, this is a fantastic option. Be sure to request a room with a view to make the most of your stay!

Hood River Hotel: Built in 1911, this historic hotel is listed on the National Register of Historic Places. This vintage gem packs plenty of character into each suite, with a legendary lobby featuring a checkered floor and a striking fireplace, adding a touch of history to your getaway.

Itinerary Outline

DAY 1

Walk the Hood River Waterfront Trail: Start at Hood River Waterfront Park and walk east along this 2.8-mile paved pathway that connects a few miniparks. Keep an eye out for kite surfers riding the white caps. Not going to lie, sometimes I feel a little nervous for them, but then again, the exhilarating energy is part of the character of Hood River.

Dinner at Ferment Brewing Company: What I remember most about this brewery is the high-spirited atmosphere, great outdoor patio views, and the delicious salmon dishes. Oh, and saying hi to a pup or two!

DAY 2

Breakfast at Broder Øst: Begin your day with a Scandinavian breakfast full of surprises in an intimate setting. The Danish pancakes with lemon curd and lingonberry jam were my personal favorite. If you're in the mood for brunch, its creative champagne cocktails are a must-try. During our stay at the Hood River Hotel, we couldn't resist this spot, which is conveniently connected to the lobby.

BRODER ØST

WAHCLELLA FALLS

Hike to Wahclella Falls: Waterfalls abound in this area, and this is a fantastic option for a day hike. This 2.4-mile trail with about three hundred feet of elevation gain is manageable and rewarding.

> **Bestie Tip:** If it has rained in the last forty-eight hours or is forecast to rain, it's best to skip this trail because of the increased risk of landslides or flooding in the recently burned forest.

Stroll downtown Hood River

- **Made in the Gorge:** Shop locally crafted goods and regional art.
- **Alpine Sea Co.:** Elevate your everyday bag game with quality gear.
- **Waucoma Bookstore:** Pick up local-interest reads and regional guides.

Lunch at the River Daze Café: My family first discovered this gem on a drive home from Bend, Oregon, and we've been hooked ever since. The made-from-scratch sandwiches are a treat, whether you prefer hot, cold, or a build-your-own option. Don't forget to try the espresso!

Enjoy Mount Hood views: Just minutes from town, Panorama Viewpoint offers stunning, unobstructed views of Mount Hood—get your cameras ready!

Hood River Fruit Loop scenic drive: Cruise south on Highway 35 to explore this scenic thirty-five-mile route dotted with more than thirty charming, family-owned farms and orchards. You can sip locally made wine, appreciate the slower pace of country roads, and soak in the springtime beauty of blooming fruit trees. Pears, apples, cherries, and peaches all show off in shades of pink and white, turning the valley into a dreamy blur of petals.

> **Bestie Tip:** For a self-guided map and to check which farm stands are open, head to hoodriverfruitloop.com.

Dinner at Riverside: As the name suggests, this restaurant offers stunning river views paired with farm-to-table food. The pasta, made with locally sourced ingredients, is especially delicious. Pair it with a selection from its extensive menu of regional wines—I recommend the Cuvée One Sparkling Rosé.

DAY 3

Breakfast at Doppio Coffee: Savor your last morning in Hood River with reasonably priced drinks, grilled panini, and 100 percent fruit smoothies on its inviting outdoor patio. If there are any downtown shops you missed, now's your chance to explore them.

Go mountain biking at Post Canyon: Hit the trails at Post Canyon, where you can enjoy world-class flow that will have you grinning from ear to ear! Keep an eye out for Mount Hood views as you zip through the forest. New to biking? Join a half- or full-day tour with Hood River Mountain Biking Adventures, which includes bike and helmet rental.

POST CANYON

DOPPIO COFFEE

Weather Backup Options

- **Brimstone Boulders:** Go bouldering in a former church turned climbing gym.
- **Hood River Distillers:** Take tours and tastings at this historic distillery, perfect for an indoor adventure.
- **Antique shopping:** Browse Hood River's charming antique stores and vintage shops along the main downtown corridor.

The Takeaway: Spring in the Columbia River Gorge doesn't whisper—it roars to life with waterfalls tumbling down ancient basalt cliffs, wildflowers carpeting meadows, and wind carving endless stories across the water. Hood River stands at the heart of it all, offering that perfect balance of adrenaline-pumping adventure and orchard-sweet serenity. Whether you're chasing mountain trails through evergreen forests, sipping wine among blooming fruit trees, or watching kite surfers dance with the wind, this vibrant riverside town delivers a season's worth of wonder in just one weekend.

20 KIRKLAND

Introduction

Known for its many waterfront parks, the eastern side of Lake Washington is a staycation spot that doesn't require traveling far from the city. In fact, it's just a bridge away from Seattle. Whether you're seeking new experiences, focusing on wellness, or reconnecting with nature, this area offers a balance of it all. Plus, it's surprisingly dog friendly. We brought our dog Lilo with us for a summer getaway, and watching the sunset over the lake by an outdoor firepit felt like we'd traveled much farther than we actually had.

During our visits over the years, we've primarily explored the small area between downtown Kirkland to the north and Carillon Point to the south, maximizing our time while taking full advantage of lakefront activities, such as swimming, kayaking, and even sauna sessions. There's something genuinely restorative about being close to the water, especially when the pace of life feels slower here.

This cozy itinerary includes these relaxing activities, along with a few exciting adventures that pushed me out of my comfort zone over the years. Kirkland is where I took my first seaplane ride, and as luck would have it, no one else booked the same flight, so I got to sit in the cockpit next to the pilot! Takeoff and landing felt like skimming across the water, and before I knew it, we were soaring above the city. The most striking moment was during a turn, when we faced the Olympic Mountains with nothing but water below us. It felt surreal, almost dreamlike.

Even with both feet on solid ground, Kirkland offers incredible experiences. I've tried virtual reality gaming, wandered through beautiful state parks, and even relaxed in a floating sauna (okay, maybe that one didn't include feet on the ground). More than anything, I've made wonderful memories in Kirkland over the years, and I hope this itinerary inspires you to create some of your own. Whether you're seeking adventure or just looking to unwind, Kirkland is a place where your imagination is the limit.

At a Glance

Location: King County, Washington
Best Season to Visit: March through May
Suggested Duration: Two nights

Getting There

Seattle to Kirkland: 11 miles, ~ 20 minutes
Portland to Kirkland: 82 miles, ~ 2 hours 40 minutes

Where to Stay

The Lodge at St. Edward Park: Hidden in a forest on slopes above the lakeshore, this historic Catholic seminary has been transformed into a quiet retreat close to the city. My favorite touches include the wallpaper featuring architectural designs for the original building, a hallway of local art, and peaceful trails—it is a state park, after all.

The Woodmark Hotel: This luxury lakefront option sits right on Lake Washington. We brought Lilo here and had a fantastic stay, though we did notice that the hotel tends to attract a more corporate clientele, creating a sophisticated but less leisurely atmosphere.

VON SAUNA

Vacation rentals: For more affordable stays, consider renting an apartment, guest unit, or small house in Kirkland. This provides cost-effective ways to experience the area while enjoying the homelike comforts.

Itinerary Outline

DAY 1

Dinner at Cedar + Elm: Located in The Lodge at St. Edward State Park, this restaurant features an aesthetically pleasing space that once served as a seminary dining hall. The menu emphasizes seasonal, locally sourced ingredients. I particularly enjoy the more casual lunch menu, so if you arrive earlier in the afternoon, it's worth sampling.

Explore Saint Edward State Park: After dinner, take a walk around the park grounds, the largest remaining natural area on Lake Washington. Don't miss the Saint Edward Grotto, a peaceful spot where priests gathered to worship.

DAY 2

Breakfast at Carillon Kitchen: This café focuses on healthy, delicious options, such as super juices and avocado toast. On a sunny day, the outdoor patio is a lovely spot to enjoy breakfast. During our stay at The Woodmark, we walked across the plaza to dine here—it was so convenient!

Get rejuvenated in Washington's first floating sauna: Kick off the day with a wood-fired sauna session at Von Sauna, located at Carillon Point. Since it's on the water, you can also take a cold plunge into Lake Washington—a refreshing experience, even for beginners. I literally took the leap, which was my first one here, and I found it a perfect complement to the sauna heat. By spring, the lake is warming up, making it more comfortable for those new to cold plunges.

Explore Marymoor Park: Walk around four miles of trails at this popular park, where you're likely to be outnumbered by dogs! The star attraction is a forty-acre off-leash dog park with Sammamish River access.

SEATTLE SKYLINE SEEN FROM A SEAPLANE

It makes me happy just walking through the dog park, even when my pup isn't with me. Keep an eye out for the heron rookery, where you might see dozens of great blue herons.

Lunch at DERU: Known for being a fast-casual eatery, this is the perfect spot to order takeout and enjoy picnic-style (though you can dine in). I can't tell you how many times we've ordered the smoked turkey sandwich—it's very shareable—and the thinly shaved apple slices are excellent.

> **Bestie Tip:** We love eating at waterfront tables at Waverly Beach Park for stunning views of Seattle as waves lap the shore. Restrooms are available.

Ride on a seaplane above Lake Washington: Flying on a seaplane is a quintessential Pacific Northwest experience. A few years ago, I got to fly with Kenmore Air for the first time. We flew over Seattle, and it was pretty surreal seeing familiar landmarks, such as the University of Washington campus and the Space Needle, from the sky.

Stroll downtown Kirkland: Just east of Marina Park Al Locke Pavilion, you'll find a few blocks of lively local businesses in a friendly setting. This area is very walkable, and we enjoyed a pleasant walk from Carillon Point.

- **Aloha Northwest LLC:** Discover authentic Hawaiian artisan goods.
- **The Whole Cat and Kaboodle:** Visit the cat lounge (reservations required) or grab treats for feline friends.
- **Bobae Coffee & Tea:** Enjoy Instagram-worthy boba drinks.

Dinner at BeachHouse: Close out the day with waterfront dining featuring fish tacos, salmon, and other American classics. Be sure to save room for dessert—either the crème brûlée or the chocolate espresso torte (gluten-free).

Evening virtual reality gaming at Sandbox VR (optional): If you still have some energy, try virtual reality gaming! I had no idea what I was getting into when I first signed up. My group got suited up and played Squid

KAYAKING AT CARILLON POINT

Game, featuring mini games similar to the Netflix show. It was a fun and fascinating experience, in which you can see yourself and your friends, but as characters.

DAY 3

Breakfast at 5 Stones Coffee Co.: Personalize your perfect slice of toast, whether sweet or savory. Pair it with a signature coffee drink or loose-leaf tea.

Go kayaking into the Yarrow Bay Wetlands: Rent a kayak at Carillon Point to explore a little-known slice of nature paradise. It requires a little bit of paddling through lily pads, but if you look closely, you should be able to spot the water "trail." We saw great blue herons, baby ducks, and a muskrat! Rentals are available from Waterfront Adventures starting in May.

The Takeaway: Seattle sits beautifully tucked between Puget Sound and the vast expanse of Lake Washington—and this weekend getaway shines a spotlight on the lake's northwest corner. Just minutes from downtown, you can soak in a floating sauna, wander fascinating forested state parks, and take off on seaplane adventures. Whether you're seeking the thrill of cold plunges and aerial views or the simple pleasure of watching the sunset over water with your dog by your side, Kirkland proves that memorable adventures don't require traveling far from home. Sometimes the most refreshing getaways happen when you discover magic hiding in plain sight, just one bridge away from the everyday.

SIUSLAW RIVER BRIDGE

21 FLORENCE

Introduction

There's nothing more satisfying than kicking off your shoes and digging your toes into the sand after a drive to the Central Oregon Coast. While Florence isn't far from Eugene and the I-5 corridor, seeing the ocean makes it feel like you've traveled much farther. After our long car ride from Washington, Lilo was eager to stretch her legs, so we rerouted to North Jetty Beach. This stretch of coastline, with its tall grasses, light-colored sand, and seashells scattered along the shore, was one of the most beautiful we'd seen. The peaceful setting, where the Siuslaw River meets the Pacific, created a serene atmosphere for unwinding.

A highlight of our trip was finally visiting the Sea Lion Caves, a place that had been on my list for years. Standing in America's largest sea cave, 215 feet below ground level, felt surreal. Our first visit taught us an important lesson about wildlife viewing—we didn't spot any sea lions and were told we might not before purchasing tickets, but the awe-inspiring ocean views and informative exhibits made the experience worthwhile anyway. Luckily, a rain check allowed us to return, and the next month, we were surrounded by nearly 150 Steller sea lions. The sight and sound of these marine mammals in their natural habitat were unforgettable, and it was probably more rewarding given that this was our second try.

Florence offers so much more than its famous sand dunes, though those are undeniably thrilling too. We discovered that the Historic Old Town, which we had driven past on previous road trips, is a lively hub of coastal culture and incredible dining. I had my first taste of the Cannonball at Mo's Seafood & Chowder, where the clam chowder in a sourdough bread bowl was the ultimate comfort food. The town's vibrant dining scene pleasantly surprised us, offering everything from Pacific fusion dishes to hearty Italian fare, with each spot more inviting than the last.

SEA LION CAVES

At a Glance

Location: Central Oregon Coast
Best Season to Visit: April through May
Suggested Duration: Two nights

Getting There

Seattle to Florence: 344 miles, ~5 hours 20 minutes
Portland to Florence: 171 miles, ~2 hours 40 minutes

> **Travel Tip:** The drive from Eugene to Florence on Highway 126 offers beautiful forest scenery before revealing dramatic coastal views.

Where to Stay

Vacation rentals: Retreat to private homes along the ocean or the Siuslaw River, where you can be just steps from the shore while enjoying the seclusion and comfort of your own space.

Best Western Pier Point Inn: Tucked in a scenic spot by the river, just across the bridge from Old Town. Indulge in omelets as part of the complimentary breakfast, and don't miss the indoor pool with its stunning views!

Super 8 Florence: Conveniently located near the main shopping and dining district, this hotel offers a comfortable stay that won't break the bank.

Itinerary Outline

DAY 1

Explore Sea Lion Caves: Visit the largest sea cave in the country by taking an elevator twelve stories down into the heart of the cave. When sea lions are present (typically from fall through early spring), you might see up to 150 Steller sea lions lounging on rocky ledges. Watching their agility as they navigate terrain that would definitely hurt us humans is impressive! Just prepare mentally for the natural aroma—these are wild animals in their authentic habitat.

SEA LION CAVES

Tour the brightest lighthouse on the Oregon Coast: From Sea Lion Caves, you'll spot the iconic Heceta Head Lighthouse. For a closer look (and because exploring lighthouses is a must on the Oregon Coast), park and take the short half-mile trail. Snap some photos and enjoy a tour of this historic beacon.

Drive to Heceta Beach: On your way back to Florence, stop by the stunning Heceta Beach for views of the postcard-worthy Cape Creek Bridge. Feeling adventurous? You can hike directly from the lighthouse—just be prepared for a seven-mile trek that will be uphill on your return trip.

Dinner at The Pono Hukilau: For a warm, Hawaiian welcome into town, head to The Pono Hukilau. It's the perfect spot to kick off your trip with Pacific fusion dishes, such as Spam *musubi*, pineapple teriyaki chicken, and kimchi fried rice.

MO'S

DAY 2

Breakfast at Little Brown Hen Café: Start your day with a classic diner-style breakfast at this cozy neighborhood gem. Be sure to bring cash—it has an onsite ATM if you forget.

Explore Oregon Dunes National Recreation Area: Get ready for an adrenaline rush! The dunes feel like a moonscape but sound like the ocean. Rent a quad or side-by-side from Torex ATV Rentals, which is conveniently located at the dunes.

Lunch at Mo's Seafood & Chowder: If you try one thing on the Oregon Coast, make it the Cannonball—a sourdough bread bowl brimming with New England–style clam chowder. I envied Kyle's choice—and, thankfully, got to help him finish it! Alongside the comfort seafood dishes, every seat offers a view of the river.

Stroll through Historic Old Town: Discover Florence's cultural heart through its charming local businesses:

- **The River Gallery:** Tap into the vibrant local art scene.
- **Kitchen Klutter:** Shop specialty kitchen accessories and coastal-themed goods.
- **Wind Drift Kites:** Pick up beach kites and toys for seaside fun.
- **Books 'n' Bears:** Peruse used books and find a perfect beach read.

▲ NORTH JETTY BEACH

Shopping Tip: Many Old Town shops offer local handmade artisan goods that make excellent souvenirs and support the coastal community.

Catch the sunset at North Jetty Beach: On our first visit to Florence, this was our go-to spot to stretch our legs (and our dog's!). You'll find where the Siuslaw River meets the ocean, making it a fantastic spot to relax. The walk through the dunes is all part of the experience.

Dinner at 1285 Restobar: For a cozy end to your day, enjoy elevated Italian cuisine in this intimate setting. Whether you choose the lasagna, chicken parmigiano, or manicotti florentine, you can't go wrong. If you're a wine lover, the selection of Californian and Oregon wines is top-notch.

DAY 3

Breakfast at Sweet Magnolia Bakery & Café: Tuck into this adorable town bakery for satisfying pastries, such as the cinnamon swirly twirly sticky buns, which are best enjoyed on the quaint outdoor patio. Or you can walk over to the Siuslaw River Bridge Interpretive Site for a scenic breakfast. Don't forget to grab a croissant sandwich for the road!

The Takeaway: Clam chowder served in warm bread bowls, caves echoing with barking sea lions, and sweeping sand dunes are just a glimpse of what makes Florence so captivating along the Central Oregon Coast. From the thrill of ATV adventures through moonscape dunes to the simple pleasure of watching the sunset where the river meets the ocean, this coastal town delivers experiences both exhilarating and restorative. Whether you're a longtime Oregon Coast enthusiast or discovering this stretch for the first time, Florence proves that some destinations reward both patience and spontaneity.

22

TRI-CITIES

Introduction

How does an underrated foodie's paradise sound? Located in Eastern Washington, the Tri-Cities are sure to surprise and delight your taste buds with bold, flavor-packed Asian street food, giant veggie sandwiches you'll dream about for weeks, and vineyards serving charcuterie boards alongside flights of wine, cider, and spirits. This region knows how to serve a meal with a side of wow.

Despite the name, the Tri-Cities actually refers to a cluster of towns—Richland, Kennewick, and Pasco—with neighboring West Richland growing rapidly too. As you drive through, it all blends together, creating the feeling of one big riverside community where life flows at the pace of the Columbia, Yakima, and Snake Rivers, which all converge here in a spectacular meeting of waters.

When I think back on my time in the Tri-Cities, I picture golden hills dotted with vineyards, wide-open skies, and winding rivers reflecting the sunset. Beyond the natural beauty, what really surprised me was how rich the region is in history, especially its connection to the Manhattan Project. Alongside Los Alamos and Oak Ridge, Hanford, Washington, played a pivotal role in developing the first atomic bombs. The B Reactor, the world's first full-scale nuclear reactor, is now a national historical site you can tour (yes, it's fascinating, and yes, it's free!). I first learned about Hanford in a college history class, but seeing it in person gave me an entirely new perspective on this pivotal moment in world history.

Another unexpected highlight? Climbing aboard the sail of the USS *Triton*, the first submarine to circumnavigate the globe underwater. It's a tight squeeze, but even if you opt for the virtual tour (I did!), imagining life underwater for sixty days is an awe-inspiring experience.

THE LODGE AT COLUMBIA POINT

At a Glance

Location: Southeastern Washington
Best Season to Visit: March through April
Suggested Duration: Two nights

Getting There

Seattle to Tri-Cities: 220 miles, ~3 hours 20 minutes
Portland to Tri-Cities: 216 miles, ~3 hours 20 minutes

Where to Stay

The Lodge at Columbia Point: Offering a warm and inviting refuge along the Columbia River, this 4-star hotel—the only one of its kind in the area—is made for celebrating special occasions. I could spend all day at the covered open-air pool and steaming jetted tub! There's also a top-rated onsite restaurant.

Hampton Inn Richland/Tri-Cities: Situated in a scenic spot along the river, this hotel provides easy access to walking paths and parks. For an extra elevated touch, opt for a room with a balcony to sip your morning coffee alfresco.

Richland Inn and Suites: This recently refreshed hotel is conveniently located within walking distance of the river and nearby restaurants. It's a well-balanced choice for travelers seeking comfort and affordability.

Itinerary Outline

DAY 1

Check out the REACH Museum: Familiarize yourself with Hanford's history and the mid-Columbia Basin's natural heritage. As someone who didn't know much about the Tri-Cities before visiting, I can say that this is the perfect place to start your adventure. Don't miss the short gravel trail to learn about wildlife in the area.

Walk through the Chamna Natural Preserve Trail: For some fresh air, head to this beautiful 276-acre riparian park along the Yakima River. With eleven miles of relatively flat trails, you can create your own adventure—whether it's a quick jaunt to see the river or an extended bird-watching hike.

CHAMNA NATURAL PRESERVE

USS *TRITON* SAIL PARK

Bestie Tip: During spring, trails closest to the river may become muddy or even flooded and might need to be avoided. Keep an eye out for beaver tracks and chew marks!

Dinner at Soi 705: Trust me—make this your first dinner stop so you have time to come back again. The food is that good. This vibrant Asian street food spot delivers bold flavors and playful twists, and the spicy K-pop bites? Easily the best chicken I've ever had. Crispy, saucy, and just the right amount of heat—pure magic.

DRUMHELLER'S

DAY 2

Breakfast at Drumheller's: Start your day with a delicious and beautifully plated breakfast at Drumheller's, located inside The Lodge at Columbia Point—just steps from our room! Kyle and I couldn't choose between the Palouse eggs Benedict and the baked apple French toast, so we ordered both to share. They totally hit the spot.

Explore USS *Triton* Sail Park: Visit this part of the Manhattan Project National Historical Park to see the sail of the record-setting nuclear-powered submarine. While impressive from the outside, a tour of the inside makes a lasting memory. Tours can be requested online, with virtual options available for those concerned about claustrophobia (like I was!).

COLUMBIA PARK

Explore the Manhattan Project National Historical Park: Dive deeper into Washington's World War II atomic history with a visit to the visitor center in Richland. From there, hop on a free, narrated forty-five-minute tour bus ride to the B Reactor in Hanford. Located within a secure area managed by the US Department of Energy, guided tours are the only way to access this site, and they provide a fascinating look at how plutonium was produced for the atomic bomb. This is truly a one-of-a-kind experience that I learned so much from!

Lunch at Graze: Sometimes simple is best, and that is true at Graze. Enjoy salad, soup, or a sandwich packed with veggies. I recommend trying the veggie torta, as it's a local favorite. You won't believe how much flavor is packed in with the chipotle dressing, jalapeños, and pickled carrots.

Visit Goose Ridge Estate Winery: Relax with your drink of choice—wine, cider, or vodka—in a beautiful vineyard setting. The spiced cranberry cider made with Yakima Valley apples is my personal favorite. On a chilly day, the Monson Ranch Cherry Brandy will warm you right up. We loved being able to bring Lilo, and she loved sharing the scrumptious charcuterie board with us. I like to say that this is my dog's favorite winery in the Pacific Northwest!

Dinner at Sterling's Restaurant: Dine riverside at this longtime local favorite known for its generous menus and premium sides, such as fettuccine Alfredo. Save room for dessert—the six-layer chocolate cake is so good you'll want to take an extra slice home with you.

GOOSE RIDGE ESTATE WINERY

DOWNTOWN ANACORTES

DAY 3

Breakfast at Ethos Bakery: Before departing, savor beautifully crafted pastries and lattes (complete with heart-melting latte art) in a chic boho space. It's the perfect send-off for your Tri-Cities culinary journey.

Explore Columbia Park: Stretch your legs one final time on the paved Columbia Park Trail. Along the way, enjoy river views of the Pioneer Memorial Bridge, bird-watching, and soaking up the sunshine before you hit the road.

> **The Takeaway:** Whether you're sipping cider at a pet-friendly winery, exploring riverside trails, or diving into the stories of the past, the Tri-Cities deliver a one-of-a-kind weekend getaway in Southeastern Washington. It's a destination that seamlessly blends exceptional cuisine, natural beauty, and profound historical significance—perfect for foodies, nature enthusiasts, and history buffs alike. Come for the weekend, and leave with a growing list of reasons to return.

23 ANACORTES

Introduction

For many years, when the temperatures become warm enough to camp comfortably, this drive-to island is one of the first places we visit. Yes, Anacortes is on an island—Fidalgo Island, to be exact! Besides the mountains, there's nowhere else that gives me that overwhelming sense of belonging to something bigger, that reminder of how the ocean connects the entire world.

During a solo spring hike in the Anacortes Community Forest Lands—a hidden gem well off the beaten path for most tourists—I experienced one of those perfect nature moments that capture why I love this place so much. It was a gorgeous day with blue skies and slight breezes as I hiked around Little Cranberry Lake on trails that hug the shoreline, sometimes coming quite close to the water.

ANACORTES COMMUNITY FOREST

Partway through, I looked up to see something unexpected—a family of geese waddling right down the trail! I stopped to give them space, watching as they wrapped up snacking and slipped back into the lake. Everything felt fresh, green, and full of new life—a splendid spring scene. Later, in a denser forested area, I rounded a bend and locked eyes with a mama deer walking toward me with her tiny spotted fawn, the smallest I'd ever seen, probably only a few weeks old. Seeing baby animals like that is a spring phenomenon, and it honestly took my breath away. After my initial surprise, I stepped behind a tree to let them pass. Moments like these remind me that nature is the ultimate shared resource—and also to always keep my camera ready!

I've said it before, and I'll say it again: I love Washington's ferries! Anacortes hosts the ferry terminal connecting passengers to the San Juan Islands. While the San Juans are covered in separate itineraries, you'll definitely spot ferries gliding by during your visit to Fidalgo Island. There are also several marinas and even a smaller ferry to neighboring Guemes Island. You might not recognize it as a ferry at first glance because it doesn't look like the others, but that's all part of the charm.

This is my happy place, offering a perfect balance between peaceful trails and connections to the wider world around me.

MOUNT ERIE

At a Glance

Location: Skagit County, Washington
Best Season to Visit: April through June
Suggested Duration: Two nights

Getting There

Seattle to Anacortes: 80 miles, ~1 hour 15 minutes
Portland to Anacortes: 254 miles, ~3 hours 50 minutes

Where to Stay

Majestic Inn & Spa: Stay in the heart of downtown at an elegant boutique hotel housed in a historic 1890s hardware store. Treat yourself to suites with balconies, fireplaces, and stunning views.

Nantucket Inn Anacortes: This charming bed-and-breakfast with coastal vibes features gourmet breakfasts and bright, beautifully designed rooms with large windows that let in plenty of natural light.

Camping at Washington Park: Perched above Rosario Strait, this city park feels like its own little island. Campsites include hookups, bathrooms with showers, and access to an epic hiking trail.

Itinerary Outline

DAY 1

Explore Mount Erie: For breathtaking views, head to the highest point on Fidalgo Island. You can drive to the top or take the scenic trail—it's a five-mile round trip with one thousand feet of elevation gain. This is also a popular spot for climbing.

Dinner at Naung Mai Thai Kitchen: Enjoy flavorful Thai classics in a cheerful family-owned restaurant. The spicy basil dish is unmatched, truly spicy, and has been a favorite of mine for years.

DAY 2

Breakfast at the Calico Cupboard Café: Pacific Northwest country breakfasts don't get better than this local institution. The made-from-scratch pastries are irresistible, especially the legendary cinnamon roll. Pair it with the homey vibes, and you're off to a great start.

Pelican Bay Books & Coffeehouse: Wander through aisles of secondhand books until you find one (or two) that spark joy. Then, settle into a cozy corner with a cup of coffee—this place does both, and it does them well. Don't miss its house-made syrups; honey-cardamom is my personal favorite.

Walk out onto the Deception Pass Bridge: Even if you've been here before, it's a must-see when visiting Anacortes. Park at Scenic Vista Parking to walk the bridge and feel the wind in your hair. On the way back, stop at Pass Island for postcard-worthy photos. If time allows, explore the rest of Deception Pass State Park—it's seriously worth it.

Lunch at Agave Taqueria: Satisfy your cravings for authentic Mexican food at this welcoming spot. Whether you're in the mood for tacos, burritos, enchiladas, or fajitas, it's got you covered.

Explore Guemes Island: Just a stone's throw away, Guemes is a small, charming island most people overlook. Take the Guemes–Anacortes ferry (less than ten minutes) and drive, bike, or walk on. I'd recommend biking as it's peaceful and scenic, and I think we saw more deer than cars!

DECEPTION PASS BRIDGE

Guemes Island Activities:

- **Hike Guemes Mountain:** Take a 1.2-mile trek each way with 550 feet of elevation gain through forest and prairie landscapes to jaw-dropping views of islands and Mount Baker.
- **Guemes Island General Store:** Find souvenirs, light bites, and meals, and stock up on drinks for your island exploration.
- **Peach Preserve:** Stroll through multiple ecosystems on your way to pristine beaches.
- **Dog Woods:** Wander this nature preserve filled with native trees and abundant wildlife.

Timing Tip: Plan your return ferry timing carefully—service is limited, and you don't want to get unexpectedly stuck on the island.

Dinner at Coconut Kenny's: A real contender for the best pizza in the Pacific Northwest, with tropical goodness in every bite. The Spicy Islander, Tiki Tan, and Waikiki are simply amazing.

Catch the sunset at Cap Sante: Overlooking the town and the marina, this is the go-to spot for a postcard-worthy sunset to end your day. We've seen a variety of wildlife here, including deer, bald eagles, and seals. You can thank me later!

DAY 3

Explore Washington Park: Go for a refreshing morning walk out to Green Point. This meadow reveals spectacular views of the San Juan Islands and Rosario Strait. If you're lucky, you might see a pod of porpoises swimming by!

Breakfast at Good Bagels: Head out of town on a high note with a hand-rolled bagel sandwich and coffee for the road.

The Takeaway: Anacortes is a sanctuary kissed by salty air. This easy-to-reach island escape offers wildlife that greets you around every corner—especially in spring, when goslings and fawns roam—and something increasingly rare: genuine peace and connection to nature just over an hour from Seattle. Whether you're walking bridges suspended over rushing waters, sharing trails with families of geese, or watching the sunset paint the marina in golden light, Anacortes invites you to unplug, reconnect with nature, and settle into a waterfront community. It's the kind of place where nature still feels like the ultimate shared resource, and every visit reminds you why some destinations become happy places that call you back year after year.

SEATTLE SKYLINE AND FERRY

24

SEATTLE

Introduction

"It's always gloomy in Seattle." That's what some people want you to believe. But as someone who went to college in the Emerald City, I promise there's more to it than meets the eye—and no, I'm not telling you to visit during summer. By the end of my freshman year of college at the University of Washington, I was totally convinced that a never-ending spring in Seattle would be heaven.

After classes, I'd find myself walking barefoot on a beach, breathing in the fragrance of blooms, and hopping on ferries just to enjoy the ride. Spring brings brilliant blue skies, snowcapped Olympic Mountains, and perfectly comfortable weather. As a journalist for *The Daily*, my college newspaper, I wrote a wellness column called "A Breath of Fresh Air," which highlighted parks while exploring research about how spending time in nature positively impacts our well-being. Between this work and my natural inclination to spend my free time outdoors, I discovered beauty beyond the famous cherry blossoms at The Quad, though those do live up to the hype.

Rain or shine, Seattle offers incredible opportunities to connect with nature on different levels. The Seattle Aquarium provides glimpses into the Salish Sea's underwater world, with the Window on Washington Waters exhibit modeled after the ocean at the northwesternmost point of the state, and what the creatures swim in is real seawater pumped from below! The underwater dome feels like being in a submarine. Plus, the aquarium houses seriously cute otters.

Seattle is the perfect place for museum hopping, whether you're exploring the rock-and-roll vibes of the Museum of Pop Culture or uncovering Indigenous art and dinosaur fossils at the Burke Museum. The city's museums showcase creativity and history while providing a cozy retreat when the weather doesn't cooperate.

First-time visitors will love this itinerary designed for car-free exploration. Flying into Seattle–Tacoma International Airport? No problem—public transport, such as Link light rail, and good walking shoes will get you everywhere you need to go, from breathtaking Sky View Observatory perspectives to fresh seafood at Pike Place Market.

At a Glance

Location: King County, Washington
Best Season to Visit: March through April
Suggested Duration: Two nights

Getting There

Portland to Seattle: 174 miles
~3 hours by car
~3 hours 25 minutes by train
~55 minutes by plane

Where to Stay:

Thompson Seattle, by Hyatt: The floor-to-ceiling views of Elliott Bay are so good, you'll be tempted to stay inside all day at this sleek spot that you can walk basically everywhere from—I'm speaking from experience!

The State Hotel: If a trendy boutique hotel is more your style, find yourself in the center of it all and snap photos of the locally inspired modern art along the way.

Homewood Suites by Hilton: This hotel is just a short walk across a pedestrian bridge to the quieter side of the waterfront. Not the bustling, touristy part, but the stretch filled with parks, pocket beaches, and locals out for a jog.

Itinerary Outline

DAY 1

Take a harbor cruise: If it's your first time in Seattle, this is the ideal way to kick things off. Hop on a cruise with Argosy Cruises to get your bearings—and take in the unbeatable combo that makes Seattle so special: the shimmering salt water of Elliott Bay, the jagged Olympic Mountains in the distance, and the iconic skyline rising above it all. My best friend and I had so much fun learning quirky facts about the city's past while snapping the best skyline photos we got on that trip. It's part city tour, part nature experience, and a great way to ease into the rhythm of the Emerald City.

Dinner at Oddfellows Café + Bar: For a romantic dinner tucked in a secret garden-style patio, make a reservation at this day-to-night café known for seasonal American dishes and expertly crafted cocktails. This place made me feel like I was in New York City!

Explore the Museum of Pop Culture: Friends, this isn't your typical museum. MOPOP is a haven for anyone who loves to geek out on fantasy (yes, Potterheads, this includes you), rock and roll, and science fiction. There's something for everyone to immerse themselves in, so prepare to lose yourself in the world of pop culture.

DAY 2

Breakfast at Six Seven: Kick off your morning with water views and a delicious breakfast at Six Seven, overlooking Elliott Bay. The food here is top-notch, but let's be honest—the view is really what makes this experience worthwhile.

PIKE PLACE MARKET

Explore the Seattle Aquarium: If you ask me, no trip to Seattle is complete without peeking into its unbelievable underwater world. The Seattle Aquarium is a curiosity-sparking gem that will leave you in awe. I still remember my first visit on an elementary school field trip, where my grandpa (chaperone of the year!) bought me a seahorse necklace from the gift shop. These days, the experience is even better with the brand-new Ocean Pavilion, which will make you marvel at just how interconnected our oceans truly are.

Lunch at Pike Place Market: When you're at Pike Place, one thing is nonnegotiable: you have to eat. The vibrant flower bouquets are amazing too—the dried ones seem to last forever! I've had a bouquet in my kitchen that I bought two years ago, and it is still going strong.

- **Old Stove Brewing:** Grab a casual meal with a waterfront view. Order a salmon BLT, and pair it with an in-house beer flight.
- **Beecher's Handmade Cheese:** See the cheese-making process live, and then cozy up with a hot cup of mac and cheese.
- **Pike Place Chowder:** If seafood chowder is calling your name, this is the place.
- **Le Panier:** End your lunch with a French treat—my go-to is a chocolate éclair.

Snap a photo with the cherry blossoms: Step into a dreamy square of pink paradise during cherry blossom season. You'll want to visit early in the morning or later in the evening if you want to avoid crowds, and get creative with your angles—sometimes crouching low helps keep people out of your shot.

> **Bestie Tip:** If you are a foodie, visit in mid-March to try special edition drinks and foods at participating restaurants in the U District for the Cherry Blossom Festival. If you want a souvenir, swing by the University Book Store for cherry merchandise such as tees and mugs.

Explore the Burke Museum: Before leaving the city, there's one more museum you must see, just a short walk from the cherry blossoms, that offers a fascinating mix of Indigenous art, dinosaur fossils, and even exhibits on human trash (trust me, it's more interesting than it sounds).

> **Bestie Tip:** Don't leave without trying the Indian fry bread at the Burke's café, Off the Rez Café—it's a fan favorite. Its fry bread tacos are so good, you'll be dreaming about them long after your visit.

Dinner at Ramen Danbo: Cap off your day with a comforting bowl of ramen at Ramen Danbo. The vegan ramen is a must-try, and the extensive customization options let you create your one-of-a-kind bowl.

CHERRY BLOSSOMS AT UNIVERSITY OF WASHINGTON

DAY 3

Breakfast at Moore Coffee: If your camera roll is full of latte art like mine is, then don't miss this pretty Latina-owned café known for its bubble waffles and drinks. There are plenty of options for non-coffee drinkers too—think taro and matcha.

The Takeaway: Seattle often gets unfairly labeled as gloomy, yet spring here bursts with vibrant energy. During this magical season, the always-bustling Pike Place Market comes alive with daffodils, tulips, and peonies, while iconic cherry blossoms paint the Emerald City pink. On warmer days that offer summer previews, you may even be tempted to walk barefoot on a beach. Whether you're cruising Elliott Bay with Olympic Mountain backdrops, getting lost in pop culture museums, or discovering the underwater wonders of the Salish Sea, spring in Seattle offers that perfect blend of urban sophistication and natural beauty that makes this city genuinely special.

SEABROOK

25

SEABROOK

Introduction

When I think of Seabrook, a.k.a. "Washington's Beach Town," I don't picture the modern, upscale retreat you see today. Instead, I remember watching it grow—home by home, business by business—slowly transforming into the vibrant coastal community it is now. Like Wenatchee, the Washington coast was one of those places my family escaped to throughout the year, whether camping in Ocean Shores or Pacific Beach or even staying in one of Seabrook's unbelievably darling beach homes. I had a front-row seat to its development. I still remember wandering through as a kid when it was just a handful of homes and imagining what it might someday become.

Returning as an adult brings a beautiful blend of nostalgia and discovery. While summer is undoubtedly a favorite time to visit the coast, it's also the busiest. I prefer late spring, when the weather often mirrors summer's warmth but without the crowds. Plus, wildflowers such as daisies are blooming! On one memorable trip in May, I walked Lilo on the wide, sandy beach for what felt like miles without seeing anyone else. The salty breeze, the crashing waves, and perfect solitude were good for the soul.

Spring trips feel wonderfully laid-back with shorter restaurant waits and plenty of space to explore the trails and shops.

Seabrook has evolved into a perfect blend of coastal charm and modern comfort, with thoughtfully designed streets and colorful homes that feel like stepping into a seaside storybook. I love wandering through town, popping into shops such as the bookstore Joie Des Livres, where I've spent way too much time sinking into the lounge chairs in its loft nook, flipping through pages.

For me, Seabrook isn't just another beach town—it's a place to escape in style and comfort. Whether you're biking through forest trails, walking the beach alongside your loved ones, or indulging in an ice cream cone from The Sweet Life, Seabrook has a way of making every visit bright. It's a town that feels like catching up with an old friend who always has a fresh adventure waiting.

At a Glance

Location: Washington Coast
Best Season to Visit: March through May
Suggested Duration: Two nights

Getting There

Seattle to Seabrook: 138 miles, ~2 hours 50 minutes
Portland to Seabrook: 172 miles, ~3 hours 15 minutes

Where to Stay

Vacation rentals: With over 250 rentable properties in Seabrook, this modern coastal town offers a wide variety of spaces to choose from, many large enough to accommodate large groups. A few days in one will have you thinking about moving to the beach yourself!

Pacific Beach State Park: Nature lovers should seriously consider this nearby park with oceanside campsites and yurts. My brother and I endlessly played in the sand and water here as kids.

SEABROOK BEACH

Itinerary Outline

DAY 1

Dinner at Frontager's Pizza Company: Ease into your trip with a casual, comforting meal here. The artisan pizzas, calzones, and garlic cheese bread are the perfect welcome to town.

Catch the sunset on the beach: End your arrival day with Seabrook's stunning sunset views from the expansive beach. The wide sandy stretches offer perfect vantage points for watching the sun dip into the Pacific.

> **Bestie Tip:** Ever since I was a kid, one of my favorite places to snap sunset photos was from the beach at Pacific Beach State Park. Walk toward Joe Creek, where you'll see old wooden pilings and capture the creek as it meets the Pacific.

SEABROOK TOWN CENTER

DAY 2

Breakfast at Blue Juice & Salad Bar: Kick off your morning with beautifully plated acai bowls, avocado toasts, and fruit smoothies. It's easily some of the best breakfast on the coast.

Stroll Seabrook: Explore the charming town center and unique local businesses:

- **Lorraine's Candle Studio:** Create your own custom candles with coastal scents.
- **The Salty Dog:** Browse pet-friendly goods and treats (perfect for traveling with furry friends).
- **Joie Des Livres: The Joy of Books:** Pick up cozy beach reads in the welcoming loft space.
- **Red Cedar Outfitters:** Gear up for outdoor adventures with quality equipment.
- **SeaWorthy Home:** Discover coastal-inspired decor that captures the beach town aesthetic.

Beach walk and exploration: Weave down one of Seabrook's charming staircases and wander the expansive sandy beaches that seem to stretch endlessly. Spring offers perfect temperatures for long walks without summer's intense heat.

Lunch at Koko's Restaurant and Tequila Bar: Modern Latin cuisine on the coast has never tasted so good on the coast! From flavorful tacos to refreshing salads, this spot delivers exceptional dishes that blend international flavors with fresh coastal ingredients.

Go mountain biking: Whether you bring your own bike or rent one from Pacific Edge Adventures, explore Seabrook's seven miles of biking-only trails, plus additional mixed-use paths. Pause along the way to capture a photo overlooking the ocean—the views are extraordinary!

Dinner at Rising Tide Tavern: Continue sampling the culinary delights that Seabook has to offer at this laid-back spot with yummy American plates.

Treat yourself at The Sweet Life: Candy stores aren't only for kids! The Sweet Life's vintage vibes and mouthwatering smells are irresistible. I always stop in for an ice cream cone—yes, even in the middle of winter.

DAY 3

Breakfast at the Surfhouse Pub & Café: Start your last morning with a hearty breakfast burrito, biscuits and gravy, or a breakfast bowl. Pair it with a warm cup of coffee, and if you feel like enjoying it on the beach, I wouldn't blame you!

Antique shopping at Sooz Rusty Nail: Hunt for treasure in this quirky antique store filled with vintage Tupperware, industrial signs, and Washington memorabilia. It's the perfect place to find a unique souvenir to take home.

The Takeaway: Need a cozy coastal escape this spring? Seabrook has been close to my heart for as long as I can remember. Whether you're chasing an adrenaline rush (hello, mountain biking) or cozy vibes with activities, such as candlemaking, this modern coastal escape lets you craft your perfect getaway. And you can bring the whole family! From watching sunsets over Joe Creek to browsing bookstore loft nooks, Seabrook offers that rare combination of relaxation and discovery that keeps families coming back, year after year.

SEABROOK DUNES

SKAGIT VALLEY TULIP FESTIVAL

26 SKAGIT VALLEY

Introduction

Have you ever noticed how it's the *imperfect* moments from your travels that stick with you the longest? That's exactly what comes to mind when I think of my first trip to the Skagit Valley, one of the most radiant and soulful corners of the Pacific Northwest. It was spring, about seven years ago—the sky was drizzly, the ground squishy with mud, and my pink rain boots were turning brown with every step.

But here's the thing: those moody gray skies made the blooms practically glow—reds, purples, and yellows shining brighter than I ever imagined possible. To this day, despite sunnier visits since, it's that first muddy, rain-soaked trip that holds a special place in my heart. So, here's my advice: don't sweat chasing *perfect* conditions. Beauty has a funny way of showing up when you're least expecting it.

The Skagit Valley Tulip Festival isn't just the largest tulip celebration in the country—it's a reminder of life's seasonal rhythms. Spring here feels alive, as winter's chill softens and the valley bursts into color: fields painted in radiant reds, sunlit yellows, blush pinks, and deep purples. And the setting? It's pure Pacific Northwest magic. The mountain-fed Skagit River meanders to meet the salty shores of the Salish Sea, creating an extraordinary harmony of nature.

But this festival transcends flowers. It's a window into the heart of Skagit Valley—a community where local farmers have shared their craft and traditions for nearly fifty years. Strolling these fields, you can't help but feel connected to something timeless: something nurtured by hard work, care, and generations of dedication.

Here's one mistake to avoid: limiting yourself to just the fields. Yes, the blooms are jaw-dropping, but the valley has so much more to offer. Think farm-to-table dining with ingredients that taste like sunshine, an under-the-radar aquarium where you can discover the creatures of the Salish Sea, and a historic waterfront town brimming with charm. Spring in the Skagit Valley isn't

just a trip—it's an experience that immerses you in the soul of the Pacific Northwest. So, grab your waterproof boots, rain jackets, and cameras and get ready to savor it all.

At a Glance

Location: Skagit County, Washington
Best Season to Visit: March through April
Suggested Duration: Two nights

Bestie Tip: Curious about whether the flowers are blooming? Check Tulips.com/bloommap to find out! In early spring, daffodils bloom. In late spring, tulips bloom.

Getting There

Seattle to Skagit Valley: 72 miles, ~1 hour 20 minutes
Portland to Skagit Valley: 246 miles, ~4 hours 30 minutes

Where to Stay

La Conner Channel Lodge: I'm a sucker for a water view, and this is the only waterfront hotel in town! Watch the sun dip below the horizon right from your room (I won't judge if you're in a bathrobe, fresh out of your personal jacuzzi).

The Wild Iris Inn: Big fan of breakfast? Check out this eighteen-room boutique hotel known for its two-course complimentary breakfast, which can even be brought up to your room for an additional fee.

Bay View State Park or Thousand Trails La Conner: The most budget-friendly option is camping, and Skagit Valley isn't a bad place to pitch a tent under the stars.

Itinerary Outline

DAY 1

Bird's-eye view at Little Mountain Park: Start with an evening adventure at this hidden gem! My jaw dropped when I saw this underrated viewpoint for the first time. Take in the breathtaking panorama of colorful tulip fields and the Skagit River framed by the San Juan Islands and the Cascade Mountains—ideal for your first impression of Skagit Valley because you can see it all. Hiking trails are also open to mountain bikes.

Dinner at Skagit Landing Restaurant: Delight in farm-to-fork dishes with ingredients sourced from local farms, as well as stunning views of small planes coming and going from the regional airport.

DAY 2

Early morning: flower fields exploration: Beat the crowds by starting early at the tulip and daffodil fields. Visit participating farms, including RoozenGaarde, Tulip Town, Garden Roslyn, and Tulip Valley Farms—check the farms' websites to find the best fit for your interests.

Festival Tip: Purchase tickets online in advance with entry time windows. Have screenshots or QR codes ready for entry. Arrive early for the best lighting and fewer crowds. With millions of tulips stretching as far as the eye can see, it's easy to get swept up in flower seas. Yet there's something magical in pausing to admire individual blooms—observing colors, comparing sizes to your hand, breathing in sweet fragrances.

Photography Tip: Consider booking special sunrise sessions for one-in-a-million lighting conditions as the sun crests over the Cascades.

Bestie Tip: I'll never forget my surprise at seeing a white field in motion—hundreds of trumpeter swans and snow geese! Snow Goose Produce Market provides perfect spots to pause, capture photos, and treat yourself to famous ice cream in waffle cones, all in down-to-earth country market settings.

Breakfast at Calico Cupboard Café & Bakery: If the only menu item here were the huge homemade cinnamon rolls, this café would still be worth visiting! Trust me, you absolutely must grab one of its legendary cinnamon rolls before setting off for a morning walk.

Padilla Bay Shore Trail Walk: For quiet nature experiences away from festival crowds, enjoy marshy views offering birdwatching opportunities galore. Explore the quiet paths and keep an eye out for herons and eagles. If you're lucky, you'll spot some seals by the shore!

Breazeale Interpretive Center & Aquarium: I never expected to find an aquarium like this! This quaint spot offers close encounters with tide pool creatures and local ecosystem education. It's a low-key stop that's fascinating for adults and kids alike. It's open from Wednesday to Saturday.

Lunch at Ristretto Coffee Lounge & Wine Bar: Cozy up among brick walls adorned with local art. Perfect for lunch or a take-out picnic to enjoy alfresco. Pop in for lunch and a cozy atmosphere, and grab a to-go coffee for your next stop.

Explore Downtown La Conner: This historic waterfront town on the National Register of Historic Places is a small-town gem full of local bookstores, vintage shops, and handmade gifts.

Bestie Tip: The best parking depends on your preference. If you don't mind being patient and circling, then you can snag free street parking. Or, if you're like me and would rather park in a less crowded area, head to the public gravel parking lot at the corner of Moore and Caledonia streets. The trade-off? This second lot requires payment and is located on a small hill above town.

Dinner at La Conner Pub & Eatery: Cross your fingers for a waterfront table at this easygoing eatery. Known for its fish and chips, burgers, and seafood appetizers, it's hard to go wrong with anything on the menu.

DAY 3

Breakfast at Whidbey Island Bagel Factory: Whenever I drive by, I can't resist stopping for a hearty bagel sandwich. You can dine indoors, outdoors, or grab-and-go. Note that this location is close to a high school, so it gets foot traffic throughout the day. Grab fresh bagel sandwiches from Whidbey Island Bagel Factory to fuel your journey home. Then hop on I-5, but don't be surprised if the valley's colors linger in your rearview mirror—and your memory—long after you've left.

The Takeaway: If you haven't experienced the magic of twenty million tulips blooming across the Skagit Valley—home to the largest tulip festival in the United States—consider this your sign to go! Beyond capturing photos worthy of your walls, you'll also have the chance to spot migrating trumpeter swans, savor the best cinnamon rolls you'll ever taste (trust me!), and connect with a farming community where people have been sharing their passion for nearly five decades. Whether your boots get muddy or the sun shines brilliantly, the Skagit Valley proves that some of life's most beautiful moments happen when you embrace whatever conditions nature provides. Sometimes the most magical travels occur when you stop chasing perfection and start celebrating the authentic, imperfect beauty that makes each experience uniquely unforgettable.

HAYSTACK ROCK

27 CANNON BEACH

Introduction

Some places just stay with you, and that definitely includes Cannon Beach, Oregon. One of my earliest travel memories involves riding in the back seat of our car, crossing what felt like an impossibly tall, bright green bridge—what I now know as the Astoria-Megler Bridge—before heading into Oregon. Not too long after, we were walking along the soft, sandy beach toward an unbelievably massive sea stack: Haystack Rock. I can still remember the birds swooping around the rock, waves lapping at my toes, the funny squawking sound the sand made underfoot, and all those adorable dogs to greet!

While most people visit Cannon Beach for Haystack Rock and the coastal small-town vibes, it's the easy access to the outdoors that keeps me coming back. Did you know that there are four state parks within a ten-mile radius? That means plenty of opportunities to explore wild areas. Summer is a popular time to visit, but I'm a huge fan of spring. You might catch stretches of sweet sunshine and mild temperatures, but even when the weather turns, there's another reason to visit in the spring: the incredible wildlife.

Birds, whales, tide pools—oh my! Between the gray whale migration, tufted puffins returning to nest on Haystack Rock, and minus tides revealing tide pools teeming with life, spring is an absolute dream for nature lovers. Plus, you never know when you might spot Roosevelt elk wandering on the beach or through town! To enhance your Haystack Rock experience, chat with the volunteers from the Haystack Rock Awareness Program, who are on the beach daily during spring low tides, ready to

ELK AT CANNON BEACH

answer your questions, point out wildlife, and help you appreciate the magic of the intertidal zone, where creatures thrive underwater at high tide and adapt to the open air during low tide.

As an adult, I've come to love strolling through town galleries, discovering everything from coastal-inspired stained glass to handcrafted ceramic whales. Whether I'm on the hunt for a meaningful gift or for something special for my own space, there's something grounding—almost therapeutic—about taking the time to admire local art in a place that's already overflowing with inspiration.

At a Glance

Location: North Oregon Coast
Best Season to Visit: March through April
Suggested Duration: Two nights

Getting There

Seattle to Cannon Beach: 206 miles, ~3 hours 40 minutes
Portland to Cannon Beach: 79 miles, ~1 hour 30 minutes

Where to Stay

Stephanie Inn: Looking for a stylish splurge? This dreamy 4-star hotel overlooking the beach is just the spot. Spacious balconies, fireplaces, and soaking tubs are all great, but it's the daily complimentary experiences, such as a brewery tour or guided beach walk, that truly make this place unforgettable.

Inn at Cannon Beach: If you're traveling with your furry friends, this hotel has you covered. After a fun day at the beach, your pup can get cleaned up at the self-wash station and then snuggle up by the fireplace. Little touches we love include fresh-baked cookies and saltwater taffy waiting at check-in, plus resident bunnies hop around the property, giving the whole place a storybook feel.

Nehalem Bay State Park: About fifteen miles from Cannon Beach, this scenic campground sits between the Nehalem River and the Pacific Ocean. You'll find access to showers as well as plenty of beautiful views. Heads up: reservations fill up fast, so plan to book six months in advance!

ECOLA STATE PARK

Itinerary Outline

DAY 1

Explore Hug Point State Recreation Site: Start off your trip with something magical—waterfalls at the beach! At low tide, take the staircase down and wander through sea caves, walk on an old stagecoach road carved into the rock, and then peer down into tide pools. Timing is everything here, so check the tide charts. Bonus: if it's been raining, the falls will be even more impressive.

> **Bestie Tip:** Hug Point is named for a reason—the old road here hugs the coastline and sits in the intertidal zone, which means it's completely underwater at high tide. If you're planning to walk along the historic road, be sure to wear sturdy shoes. It's usually wet and can be slick with barnacles and other tide pool creatures, so it's definitely not a spot for bare feet or flip-flops!

Dinner at Tom's Fish & Chips: Ease into your adventure with some classic coastal eats. Go for the fish and chips or try the blackened salmon Caesar salad. Kyle and I usually get both to share. Also, the dog-friendly patio is a nice bonus!

DAY 2

Breakfast at The Lazy Susan Café: For a cozy, seasonally inspired breakfast, settle into this café. The seasonal waffles are amazing, but if you're in the mood for something savory, the famous omelets with fresh fruit are always a hit. Don't forget to bring cash—cards aren't accepted here.

Tide pooling at Haystack Rock: The 235-foot Haystack Rock isn't just an Instagram-worthy landmark—it's teeming with life! You'll find colorful sea stars, tiny hermit crabs, and even tufted puffins (from April to July). To protect the sea life, be careful where you step; when in doubt, stick to the sand.

> **Bestie Tip:** Keep an eye out for volunteers in red jackets. They're part of the Haystack Rock Awareness Program and can help you learn about the intertidal zone. The volunteers are there every day from mid-February through November at low tide, so don't be shy—ask them questions!

Coffee at Insomnia Coffee: Warm up post-beach-exploration at this cozy coffee shop. Sip on a beautifully crafted Aztec mocha or real caramel latte while checking out local art on the walls—there's a new featured artist every month.

Hike Neahkahnie Mountain: For an unforgettable adventure, head to the south trailhead. The hike is roughly a three-mile round trip with a one-thousand-foot elevation gain, and the views are worth it. At the top, you'll get a sweeping view of the Pacific, Nehalem Bay, and layers of mountains in the distance.

Picnic lunch at Ecola State Park: Pick up a burger or flatbread to go from Pelican Brewing and enjoy it at one of the most scenic spots on the Oregon Coast. During spring, keep an eye out for migrating gray whales!

> **Bestie Tip:** The forested, winding road into the park feels delightfully off the beaten path, so take it slow and keep your eyes peeled for the resident Roosevelt elk herd. We got lucky once and spotted them near Ecola Creek right around sunset. I still can't believe it.

Stroll through town: Explore the artistic soul of Cannon Beach through its charming galleries and shops:

- **Shearwater Studio & Gallery:** Discover surfer-themed ceramic mugs, stained glass tulips, and locally crafted jewelry.
- **Cannon Beach Bookstore:** Grab beach reads and unique tote bags made from upcycled table linens (fair warning: picking just one is challenging!).
- **Cannon Beach Soap and Candle:** Treat yourself to bath truffles and luxurious bubble baths.
- **Cannon Beach Chocolate Café:** Satisfy your sweet tooth with literal spoonfuls of chocolate.
- **FOUND:** Search for secondhand gems and vintage treasures.

> **Shopping Tip:** Many galleries feature local artists whose work captures the coastal spirit—perfect for meaningful souvenirs.

Dinner at The Wayfarer Restaurant & Lounge: For the perfect seafood dinner with a view of Haystack Rock, head to this woodsy-chic eatery. Save room for the signature dessert—the Haystack Heaven is a chocolate lover's dream come true.

DAY 3

Breakfast at Crêpe Neptune: Before saying goodbye to the coast, grab a crepe from this walk-up spot. Whether you're craving sweet or savory, it's got you covered. My go-to picks? The Fort Stevens (smoked salmon) and the Haystack Rock (Nutella and banana).

> **The Takeaway:** You've likely seen those scroll-stopping photos of Haystack Rock—and for good reason. It's truly something special, home to fascinating creatures, such as tufted puffins and starfish that bring the scene to life. But Cannon Beach offers so much more than its iconic landmark. From beach waterfalls that appear at low tide to whimsical art galleries and a welcoming dog-friendly vibe, this beloved Pacific Northwest spot has captured the hearts of people of all ages, including mine since childhood.

SUMMER *GETAWAYS*

PORT TOWNSEND WATERFRONT

VICTORIAN ARCHITECTURE IN PORT TOWNSEND

28 PORT TOWNSEND

Introduction

If you're planning a trip to the Olympic Peninsula, you might miss one of the country's only Victorian seaports if you're not careful: Port Townsend. Just a short detour off Highway 101, this artsy town sits on the northeastern tip of the peninsula, right across the water from Whidbey Island's Fort Ebey and Fort Casey. From the moment you arrive, Port Townsend makes a grand first impression. Think steeped roofs, ornate carvings, and crown molding that feels straight out of a storybook.

My first memory of Port Townsend is taking the ferry over from Whidbey Island. I didn't know what to expect, but I certainly wasn't prepared for how downright delightful it is. The ferry drops you off right in the heart of downtown, and it's the kind of place where you can easily explore on foot. I remember thinking it didn't even feel like Washington—at least not the Washington I was used to. The historic architecture reminded me of what I imagine older East Coast towns look like, with most of the stunning buildings dating back to the nineteenth century and lovingly preserved as part of a National Historic Landmark District.

But beyond the charm of the town itself, the other compelling reason to visit is the water. Port Townsend feels almost like an island, as it's surrounded by salt water on three sides. It's a paradise for anyone who loves to get out on the water—whether by boat, kayak, or paddleboard. And, yes, you might even spot a brave soul or two swimming in the bay!

Every September, the town celebrates its maritime culture with the Wooden Boat Festival, drawing sailing enthusiasts from across the region. But there are plenty of opportunities to admire boats—or hop aboard one—all summer long. Summer is the best time to experience Port Townsend, as you can spend days soaking up the sun on one of the many beaches, catch a dreamy sunset at Point Wilson Lighthouse, and take your time wandering through the idyllic streets. It's a destination that welcomes everyone—families, solo travelers, and even your furry companions.

PORT TOWNSEND BEACH

At a Glance

Location: Olympic Peninsula, Washington
Best Season to Visit: May through September
Suggested Duration: Two nights

Getting There

Seattle to Port Townsend: 111 miles, ~2 hours

- **Ferry shortcut:** Take Seattle–Bainbridge or Edmonds–Kingston ferry to reduce mileage (travel time roughly the same)

Portland to Port Townsend: 219 miles, ~3 hours 35 minutes

Where to Stay

Palace Hotel: If you're into historic stays that match Port Townsend's Victorian vibes, the Palace Hotel is the best option. Each of its twenty-six rooms is one of a kind. Since the building dates back to 1889, modern conveniences, such as air-conditioning and elevators, aren't available—but that's part of the old-timey experience.

Vacation rentals: For a more modern stay just outside of town, check out vacation rentals. You'll find some adorable tiny houses and cottages, some with water views that make you want to cozy up and stay awhile.

Camping at historical state parks: Almost every time I've visited Port Townsend in the summer, I've camped—it's such a fun way to see more than just the town. With several state parks nearby, you've got great options. If you're planning a last-minute trip, consider Fort Townsend—it's a bit of a hidden gem compared to the more popular Fort Worden.

Itinerary Outline

DAY 1

Soak on the Sound: I don't know about you, but I welcome any opportunity to soak. There's nothing better than feeling the stress melt away as you sink into a saltwater tub and enjoy a sauna's steamy bliss. Honestly, I can't think of a more satisfying way to kick off a weekend of relaxation.

Dinner at Siren's Waterfront Gastropub: This speakeasy with a cozy outdoor deck is my go-to spot in Port Townsend. One bite of the Black Bean Burger while watching the sunset, and you'll see why I keep returning. The drink menu is generous, with plenty of spirit-free cocktails.

Whale on the Wharf: If you're dining on Siren's patio, look down—you might spot Gunther, the forty-two-foot gray whale skeleton on Union Wharf below. Visit him up close! While most people stop by during the day, I think Gunther looks even cooler lit up at night.

DAY 2

Coffee at Better Living Through Coffee: This is the place you'll wish you could start every morning! Whether you score a window seat or wander to the pocket beach next door, the organic coffee here is next level, and gosh, the views of Port Townsend Bay give me life.

> **Bestie Tip:** Love salted caramel? Grab a jar of the perfectly balanced homemade sauce—it makes my at-home coffees a hundred times better.

Breakfast from Lighthouse Café: Right next to Better Living Through Coffee, this spot serves up delightful avocado toast, breakfast sandwiches, and pastries. Grab your breakfast to go and enjoy it outside while you watch the ferries sail by.

Tour the Point Wilson Lighthouse: This windswept lighthouse has stood watch since 1879, and it remains a main attraction. If volunteers are present, you can climb the narrow staircase to the top for a peek at the light in action.

POINT WILSON LIGHTHOUSE

> **Bestie Tip:** Traveling with a lighthouse lover? Surprise them with a stay in the lighthouse keeper's quarters. It's a splurge, and the decor isn't the most modern, but the beach access and views are unforgettable.

Glass Beach Adventure: If you never turn down the opportunity to take a long walk on the beach, then this is one you can't miss. Start at North Beach County Park and walk about three miles west along the shore to McCurdy Point. The area used to be a dump site, so now it's a treasure trove of smooth sea glass. I thought this long walk or hike, whichever you want to call it, was totally worthwhile. But be mindful of the tides—you don't want to get stuck when they come in!

Lunch at Tommyknocker's Cornish Pasty: This restaurant serves tasty mac and cheese, salmon clam chowder, and delectable British pasties. It's one of the most unique dining experiences in town! I love snagging a table outside, partially to say hello to all the cute pups passing by.

POINT WILSON LIGHTHOUSE

Kayaking on Port Townsend Bay: Home to the Northwest Maritime Center, Port Townsend is nothing if not a water-lover's town. To dip your toes in, rent a kayak or paddleboard from Olympic Kayak Tours. First timer? Join a guided tour to help you feel more comfortable on the water.

Stroll Victorian downtown: Explore the historic district's charming attractions:

- **Port Townsend Marine Science Center:** Dive into Salish Sea wonders.
- **Imprint Bookshop and William James Bookseller:** Visit two excellent bookstores across the street from each other.
- **Port Townsend Antique Mall:** Get lost in vintage treasures.

> **Architecture Tip:** Look up while walking—the Victorian details in upper stories and cornices are often the most spectacular.

Dinner at Salish Grill: Perched at the marina's tip, this seafood gem will satisfy your cravings. Whether you're into ahi tuna Nicoise or Thai curry mussels, everything is delicious, with waterfront ambiance to match.

Catch the sunset at Point Wilson Lighthouse: From a photography perspective, the sunset behind this lighthouse with wildflowers in the foreground is magical. The combination of historic architecture, natural beauty, and golden light creates perfect Pacific Northwest moments.

DAY 3

High tea at Café Tenby: Sleep in and start your day slowly with proper high tea: think loose-leaf teas, pastries, fruit, scones, and sandwiches. Be sure to book a reservation online—this popular experience fills up quickly!

Explore the military history of Fort Worden Historical State Park: Hidden within the park are trails (open to cyclists and hikers) that lead to old gun batteries, a searchlight shelter, and other military relics. I felt like my imagination was free to run wild here, as I was never sure what was around the corner. Along the way, keep an eye out for grazing black-tailed deer and enjoy stunning views of the coastline below.

BURROUGHS MOUNTAIN TRAIL

The Takeaway: To step into a seafaring fairy tale, all you need to do is experience summer in Port Townsend, where Victorian architecture lines the streets, and the boats anchored in the harbor tell tales of the town's maritime past. By day, you can beachcomb for sea glass treasures, climb up inside historic lighthouses, or kayak through glittering bay waters. By evening, you can soak in saltwater spas, dine on waterfront patios, and watch spectacular sunsets paint the sky behind century-old beacons. Whether you arrive by ferry like I first did or drive through the scenic Olympic Peninsula, Port Townsend offers that rare combination of historical authenticity and natural beauty that makes every visit feel both educational and restorative.

29 MOUNT RAINIER NATIONAL PARK

Introduction

The mountain in my backyard—growing up in the South Sound, that's how I've always thought of Mount Rainier. Traditionally known as Tahoma, it's the largest mountain in the Cascade Range, standing at 14,441 feet. But if you live here, it's so much more than that—it's like a compass, something steady and familiar. It provides the most breathtaking sunsets when it glows bright pink for just a few fleeting moments. Other days, it blends into the clouds with only its peak visible. When I fly home to Seattle–Tacoma Airport, seeing the mountain from the plane window is the warmest welcome home. If you hear someone say, "The mountain is out," you just know it's going to be a good day.

HOARY MARMOT

Between summertime wildflowers, massive glaciers (the most in the contiguous United States!), and abundant wildlife—think black bears, mountain goats, and marmots—Mount Rainier is one of the most unforgettable weekend getaways in the Pacific Northwest. It's also one worth repeating. Out on trails, I've lost count of how many different languages I've heard, with people coming from all over the world to visit this place.

Since some roads, trails, and visitor centers are only accessible from mid-to-late summer, that's the optimal time to visit. Just be prepared to share the experience with others, especially on weekends. If you can, visit midweek and get an early start, as this helps avoid long entrance lines and crowded parking lots. In 2024, the park introduced a timed-entry reservation system for the most popular areas, so check the park's website for current requirements. Planning a last-minute trip? You can usually skip the reservation by arriving early in the morning.

For first-time visitors, make sure both the Paradise and Sunrise areas are on your radar. You can have an adventure-packed trip by sticking to just one, but if you can, it's worth squeezing in both. Paradise offers scenic drives with roadside pull-offs that showcase waterfalls, rivers, and old-growth forests. Sunrise, on the other hand, takes you to the highest drivable point in the park with incredible panoramic views. Both have visitor centers with trail access, educational exhibits, and gift shops.

For those who have already hit the main highlights, there's so much more to explore. Lesser-known areas, such as Westside Road, Ohanapecosh, and the Tatoosh Range, offer quieter experiences. The surrounding national forest lands also have stunning trails with epic mountain views.

At a Glance

Location: West-central Washington
Best Season to Visit: July through October
Suggested Duration: Two or three nights

Park Information

- **Entrance fee:** $30 per vehicle (seven days) or $55 annual America the Beautiful Pass
- Main entrances, including Nisqually, Stevens Canyon, and White River/Sunrise, are open in summer
- **Check current conditions:** nps.gov/mora or call (360) 569-2211

Getting There

Seattle to Mount Rainier (Nisqually Entrance): 90 miles, ~2 hours
Portland to Mount Rainier (Nisqually Entrance): 138 miles, ~2 hours 25 minutes

Where to Stay

Lodges in the park: For a rustic retreat within the national park, check out the Paradise Inn (Paradise) and National Park Inn (Longmire). These historic buildings offer excellent locations but feature simple accommodations that may include shared bathrooms—part of the authentic national park experience.

Vacation rentals: Since the park is remote, having kitchens for cooking meals with your own groceries proves very useful. Try Ashford for Paradise area access or Enumclaw for Sunrise area convenience.

Campgrounds in the park: With advance planning (or luck with walk-in sites), the three main campgrounds—Cougar Rock (near Paradise), White River (near Sunrise), and Ohanapecosh—are my favorite places to stay. A great nearby alternative is Alder Lake Park.

Itinerary Outline

DAY 1

Discover Northwest wildlife at Northwest Trek Wildlife Park: While there's no guarantee you'll spot all the wildlife that calls Mount Rainier home, Northwest Trek gives you a chance to see native species up close. Their free-roaming area includes moose, elk, bison, and mountain goats. Opt for a tram tour or, for a more one-on-one experience, book the Keeper Adventure Tour, in which you ride in an off-road jeep with a wildlife expert.

Check out Ashford Creek Pottery: This art gallery is secretly the best place to pick up locally made souvenirs, especially if you love ceramics, paintings, and vintage postcards. Every time I step inside, I lose track of time—trust me, you don't want to skip this hidden gem!

NORTHWEST TREK

DAY 2

Explore Paradise

- **Enter through Nisqually Entrance:** Drive toward Paradise, stopping at roadside attractions, such as Longmire (don't miss the Longmire Museum), Christine Falls, Narada Falls, and Ricksecker Point. These stops provide an excellent introduction to the park's diverse ecosystems and geological features.
- **Visit Henry M. Jackson Memorial Visitor Center:** Watch the park film, browse the gift shop, and check current trail conditions. The visitor center provides essential context for understanding Mount Rainier's glacial and volcanic history.
- **Hike the Skyline Loop Trail (or East Skyline to Myrtle Falls):** There's a good chance you'll discover a new favorite trail hiking this iconic loop. With waterfalls, wildflowers, and jaw-dropping Mount Rainier views, it really has everything. As one of the park's most beloved hikes, Skyline Trail tends to be busy, so plan to share paths and yield to uphill hikers. Keep your eyes peeled for marmots cooling off on lingering snow patches—they're the local celebrities!

MOUNT RAINIER

- **Full loop option:** 5.5 miles with 1,700 feet elevation gain (moderately challenging, allow four to five hours).
- **Shorter option:** East Skyline Trail to Myrtle Falls (an easier trail at 2.5 miles—allow two to three hours).
- **Wildflower etiquette:** Keep feet on trails to protect fragile meadows. Every off-trail step damages these delicate ecosystems, but you can capture amazing photos from designated paths!
- **Photography at Reflection Lakes:** This classic Mount Rainier photo opportunity offers stunning mountain reflections when conditions cooperate.

Bestie Tip: For the most favorable photography conditions, arrive for sunrise when the water tends to be at its calmest. You'll likely meet other photographers sharing unforgettable dawn experiences.

- **Alternative Afternoon Hike: Pinnacle Peak Trail**—For moderately challenging trails that are quieter than Skyline, head into the beauty of the rugged Tatoosh Range. The trail begins across from Reflection Lake and climbs through rocky, exposed terrain, gaining about 1,050 feet in elevation before rewarding you with sweeping Paradise views and Mount Adams vistas.

Weather Alternative: The Bench and Snow Lakes Trail offers easier options (2.5 miles, six hundred feet of elevation gain) with more shade and peaceful lake access.

DAY 3

Explore Sunrise

Catch the sunrise at Sunrise Point Lookout: Start early to experience the park's highest drivable point during golden hour when the mountain often emerges from morning clouds in spectacular fashion.

Choose your Sunrise area hike

- **Option 1: Mount Fremont Lookout and Burroughs Mountain Loop (challenging)**—My favorite trail combination! This demanding loop links Mount Fremont Lookout and Burroughs Mountain trails, connecting back via Shadow Lake. It's a serious workout offering comprehensive area tours, wildlife viewing opportunities (we've seen mountain goats and a mama black bear with cubs!), and incredible mountain views. Expect approximately 9.4 miles with two thousand feet elevation gain—plan for six to eight hours in total.
- **Option 2: Sunrise Nature Trail (easy)**—For shorter adventures or a gentle start to the day, try this mellow 1.5-mile loop, climbing about three hundred feet while offering big views with minimal effort. It's perfect for getting terrain feels, stretching your legs, and catching stunning Rainier vistas with surrounding alpine landscapes.

Weather Backup Options

- **Visitor Center programs:** Both Paradise and Sunrise Visitor Centers offer ranger programs, films, and exhibits that are perfect for learning during inclement weather.
- **Scenic driving:** The roads themselves offer spectacular views even when hiking isn't possible, with numerous pull-offs for safe viewing and photography.

FREMONT LOOKOUT

Safety Tip: Bring layers, plenty of water, and snacks for longer hikes. Weather can change rapidly at elevation, and afternoon thunderstorms are common in summer.

Wildlife Tip: Early morning and late afternoon provide the best opportunities for spotting mountain goats, marmots, and occasionally, black bears.

The Takeaway: Some places take your breath away the first time you see them—Mount Rainier takes it every time. Whether it's glowing pink at sunset, rising above a sea of clouds, or towering over a meadow full of wildflowers, it never looks the same twice. For those of us who grew up nearby, it's more than a peak—it's a landmark, a memory, a steady companion in the distance that anchors our sense of place in the Pacific Northwest. Come and discover why we love it so much by taking scenic drives, hiking among marmots and wildflowers, and creating your own memories in the shadow of this magnificent volcano.

30

TACOMA

Introduction

When my grandparents settled in the Pacific Northwest—coming from the Philippines, South Korea, North Dakota, and Minnesota—they all chose Tacoma as their home. It was the largest urban area near Mount Rainier, with a deep connection to the water thanks to its prime location along the Puget Sound. This is where my parents grew up, where so many of my family's stories are rooted, and where I still love spending time today.

Tacoma wears its character proudly as a city that's artsy, historic, and naturally beautiful all at once. It's home to the renowned Museum of Glass and the Chihuly Bridge of Glass, where you can walk beneath a kaleidoscope of blown-glass masterpieces. Downtown ghost signs—those beautifully faded, hand-painted advertisements on old brick buildings—tell stories of the past, while landmarks, such as the Washington State History Museum, keep the heritage alive. Above all, Tacoma seamlessly blends nature, art, and history into one compelling destination.

While Tacoma makes for a great year-round getaway, some of the most unforgettable outdoor experiences, such as hot-air ballooning and seaplane rides, are only available in the summer.

At the heart of this trip is something I grew up with: the Washington State Fair. Once known as the Puyallup Fair, it was a rite of late summer for my family and me. I remember my best friend daring me to ride the Zipper, our hearts pounding as we tumbled upside down time after time, and the thrill of trying my luck at the frog ring toss—always hoping to win one of those giant stuffed animals—and the sheer disbelief when I finally won.

Even now, there's something magical about seeing it all from the High Swing—like flying through warm evening air, breeze brushing your face as the world spins gently below in a blur of lights and laughter. The fair runs from late August through September and feels like the ultimate way to say goodbye to summer and welcome fall. The scent

RUSTON WAY WATERFRONT

of buttery, raspberry-filled scones drifts through the air, mingling with the savory aroma of curly fries and the sugary sweetness of freshly fried elephant ears. It's the kind of nostalgic magic that brings out the kid in all of us.

So many Washington residents talk about going, but not everyone has made it yet—so I designed this itinerary around that experience. Take it from me: dive in, soak it up, and savor every colorful moment.

At a Glance

Location: Pierce County, Washington
Best Season to Visit: September
Suggested Duration: Two nights

Getting There

Seattle to Tacoma: 35 miles, ~40 minutes
Portland to Tacoma: 144 miles, ~2 hours 15 minutes

Where to Stay

Silver Cloud Hotel Tacoma at Point Ruston Waterfront: The waterfront along Ruston Way has really leveled up in the past few years. It's now a dreamy, walkable area lined with fantastic restaurants, charming shops, and some of the best sunrise views over Commencement Bay. This 4-star hotel is the crown jewel of the area, offering modern luxury, spacious rooms, and stunning water and Mount Rainier views from your window. If you're looking for a stay that feels like a mini vacation in itself, this is the spot.

Silver Cloud Hotel Tacoma - Waterfront: Just a little east of its newer sister property, this 3-star hotel has been a staple along the Tacoma waterfront for years. It's a great option if you're looking for something a bit more budget friendly without giving up those gorgeous Puget Sound views. Plus, staying here puts you closer to downtown Tacoma, making it easy to explore the city's museums, coffee shops, and arts scene.

Vacation rentals: For a more local, lived-in experience, consider staying in a vacation rental. Tacoma's neighborhoods each have their own personality—whether it's the historic charm of the North End, the artsy vibes of Hilltop, or the peaceful, tree-lined streets of Proctor. A rental home lets you settle in like a local, away from the more touristy areas, while still keeping you close to all the must-visit spots.

Itinerary Outline

DAY 1

Dinner at Harbor Lights: Settle in for a cozy, waterfront meal at Harbor Lights, a beloved Tacoma institution with stunning views of Commencement Bay. Its three-course dinners are fantastic value, offering a starter (I highly recommend the clam chowder), a fresh seafood entrée, and a sweet treat to round out your meal. This longtime favorite has been serving the community for decades.

Washington State History Museum: If you appreciate a well-curated museum, this stop is essential. With detailed exhibits on Washington's past, rotating special collections, and intricate model railroads (my grandpa's brother used to work on these displays!), the museum brings the state's story to life. I remember coming here on a field trip as a kid, and I still find myself equally fascinated today.

Explore the Museum of Glass: End the night with a visit to the largest glass museum on the West Coast. The highlight? The Hot Shop, where you can watch live glassblowing demonstrations. Seeing artists craft delicate, intricate pieces from molten glass is mesmerizing—it's like watching magic happen before your eyes.

DAY 2

Breakfast at Hob Nob restaurant: Start your morning with a hearty breakfast at Hob Nob, a charming eatery housed in a historic building listed on the National Register of Historic Places. It's the kind of place where you feel like a local the moment you walk in. My go-to is Lily's Apple Pie Waffle, but honestly, you can't go wrong with anything on the menu.

Explore Point Defiance Park: Point Defiance is one of the most stunning urban parks in the country, blending 760 acres of towering forests, saltwater beaches, and lush gardens. It's a local favorite for walking, biking, and running, offering almost any outdoor activity you can imagine:

- **Owen Beach:** Rent kayaks or go tide pooling during low tide.
- **Five Mile Drive:** Walk, run, or cycle this former scenic road now closed to traffic.
- **Rose Garden:** Stop and smell the flowers in this beautifully maintained space.
- **Off-Leash Dog Park:** Let pups run free in designated areas.

> **Activity Tip:** Check tide charts for optimal tide pooling conditions, and consider renting bikes at Point Ruston for easier Five Mile Drive exploration.

Lunch at Woven Seafood & Chophouse: This fresh ocean-centered restaurant delivers Pacific fusion cuisine, such as poke bowls, spicy tuna rolls, and seafood pillows. It's a delicious blend of Hawaiian and Japanese flavors, served with a side of scenic bay views.

> **Bestie Tip:** Looking for a unique way to see Pierce County from above? Book a South Sound Scenic Flight with Kenmore Air, which takes off right next to Woven! You'll get bird's-eye views of the islands, the Narrows Bridge, and beyond—a short, sweet, and unforgettable experience (available through mid-September).

Explore the Washington State Fair: If you're visiting in September, you're in luck—the Washington State Fair (formerly the Puyallup Fair) is in full swing! A tradition for over 125 years and located in neighboring Puyallup, the fair celebrates agricultural heritage, live music (this is where I attended my first concert—Hilary Duff!), and pure fun. With over seventy-five rides, countless carnival games, and exhibit halls, plan for at least a few hours of exploration.

Fair food essentials include elephant ears, earthquake burgers, and krusty pups, but get a baker's dozen of Fisher scones to take home with you! I've been coming here since I was a kid, and I love how little it changes—there's something nostalgic about watching new generations experience the same fair magic for the first time.

Dinner at Matador Tacoma: End the day at this vibrant spot known for its Mexican-inspired dishes and craft tequila cocktails. The ambiance is lively, the flavors are bold, and happy hour is a steal if you time it right. Whether you go for the street tacos, sizzling fajitas, or one of the famous margaritas, this is the perfect way to wrap up your second night in Tacoma.

DAY 3

Sunrise hot-air balloon ride: One of the most unforgettable mornings of my life was seeing sunrise over Pierce County from a hot-air balloon with Seattle Ballooning. The early wake-up call is *so* worth it for the peaceful, dreamlike experience of floating above the landscape. From this vantage point, you'll see Mount Rainier towering in the distance, as well as winding rivers and lakes, plus unique perspectives of Tacoma and beyond.

WOVEN SEAFOOD & CHOPHOUSE

WASHINGTON STATE FAIR

SUNRISE HOT-AIR BALLOON RIDE

Breakfast at Howdy Bagel: After your morning flight, cozy up with breakfast at this cheery neighborhood favorite known for its fresh bagels, cream cheese, and mouthwatering sandwiches. The line might be out the door, but trust me, it is worth the wait.

Explore Vashon Island: If you have a little extra time before heading home, hop on the ferry to Vashon Island, a quiet, rural escape just a short ride from Tacoma. Some of my favorite places to stop are the Point Robinson Lighthouse, Vashon Island Coffee Roasterie, and the Dockton Forest (popular for mountain biking).

The Takeaway: Feel like a kid again riding roller coasters at the Washington State Fair, drift through the sky on a sunrise hot-air balloon ride, and soak up every moment along the shores of the Puget Sound. The greater Tacoma area has always held a special place in my heart, as it's where my family's Pacific Northwest story began and continues to unfold. Whether you're drawn by world-class museums, coastal adventures, or that magical fairground nostalgia that connects generations, Tacoma delivers urban adventure with a distinctly Pacific Northwest style. It's a place where past and present blend seamlessly—where you can trace family history through historic neighborhoods one day and soar above it all in a balloon basket the next, creating new memories while honoring the old ones that make this place feel like home.

FALLS CREEK

31

WINTHROP

Introduction

When summer rolls around, it's hard to imagine a better escape than Winthrop. With sun-soaked days and temperatures climbing to the eighties, mountain views in every direction, and plenty of lakes and rivers to cool off in, the Methow Valley feels like it was made for outdoor adventurers. It's remote enough to truly disconnect from city life, yet full of ways to reconnect with nature—whether by hiking through quiet forests, paddling across glassy waters, or simply soaking in the golden glow of a summer sunset.

Sitting at 1,768 feet and nestled against the North Cascades, Winthrop is a gateway to diverse landscapes—meadows bursting with wildflowers, pine forests scented with fresh mountain air, and lakes that shimmer under the summer sun. But beyond its natural beauty, Winthrop is a town with undeniable charm. This isn't just another small town; it's a place that transports you back in time to the Old American West. Think cowboys, wooden boardwalks, and swinging saloon doors. The storefronts along Riverside Avenue fit the theme perfectly, with vintage gas pumps, rustic facades, and even the most elegant bank you've ever seen. It's the kind of place that makes you want to slow down, take it all in, and maybe even trade in your hiking boots for cowboy boots—at least for the weekend.

Summer is when Winthrop feels most alive—but it's also wildfire season, so stay mindful. Each year, wildfires seem more frequent, and Winthrop's proximity to dense forests means smoky conditions can be a real possibility. I've been here during thick smoke, and it's no joke—especially since many trails are remote with spotty cell service. I highly recommend monitoring current fire conditions and air quality reports before heading out.

When the skies are clear and summer sun is shining, though, Winthrop is pure magic. One of my favorite ways to beat the heat is

PEARRYGIN LAKE

paddleboarding and swimming at Pearrygin Lake. Mornings are especially peaceful with still waters and birdsong creating perfect settings for sunrise paddles. By afternoon, when temperatures rise, jumping into the lake feels like the best decision you'll make all day.

Whether you're hiking, paddling, or wandering Old West streets with ice cream cones in hand, Winthrop makes summer feel endless in the most wonderful way.

At a Glance

Location: North Central Washington
Best Season to Visit: July through August
Suggested Duration: Two or three nights

Getting There

Seattle to Winthrop: 241 miles, ~4 hours 20 minutes
Portland to Winthrop: 384 miles, ~7 hours

Where to Stay

Sun Mountain Lodge: If you're looking for a luxury stay with views that will leave you breathless, this is the place. Located ten miles outside of town, it's the perfect escape into nature.

Methow River Lodge & Cabins: Stay close to town while soaking in riverfront views at this cozy lodge. Opt for a private cabin with a hot tub for a rustic yet comfortable getaway.

Camping at Pearrygin Lake State Park: For a budget-friendly stay with unbeatable water access, it doesn't get better than this campground. Many sites even have lakeside spots for swimming, kayaking, and paddleboarding.

Itinerary Outline

DAY 1

Stroll through the Old West town: Similar to themed towns such as Leavenworth or Poulsbo, much of Winthrop's charm is in its Old Western–style design. Strolling through town feels like stepping into a movie set—just like the classic Westerns my grandpa used to love.

- **Cascades Outdoor Store:** Whether you need a new hiking layer or just want to browse, this locally loved shop has all the essentials for your North Cascades adventures.
- **Trails End Bookstore:** This cozy indie bookstore with a well-curated selection is perfect for picking up a road-trip read or a book about the region.
- **Sheri's Sweet Shoppe:** Ice cream cones, pastries, and nostalgic candy—this place is pure joy.

Drinks at Methow Valley Ciderhouse: Grab a cider flight and settle in on the patio, where the drinks are crisp and the views are serene. The cider is made from a local orchard just a few miles outside Winthrop, and the Black Raven (a blackberry cider) is a favorite.

TRAILS END BOOKSTORE

Dinner at the Old Schoolhouse Brewery: Housed in—you guessed it—an old schoolhouse, this spot serves up burgers, fish and chips, and craft beer, and it has unbeatable river views.

DAY 2

Breakfast at Rocking Horse Bakery: It was love at first sight for me and the cinnamon rolls here. While sipping your coffee, take a look around—the walls display historic artifacts offering glimpses into Winthrop's past. If the weather's nice, grab a seat outside by the river.

Morning paddleboarding at Pearrygin Lake: Winthrop is where I first tried stand-up paddleboarding, and I loved it so much that I returned the next summer! Rent from Methow Cycle & Sport and take your board to Pearrygin Lake State Park.

> **Bestie Tip:** Pick up your rental the night before so that, the next day, you can get out on the water before the boats create wakes.

Hike around Pearrygin Lake: For peaceful shrub-steppe scenery and a glimpse into the past, take the three-mile Rex Derr Trail, where remnants of old farmsteads dot the landscape. To complete a full loop around the lake, plan for about five miles, with a short stretch along the road. We spotted plenty of deer along the way! If you're into mountain biking, this trail is also bike friendly.

Lunch at Jupiter: For fresh, colorful, and globally inspired dishes, Jupiter is a must-visit. The bowls, salads, and kimchi fried rice are as flavorful as they are Instagram-worthy—plus, many dishes are vegan friendly!

PEARRYGIN LAKE

Hike Falls Creek Falls: If you're looking for a way to cool off, this easy, quarter-mile paved trail leads to a gorgeous waterfall. For a bit more adventure, hike up to higher viewpoints—the full trail is 2.6 miles with 750 feet of elevation gain. Keep an eye out for wildflowers and be sure to bring plenty of water.

Dinner at East 20 Pizza: Order a pie to go and enjoy it at a picnic table along the Methow River at Mack Lloyd Park. The creative pizzas alone, such as the Thai-inspired one with roasted bell peppers, cilantro, and curry sauce, are worth the trip.

Evening at The Barnyard Cinema: If the summer heat has you seeking air-conditioning (which is exactly how my friends and I ended up here), this indie movie theater is the perfect place to unwind. Arrive early to snag your seat and take in the mountain views before the window curtains close.

DEER AT PEARRYGIN LAKE

SHAFER MUSEUM

DAY 3

Breakfast at Three Fingered Jack's Saloon: For a classic country breakfast, this spot is a must. As Washington's oldest legal saloon, it serves up homemade buttermilk biscuits and gravy, steak and eggs, and pancakes that will fuel you for the day ahead.

Explore the Shafer Museum: Tucked just a street back from the main street, this hidden gem offers a well-detailed glimpse into Winthrop's past. From old mining equipment to antique household wares, it's a fascinating look at frontier life. Even if the indoor exhibits are closed, the outdoor displays—featuring farming and mining artifacts—are usually open to explore.

The Takeaway: Summer in Winthrop reveals a sun-warmed Western daydream where saloon-style storefronts meet shimmering lakes, and every breeze carries a hint of pine and nostalgia. Mornings invite paddleboarding on still waters, afternoons are made for chasing waterfalls or flipping pages in a trail-worn paperback, and evenings end with cider in hand under a sky set ablaze. It's a place where the pace slows, the days seem longer, and the line between adventure and relaxation fades into a dusty horizon. Whether you're cooling off in mountain lakes, exploring frontier history, or simply savoring ice cream on wooden boardwalks, Winthrop proves that sometimes the most magical summer escapes happen when you step back in time while stepping forward into adventure.

COLDWATER LAKE

32 VANCOUVER

Introduction

Can you imagine a volcano erupting in your backyard on your birthday? That's exactly what my dad experienced in 1980 when Mount St. Helens erupted, leaving lasting marks on the landscape that reached far beyond Washington. Although this happened before my time, I've always been fascinated by the sheer power of Mother Nature, the resiliency of plants and animal species, and how the mountain is actively rebuilding itself with its lava dome—something you can witness with your own eyes when visiting.

Today, the area is a National Monument offering incredible outdoor recreation opportunities. Compared to its sister mountain, Mount Rainier, located about fifty miles away, Mount St. Helens receives far fewer visitors. Yet I'd argue it's just as bucket-list-worthy, offering a one-of-a-kind story you won't soon forget.

Vancouver, Washington's fourth-largest city, sits along the scenic Columbia River and serves as the perfect base camp for volcanic exploration. If you've only ever driven through (and I've been guilty of this), you're missing a city full of history, amazing food, and abundant nearby nature spaces—oh, and fantastic coffee! While I've enjoyed peaceful winter visits here, summer is ideal for exploring the greater Vancouver area when mountain trails and scenic drives at Mount St. Helens become fully accessible.

Using Vancouver as your home base positions you perfectly to explore Mount St. Helen's powerful story of resilience, regrowth, and raw natural force, then return to a city that balances creature comforts and foodie-approved restaurants with historic roots dating back to fur trading posts.

At a Glance

Location: Clark County, Washington (across the river from Portland, Oregon)
Best Season to Visit: June through September
Suggested Duration: Two or three nights

Getting There

Seattle to Vancouver: 174 miles, ~2 hours 45 minutes
Portland to Vancouver: 10 miles, ~15–30 minutes

Where to Stay

AC Hotel Vancouver Waterfront: Looking for a luxe getaway? Treat yourself to a corner suite, complete with a private balcony and cozy patio furniture—perfect for soaking in those river views.

Hotel Indigo Vancouver Downtown: Portland Area—Traveling with your pup? This stylish waterfront hotel is as pet friendly as it is chic, offering a warm welcome for you and your furry friend.

Half-Giant Hut: If you don't mind being about an hour outside Vancouver (but closer to Mount St. Helens), then I've got a spellbinding secret for you. You can stay in a home crafted just like Hagrid's hut—giant wooden furniture fit for a half-giant, a dragon overhead, and authentic wizarding touches that make you feel like you've wandered straight out of the pages of the Harry Potter books.

HALF-GIANT HUT

HALF-GIANT HUT

Itinerary Outline

DAY 1

Explore Fort Vancouver National Historic Site: This landmark tells the story of trade in the area, from Indigenous communities to the Hudson's Bay Company's fur trading post built over two hundred years ago. It also tells a story you might not expect: the production of airplanes during World War I for the US Army. Be sure to stop off at these points to get the full experience:

- **Fort Vancouver Visitor Center:** Get oriented by watching a documentary film, strolling through educational exhibits, and picking up a local-interest book.
- **Reconstructed British fur trading fort:** Wander through a beautiful garden, an impressive bastion (three-story tower), and check out the old jail.
- **Pearson Air Museum:** Discover historic aircraft from World War I.

Dinner at Wahi Hana Tiki Bar: This tropical-themed spot is a welcoming place to settle in with a fun drink in hand. The Polynesian cuisine—such as kalua pork, *lumpia*, and Spam fried rice—nails it every time. Don't skip the Dole Whip for dessert!

DAY 2

Breakfast at Syrup Trap: Think you know waffles? Think again. This is *the* spot to treat yourself to *Liège* waffles. I can't resist the apple pie filling, streusel, caramel, and whipped cream. In a savory mood? Try a breakfast sandwich—on a waffle, of course.

Grab coffee from Relevant Coffee: Fuel up before hitting the road at my favorite coffee shop in Vancouver. The seasonal lattes are a must-try, and there's also a great matcha on the menu, all to enjoy in this cozy, bright space.

Explore Mount St. Helens National Volcanic Monument

At the time of writing, Johnston Ridge Observatory (the furthest drivable point in the park) was closed due to a landslide but is scheduled to reopen in 2027. That said, there's still plenty to explore!

- **Mount St Helens Visitor Center (Castle Rock):** Discover exactly what happened on May 18, 1980, when Mount St Helens erupted, the far-reaching impacts, and how the landscape has recovered.
- **Coldwater Lake:** Marvel at this intensely blue lake, formed by the eruption.
- **Hummocks Trail:** Hike a 2.4-mile loop through distinctive terrain with excellent views of the mountain and North Fork Toutle River. Keep an eye out for elk, mountain goats, and wildflowers (*reminder to stay on the trail to protect fragile plants!*) Expect around one hundred feet of elevation gain.

Lunch at Heathen Brewing Feral Public House: After your volcanic adventure, kick back on the outdoor patio with locally made cider or beer. As a cider fan, I love the selection—my favorite is the pineapple dream, which tastes like island time in a glass. The generous food menu includes pizza, tacos, and burgers.

Explore Beacon Rock State Park: Get a bird's-eye view of the Columbia River Gorge by hiking a steep mile up the ancient volcano known as Beacon Rock. This trail is unlike any other, zigzagging up the rock face with stunning views along the way. Not a fan of heights? Opt for the Doetsch Walking Path instead—a peaceful, picturesque trail with no elevation gain.

Go shopping

- **Vancouver Farmers' Market:** From pottery to handmade soaps to fresh flowers, you never know what treasures you'll find at this vibrant market.
- **Pop-Local:** Browse over 250 local brands from the Vancouver and Portland Metro area—all in one space! No trip to Vancouver is complete without tapping into what the community here is up to.
- **Persnickety:** Discover gorgeous vintage furniture—it reminds me of my grandparents' house (in the best way!)

Dinner at Grassa: Wind down with a comforting bowl of handcrafted pasta and meatballs at this laid-back spot near the waterfront.

MOUNT ST. HELENS

Catch the sunset over the Columbia River: After dinner, walk a couple of steps to the lively Vancouver waterfront, where you can catch the sunset with a few bridges and Mount Hood in the distance.

DAY 3

Breakfast at Seize the Bagel: Bagels for breakfast? Always a good idea. This local, family-owned spot offers build-your-own egg sandwiches, seasonal specials, and classic bagels with spreads. It's so good, you might want to grab a baker's dozen to take home!

Chase waterfalls: Follow the East Fork Lewis River for not one, but two easily accessible waterfalls. You can drive to each or connect them by trail. Up for a challenge? Extend your adventure on the Bells Mountain Trail.

- **Lucia Falls Regional Park:** 1.1 miles with two hundred feet of elevation gain
- **Moulton Falls Regional Park:** four miles with ninety feet of elevation gain

Bestie Tip: Download a trail map ahead of time—this area isn't known for the best signage, and you don't want to get lost!

The Takeaway: Did you know that you can stand in the shadow of a volcano that changed the course of history in 1980? Using Vancouver as your home base positions you perfectly to explore Mount St. Helen's powerful story—one of resilience, regrowth, and raw natural force. Spend your days exploring lunar-like landscapes and gazing into deep blue lakes born from the blast, then return to a city that balances creature comforts and foodie-approved restaurants with historic roots such as old fur trading posts. Vancouver proves that some of the most fascinating adventures happen when geological drama meets Pacific Northwest hospitality. It's a destination where every vista tells stories of both catastrophe and renewal, reminding us of nature's incredible ability to both destroy and create anew.

OLYMPIC NATIONAL PARK

HURRICANE RIDGE

33

PORT ANGELES

(OLYMPIC PENINSULA PART 1)

Introduction

I'm not sure when it started, but spending early summer on the Olympic Peninsula has become a tradition for Kyle and me. There's something magical about watching baby ducklings paddle across Lake Crescent, standing beneath towering old-growth trees, and witnessing the sun set over a wildflower-strewn meadow with snow-capped peaks in the background. These are the moments that keep drawing us back.

The Olympic Peninsula is one of the last places where you can truly immerse yourself in raw, untamed beauty. It's a place that taps into that deep human instinct to connect with nature. And honestly? It's far too vast to experience in just one weekend. That's why I've put together three separate itineraries, each exploring a different corner of this rugged wonderland. You can tackle them one at a time or string them together for an epic weeklong road trip.

While there's a special charm to visiting in the offseason (especially if you love those moody, misty PNW days straight out of *Twilight*), summer is the undisputed best time to go. Long daylight hours make for adventure-filled days, and cooler coastal temperatures offer a refreshing break, especially if, like me, you're escaping a home without air-conditioning.

SALT CREEK RECREATION AREA

This itinerary is centered around Port Angeles, the gateway to Olympic National Park. With the most dining and lodging options in the region, chances are you'll pass through here even if you opt to sleep under the stars. Summer also brings the most reliable access to Hurricane Ridge—one of the crown jewels of the park. Perched at 5,242 feet, this alpine area is often cloaked in snow and subject to unpredictable closures the rest of the year. But come summer, the road is usually clear and open daily, making it much easier to reach those panoramic mountain views and high-elevation wildflower meadows. If seeing the Olympic Mountains in all their glory is on your list, this is the time to go.

At a Glance

Location: Olympic Peninsula, Washington
Best Season to Visit: June through September
Suggested Duration: Two or three nights

Park Information

- **Entrance fee:** $30 per vehicle (seven days) or $55 annual America the Beautiful Pass
- Main entrances, including Hurricane Ridge, Sol Duc, and Lake Crescent, are open in summer
- **Check current conditions:** nps.gov/olym or call (360) 565-3130

Getting There

Seattle to Port Angeles: 138 miles (without ferries), ~2 hours 30 minutes

- **Ferry option:** Seattle–Bainbridge or Edmonds–Kingston ferries shorten mileage but maintain similar travel times

Portland to Port Angeles: 230 miles, ~4 hours 25 minutes

Where to Stay

Lake Crescent Lodge: If you're looking to unplug, this historic lakeside retreat is pure magic. Stay in a lodge room, a cozy cottage, or a spacious cabin—all just steps from the deep, vividly blue waters of Lake Crescent. Its sister property, the Log Cabin Resort, is another fantastic option, tucked away on the opposite shore.

Salt Creek Recreation Area: For jaw-dropping views of the Strait of Juan de Fuca, this scenic campground is unbeatable. At high tide, Tongue Point becomes an island; at low tide, the tide pools are teeming with life. Campsites aren't the most private, but the waterfront views make up for it. Book in advance! If you're planning a last-minute trip, try Heart O' the Hills Campground—a first-come, first-served forested site surprisingly close to town.

Red Lion Hotel Port Angeles Harbor: Located in the heart of downtown, this waterfront hotel is a convenient base camp. Opt for a premium room to enjoy sunset views from your balcony. Bonus: It's dog friendly, and there's a small beach just steps away.

Itinerary Outline

DAY 1

Catch the sunset at Hurricane Ridge: Drive from sea level in Port Angeles to 5,242 feet at Hurricane Ridge, the highest point accessible by car in Olympic National Park, and you'll reach the mountainous side of the park. The panoramic mountain views are unreal, and you never know what wildlife might make an appearance—we've spotted deer and the Olympic marmot, which is a species unique to this area. In summer, visit in the evening to avoid crowds.

CAPE FLATTERY

Dinner at Frugals: Hit this local favorite drive-through for great rotating milkshakes and perfectly crispy fries. My family has been going to Frugals for as long as I can remember!

> **Bestie Tip:** Check the website for a hidden menu—my go-to is the spicy chicken club.

DAY 2

Morning

Northwestmost corner adventure

- Scenic drive and Cape Flattery exploration
- Morning: Drive to Neah Bay: Head west along the Strait of Juan de Fuca Highway, stopping at roadside pull-offs to admire ocean views. On sunny days, the water almost looks tropical!

Breakfast at Native Grounds Espresso (Neah Bay): Enjoy made-to-order breakfast staples, such as burritos, sandwiches, and pancakes. My recommendation is the loaded sriracha sandwich that will keep you full for morning adventures! For sweet treats, don't miss the incredible ube cheesecake.

Makah Cultural & Research Center Museum: Step into the Makah Tribe's story through this unique museum, revealing village artifacts preserved beneath mudslides for hundreds of years. While here, purchase a Makah Recreation Pass for Cape Flattery parking ($10 daily, $30 annual) or buy online ahead of time.

> **Cultural Note:** Allow time to fully appreciate the museum's artifacts and cultural significance—this isn't just a quick stop before hiking.

Hike to Cape Flattery: Reach Washington's northwesternmost point via this forested trail transitioning to wooden boardwalks. Dramatic views of tree-topped sea stacks and vibrant blue-green waters create magical moments. The trail covers about three-quarters of a mile each way with minimal elevation gain.

> **Safety Tip:** Boardwalks can be slippery when wet, and cliff edges lack barriers—stay on designated paths and supervise children closely.

Lunch at Pat's Place: I remember my first Indian taco like it was yesterday—eagles soared overhead, seals swam in the water, and the sun was shining. This is where I first tried Indian Fry Bread as part of a taco, and it was delicious! Enjoy meals at picnic tables overlooking the marina.

Afternoon

Hike to Sol Duc Falls: This waterfall adventure meanders through old-growth forest to a wooden bridge overlooking cascading waters. Explore different viewpoints and prepare to get sprayed! The trail covers a 1.6-mile round trip with two hundred feet of elevation gain.

> **Timing Note:** This location is about forty-five minutes from Neah Bay, so plan accordingly for afternoon activities.

Explore Lake Crescent: Hike to Marymere Falls. Don't miss this fairylike waterfall that exceeds expectations. The easy trail offers incredible old-growth tree photo opportunities along the way.

Paddle from Lake Crescent Lodge: Rent kayaks, canoes, or paddleboards from Lake Crescent Lodge and soak in the scenery. Fair warning—the water stays icy cold year-round!

SOL DUC FALLS

Advanced Option: Experienced hikers comfortable with heights can continue to Mount Storm King for amazing Lake Crescent views from above. However, this Instagram-popular trail involves ropes and sheer drop-offs at the top—it's more dangerous than expected and requires serious caution.

Dinner at Midtown Public House: Give your taste buds something to rave about at this vibrant Asian fusion pub. Whether choosing Korean street tacos with bulgogi, lemon-grass tofu, chili sesame noodle bowls, or perfectly crafted banh mi sandwiches, every bite packs bold flavors.

DAY 3

Breakfast at Fogtown Coffee Bar: Kick off the day with a breakfast burrito or sandwich—don't forget to say yes to the sriracha mayo. Pair it with your favorite drink—be it coffee, tea, or an energy boost. This is my favorite coffee shop in Port Angeles!

Explore the Ediz Hook: Drive out onto the three-mile sand spit, stopping at Harborview Park to look for birds and seals. Bring a windbreaker—the wind can be strong here.

Learn about the Salish Sea at the Feiro Marine Life Center: This small but mighty aquarium will surprise you. And it's not just about looking—it's about doing. There are touch tanks that can help you become more familiar with the creatures that live in tide pools.

Tide pooling at Salt Creek Recreation Area: Put your new marine life knowledge to the test and explore real tide pools at low tide at this picturesque beach! Check tide charts ahead of time for optimal low-tide timing.

The Takeaway: Sample what makes the Evergreen State so jaw-droppingly beautiful in a weekend that takes you from salt-sprayed beaches to glacier-capped peaks, all while exploring the very edge of the continental United States at Washington's northwesternmost corner. From watching the sunrise paint Olympic peaks in alpenglow to discovering ancient Makah artifacts preserved by mudslides, this corner of the peninsula offers experiences that connect you to both natural wonder and cultural heritage. This is part one of three Olympic Peninsula itineraries, each offering its own slice of this extraordinary wilderness where mountains meet sea in ways that will leave you planning your return before you've even left.

RUBY BEACH

34 OLYMPIC COAST

(OLYMPIC PENINSULA PART 2)

Introduction

One of the first places Kyle and I explored together was the remote and untamed Olympic coastline. We both grew up spending summers camping farther south along Washington's beaches, where small coastal towns and developed campgrounds made the area feel more accessible. But something about the Olympic Peninsula pulled us in: its dramatic landscapes of jagged sea stacks rising from the surf and moody fog drifting through ancient rainforests felt almost otherworldly.

Olympic National Park is one of the few places where you can experience a misty, driftwood-strewn shoreline and moss-draped forest, and we were eager to experience it for ourselves. What we didn't expect was finding some of the largest trees in the world hidden among the Peninsula's temperate rainforests—giants that have stood for centuries, weathering Pacific storms. We also didn't anticipate the added charm that Forks would bring to our trip. Forever linked to the *Twilight* saga, this small town embraces its vampire lore with quirky photo ops and themed attractions that delight fans like me (someone who owns multiple copies of the books and still rereads them to usher in fall).

Forks also serves as a convenient stop for groceries, coffee, or warm meals while exploring this rugged stretch of coast. Our very first trip out here was a day trip—big mistake! Olympic National Park deserves more than a rushed visit, and ever since, we've taken our time to soak it all in.

Whether it's camping along the coast, pitching a tent deep in the rainforest, or staying in a cozy lodge near the surf, summer and the shoulder seasons are ideal for making unforgettable memories here. If you're planning to camp, summer is by far the most comfortable time to visit. Most of the lodging options out here are rustic—think tent sites and no-frills cabins rather than resorts—so having longer daylight hours, drier weather, and warmer temperatures can make a big difference in your experience. Coastal mornings can still be misty, and evenings can get chilly, but summer gives you the best shot at sunny stretches and those magical golden hours on the beach. If you've ever dreamed of falling asleep to the sound of crashing waves, summer is the season to make it happen.

A few essential reminders: this area is remote. Cell service is spotty at best, so download maps ahead of time. Grocery stores and restaurants are few and far between, so pack extra food. And, above all, embrace the wildness of it all. Out here, the waves crash a little louder, the trees stand a little taller, and time slows down. Let it.

TREE OF LIFE

At a Glance

Location: Olympic Peninsula, Washington
Best Season to Visit: May through September
Suggested Duration: Two nights

Park Information

- **Entrance fee:** $30 per vehicle (seven days) or $55 annual America the Beautiful Pass
- **Main entrances,** including Quinault and Hoh Rain Forest, are open in summer
- **Check current conditions:** nps.gov/olym or call (360) 565-3130

LILO AT KALALOCH

Getting There

Seattle to Kalaloch: 177 miles, ~3 hours
Portland to Kalaloch: 211 miles, ~3 hours 40 minutes

Where to Stay

Kalaloch Lodge: If you dream of falling asleep to the soothing sound of crashing waves, Kalaloch Lodge is your spot. These cozy, rustic cabins are pet friendly and offer the perfect home base for exploring both the beaches and rainforests of the Olympic Peninsula.

Kalaloch Campground: This beachfront campground within Olympic National Park is one of Washington's most coveted spots for camping. Book your site well in advance—you might just score an ocean-front view! Looking for another option? South Beach Campground is just down the road, but its sites are a bit less private.

Vacation rentals: With limited hotel options in this remote region, a vacation rental is a great alternative. For a more modern and private stay, check out options on Airbnb. If you want to be close to a town with grocery stores, restaurants, and shops, look for rentals near Forks.

Budget Tip: Dispersed camping is available in Olympic National Forest areas—just come prepared for self-sufficiency and practice Leave No Trace to keep the wilderness wild.

Itinerary Outline

DAY 1

Quinault Valley and coastal introduction—Explore the Quinault Valley: Morning: Quinault Rainforest—Step into lush worlds of towering trees, moss-draped branches, and emerald ferns. For quick adventures, try the half-mile nature trail loop. Ready for more? Extend the hike along the lake for longer scenic routes.

Practical Stops

- **Quinault Rain Forest Ranger Station:** Get trail recommendations and area history.
- **World's Largest Sitka Spruce:** A short detour brings you face-to-trunk with this massive, centuries-old giant.
- **Merriman Falls:** This picturesque roadside waterfall is worth a quick photo stop.
- **Kestner Homestead Trail:** See remnants of nineteenth-century life in this remote area with peaceful strolls on the 1.3-mile loop trail through historic homestead sites.

> **Bestie Tip:** If coastal campsites are full, check out Graves Creek Campground—a peaceful, lesser-known spot nestled deep in rainforest along the Quinault River.

Picnic by Lake Quinault: Take breaks and enjoy packed lunches with serene lakeside views. This is also an excellent spot for photography with reflections of the surrounding peaks.

Dinner at Creekside Restaurant: This is of the few dining options on this part of the coast, and you might be surprised by the quality American seafood dishes at Kalaloch Lodge's restaurant. The menu isn't huge, but each entrée delivers. Save room for dessert!

Catch the sunset at Kalaloch Beach: One of the most popular and easily accessible parts of the park is Kalaloch. For shorter hikes, check out access points along Highway 101 between South Beach Campground and Kalaloch Beach 4. I love the Spruce Burl Trailhead—the knotty trees are fascinating and unique! Note that driftwood conditions might make reaching sandy beaches tricky or impossible.

DAY 2

Forks & Ruby Beach, Baby! Visit Forks—the *Twilight* Town: If you're anything like me and have been obsessed with the *Twilight* saga since your teens, it's worth visiting the town where the books are set. While the movies weren't filmed here, the town fully embraces its vampire and werewolf fame!

Forks Timber Museum: Driving into town from Kalaloch, the first thing you'll see is Bella's iconic orange truck! Pull in to snap photos and explore the museum showcasing the region's logging roots. There's a small admission fee, and hours vary seasonally.

Breakfast at A Shot In the Dark: Grab quick, tasty breakfast sandwiches (croissant or bagel—your choice!) and strong coffee. The seasonal specials are always worth trying.

Forever Twilight in Forks Collection: This small but passionate museum overflows with movie props, costumes, and behind-the-scenes memorabilia. Volunteers here are super friendly and happy to chat about all things *Twilight*! Donations are appreciated.

Photo Ops

- Forks Welcome Sign (obviously!)
- Forks High School
- Forks Community Hospital—Dr. Cullen's reserved parking space

HOH RAIN FOREST

Bestie Tip: Hardcore *Twilight* fans should time visits during the annual Forever Twilight in Forks Festival (usually mid-September) for chances to meet actors and get autographs.

Explore Ruby Beach: One of the most ruggedly beautiful beaches on the Olympic Peninsula, Ruby Beach delivers sea stacks, tide pools filled with starfish, and epic sunsets. From the parking lot, expect a short but somewhat steep trail, including stairs, to reach the beach.

Best Timing: Visit at low tide for optimal tide pool exploration. Check tide charts ahead of time.

Safety Note: Never turn your back on the ocean—sneaker waves can be dangerous. Stay aware of rising tides when exploring tide pools.

Photography Tip: Golden hour here casts the sea stacks and driftwood in a dreamy glow, perfect for silhouettes. Arrive about thirty minutes before sunset for the best light—and if you can, get low! Shooting from a low angle near tide pools or streams is one of my favorite ways to capture the magic.

DAY 3

Breakfast at the Creekside Restaurant: Treat yourself to marionberry-stuffed French toast or a classic breakfast platter on your final morning at the coast—get a table by the window to soak up the views while you eat.

Explore the Hoh Rain Forest: Before leaving the Olympic Coast, there's one more rainforest you need to experience! Known for having one of the quietest spots in the country, it's worth getting as early a start as you can to get here (as the lines get long to enter the national park).

The Hall of Mosses Trail: If you've ever seen a picture of the Hoh Rain Forest, it was probably taken along this 0.8-mile loop. With massive moss-draped maples, it feels like stepping into a fairy tale.

After completing the Hall of Mosses, it's worth seeking solitude on one of the area's other trails, such as the Spruce Nature Trail or the Hoh River Trail: the latter is a lengthy trail at almost twenty miles, which you can make more of an adventure.

The Takeaway: Rugged beauty takes on a whole new depth after standing beneath the moss-draped giants of the Hoh Rain Forest and catching the final flickers of daylight over the Pacific Ocean—golden hour here feels like something straight out of a dream (or a vampire saga). From tide pool discoveries that reveal hidden underwater worlds to moments of stillness among ancient trees that have weathered centuries of coastal storms, this stretch of the Olympic Peninsula is pure magic. And, yes, it's the perfect place to let your inner *Twilight* fan run free—this is the land of brooding skies, mysterious forests, and the kind of moody beauty that inspired an entire supernatural world. This is part two of three Olympic itineraries, focused on the untamed majesty where ancient forests meet the endless ocean—a place where time moves differently and nature still writes the rules.

35

SEQUIM

(OLYMPIC PENINSULA PART 3)

Introduction

If there's one underrated town on the Olympic Peninsula, it's Sequim. Every time I visit, I feel an unmistakable warmth, both from the friendly community and the abundant sunshine. Thanks to its location in the rain shadow of the Olympic Mountains, Sequim enjoys more sunny days than many surrounding areas, making it a perfect destination for a Pacific Northwest weekend getaway when you're craving vitamin D.

My first impression of Sequim was spectacular natural beauty perched above the serene waters of Dungeness Bay. One of its most striking landmarks is the Dungeness Spit—a narrow, five-mile stretch of land reaching into the water. Home to the historic New Dungeness Lighthouse and a protected refuge for wildlife, this unique feature is a must-see, especially for bird-watchers and beachcombers.

Unlike some of the more rugged spots along the Olympic Coast—where the best campsites often book out months in advance—Sequim is refreshingly easy to plan for. It's one of the most laid-back stops on this stretch of the Peninsula. With a wider variety of vacation rentals and accommodations, it's especially well-suited for spontaneous trips or last-minute getaways. That flexibility, paired with all the sunshine, makes it a breath of fresh air.

Our first visit to Sequim was actually a spontaneous detour for brunch. I had seen a photo of a cozy Bavarian-style cottage, followed by a snapshot of a coffee drink that instantly stole my heart. That was all it took to reroute our trip straight to The Oak Table Café. Once inside, I showed our waitress the coffee photo and learned it was called a Viennese—a rich, cinnamon- and vanilla-infused drink topped with house-made espresso whipped cream. I don't always go for hot coffee, but this one is simply irresistible (and picture-perfect!).

The food proved equally spectacular. From the airy, soufflé-like apple pancakes to the creamy blintzes and indulgent smoked salmon eggs Benedict, every bite at The Oak Table Café feels like a treat. Believe me—this place alone is worth the trip to Sequim.

But Sequim isn't just about exceptional food. It's also an invitation to slow down, breathe in the fresh air, and immerse yourself in nature. Whether it's strolling through the many green spaces, exploring the iconic lavender fields in the summertime, or simply savoring a peaceful moment by the water, this charming town is the perfect place to relax and recharge. Come to Sequim, step outside, eat well, and soak up that precious Pacific Northwest sunshine.

At a Glance

Location: Clallam County, Washington
Best Season to Visit: May through September
Suggested Duration: Two nights

Getting There

Seattle to Sequim: 122 miles (with no ferries), ~2 hours 30 minutes

- **Ferry option:** Seattle–Bainbridge or Edmonds–Kingston ferries shorten mileage, though travel time is roughly the same

Portland to Sequim: 214 miles, ~3 hours 45 minutes

Where to Stay

Juan de Fuca Cottages: For a relaxing, romantic stay with some of the best views in Sequim, this is the spot, and it's dog friendly! Splurge on a cottage with a private hot tub—perfect for watching the sunset.

Holiday Inn Express & Suites Sequim: If you want to stay close to town, this hotel gets the job done. Enjoy free breakfast, electric vehicle charging, and an indoor pool.

Camping at the Dungeness Recreation Area: Refresh your soul at this forested campsite perched on a bluff overlooking the water. It's just a short (but steep) walk to the beach. Showers are available.

Itinerary Outline

DAY 1

Explore the Dungeness Recreation Center: If you're a nature lover, this spot will seal the deal on Sequim for you. We spontaneously stopped here to stretch our legs, and I was immediately won over by the hyper-local educational exhibits, which tell the story of the Dungeness River watershed—from its origins in the Olympic Mountains all the way to the Strait of Juan de Fuca. Learn about the native species that call this area home, then step outside and experience the beauty firsthand with a walk through the park. If you have a furry friend, this is a fantastic place to explore, especially the scenic stretch across the Railroad Bridge.

Dinner at Salty Girls: Tap into coastal vibes at this fresh seafood spot, which is best known for its raw oyster bar (you can even do a flight!). You also can't go wrong with the comforting clam chowder or perfectly grilled sandwiches. Pair your meal with a locally crafted cider, wine, kombucha, or beer on tap.

DUNGENESS LIGHTHOUSE

DAY 2

Breakfast at The Oak Table Café: For a breakfast you'll never forget, cozy up inside this Bavarian-style cottage. If you're anything like me, choosing just one dish will be nearly impossible—every item on the made-from-scratch menu is crafted with love. You have to try the apple pancake at least once—it's the café's specialty!

THE OAK TABLE CAFÉ

Explore the Dungeness National Wildlife Refuge

- Follow the paved walking path through a windswept forest that leads to a breathtaking sandy beach. Along the way, stop at the viewpoint to take in the full scale of the Dungeness Spit—it stretches much farther into the water than you might expect! At its very tip stands the New Dungeness Lighthouse.
- **Lighthouse hike option:** For those who enjoy really long beach walks (and time it right with the tides), you can hike all the way out to it and even take a tour to the top. It's a serious trek—one that Kyle and I tackled on a day with 40 mph winds! But even if you don't venture all the way, the beach itself offers jaw-dropping views of the Olympic Mountains rising over the water. I could hardly believe my eyes.

Lunch at Baja Cantina: This family-owned Mexican grill is the place to go for flavorful, generously portioned platters and refreshing margaritas. I'm never not in the mood for authentic, homey Mexican food like this!

OLYMPIC DISCOVERY TRAIL

Bike on the Olympic Discovery Trail: This epic rail trail spans over 135 miles across the Olympic Peninsula, welcoming both walkers and cyclists. While you don't need to tackle the entire stretch, exploring even a small section offers a fun off-the-beaten-path adventure. From Sequim, try starting at Sequim Bay State Park or the Dungeness River Nature Center for a scenic ride.

Dinner at Alder Wood Bistro: Savor some of the best wood-fired pizza in the Pacific Northwest in this cozy garden setting. This spot elevates pizza to fine-dining levels, featuring house sourdough made with local organic flour. It's so good you might want to take a loaf of the sourdough home with you! Pair your pizza with one of the fresh, creative salads for the ultimate meal.

DAY 3

Breakfast at Hi-Way 101 Diner: Step back into the 1950s at this charming diner, which instantly reminded me of *Grease.* The hearty breakfast plates will leave you fully satisfied, and the milkshakes are so good you'll be tempted to have one before lunch.

Explore lavender fields: Before heading home, stop by one of Sequim's famous lavender fields for stunning photo ops and locally made lavender products—the lemonade is my absolute favorite! B&B Family Lavender Farm is a third-generation, family-run operation with over fourteen thousand lavender plants, and it's completely free to visit. Don't miss the brief but fascinating tours, where you can learn about the lavender farming process.

The Takeaway: Savor a silky Viennese latte, pedal along a scenic rail trail, and wander out to a windswept lighthouse in the "Lavender Capital of North America." From sun-drenched lavender fields that paint the landscape purple each summer to pristine beaches where you can walk for miles without seeing another soul, Sequim represents the gentler side of Olympic Peninsula exploration. Whether you're discovering the intricate ecosystem of Dungeness Spit, indulging in farm-to-table cuisine that celebrates local ingredients, or simply enjoying reliable sunshine that makes every outdoor adventure more appealing, this charming town proves that some of the best Pacific Northwest experiences happen when you slow down and savor the moment. This is part three of three Olympic Peninsula itineraries, spotlighting the easygoing charm and unexpected sunshine of a place that feels like the region's best-kept secret.

MOUNTAIN BIKING AT OAKRIDGE

36 EUGENE

Introduction

You've probably heard of Eugene for its track-and-field legacy, Nike connections, and as home to the University of Oregon. But what you might not know is that it's also an ideal weekend getaway for anyone who loves a mix of outdoor adventure, incredible local food, and a sense of history that deepens your connection to place. With its convenient location right off I-5, getting here is a breeze—and once you arrive, you'll realize just how much more Eugene has to offer beyond its college-town reputation.

My first few visits were just quick coffee breaks en route to the coast, but even then, I could feel the city's friendly energy and see how lush and green everything was. On this trip, I finally carved out a full weekend to explore—and I'm so glad I did. One of my favorite finds was Farmers Union Coffee Roasters, tucked inside a historic egg warehouse with pink roasting equipment, warm wood beams, and strong, sustainably sourced coffee that made me want to stay and linger. From there, I wandered to a dreamy romantasy bookshop, climbed to sweeping views atop Spencer Butte, and discovered that Eugene has hiking trails in nearly every direction—including a few right in the heart of downtown.

What really sealed the deal, though, was the nearby mountain town of Oakridge. Kyle and I planned this trip around his birthday to take advantage of the region's hundreds of miles of mountain biking trails—even in winter! While he rode the legendary Alpine Trail, I chased waterfalls and explored charming covered bridges nearby. Between Eugene's vibrant downtown and Oakridge's wild spirit, our weekend struck the perfect balance of cozy, adventurous, and unforgettable.

At a Glance

Location: Southern Willamette Valley, Oregon
Best Season to Visit: May through September
Suggested Duration: Two nights

Getting There

Seattle to Eugene: 283 miles, ~4 hours 30 minutes
Portland to Eugene: 110 miles, ~1 hour 45 minutes

> **Bestie Tip:** Plan around University of Oregon events—football weekends and graduation can impact accommodation availability and downtown crowds.

Where to Stay

The Gordon Hotel: Right in the heart of Eugene, this stylish downtown stay defines modern luxury. Upgrade to a suite for extra space and cozy amenities, such as a fireplace and soaking tub. Bonus: it's pet friendly!

Home2 Suites by Hilton: For a classic stay in a recently renovated building, this dog-friendly hotel is a solid pick. Enjoy the indoor pool for relaxation and take advantage of the walkable location—it's just steps from downtown's best restaurants and shopping.

Vacation rentals: For a comfortable stay that won't break the bank, I love checking out the Airbnb rentals in the neighborhoods of Eugene. One area we really enjoyed was Whiteaker, there were definitely some hidden gem restaurants that we walked to!

Itinerary Outline

DAY 1

Coffee at Farmers Union Coffee Roasters: One of my favorite finds in Eugene—discovered completely by chance—is this charming café with a pretty pink roasting machine and seriously good coffee made from sustainably sourced beans. Housed in a historic former egg warehouse, the space has an airy, farmhouse feel with high

FARMERS UNION COFFEE ROASTERS

DAFFODIL ROMANTASY BOOKS & GIFTS

ceilings, exposed wooden beams, and a handful of outdoor tables tucked away on the patio. While you wait for your drink, take a moment to admire the vintage details, such as the old black-and-white aerial photo of Eugene and the playful nods to the building's past.

SPENCER BUTTE

Daffodil Romantasy Books & Gifts: Just around the corner, step into a magical little bookstore made for lovers of romantic fantasy. Whether you're popping in to pick up your next otherworldly read or lingering to cozy up in the beautifully curated space, you'll feel the heart and intention poured into every detail. With weathered book pages suspended from the ceiling and the glow of antique lamps lighting the shelves, it's a place that stays with you long after leaving.

Sunset hike at Spencer Butte Trail: Kick off your adventure with a pup-friendly hike to the highest point in Eugene, where you'll be rewarded with sweeping valley views—and on a clear day, you might even spot the Three Sisters peaks in the distance. The 1.7-mile round-trip trail climbs about 730 feet, making for a satisfying but doable workout. I couldn't believe this gem was less than twenty minutes from the city!

Dinner at Nelson's in the Whit: After working up an appetite, settle into a seat at a picnic table at one of the most welcoming spots I've had the pleasure of visiting. Nelson's serves up authentic Latin fusion in a laid-back, community-centered setting that makes you feel right at home. During happy hour, don't miss the $7 lime margarita with a *Tajín* rim—it's the perfect mix of spicy and refreshing. We couldn't resist the birria tamales (made fresh daily), and they absolutely hit the spot.

> **Bestie Tip:** Our server, Jordan, tipped us off to a local favorite—Prince Puckler's Ice Cream. If you're a mint chip fan, order the Obama, named after President Obama's spontaneous visit in 2008 when he picked that very flavor. Huge thanks to Jordan for the warm hospitality and spot-on recs—you made our night!

DAY 2

Breakfast at Morning Glory Café: Start your morning on a cheery note at this beloved plant-based café. Whether you're in the mood for sweet waffles and French toast or a savory omelet, you'll find plenty to love—including lots of vegan-friendly options! For me, the chiliquiles hit the spot every time.

OWEN ROSE GARDEN

MORNING GLORY CAFÉ

Stroll through Owen Rose Garden: Just a short walk from downtown, this peaceful garden is the perfect place to slow down and let your worries melt away among the blooms. It's easy to see why locals love it for picnics, bike rides, and leisurely walks. Honestly, I didn't make it more than a few steps from our car before I started snapping photos of the flowers. In the summertime, over four hundred varieties of roses burst into bloom.

Explore the Castle on the Hill: Tucked right in downtown Eugene, the Shelton McMurphey Johnson House (or Castle on the Hill) is an architectural gem. This grand Victorian home from the late eighteen hundreds is open for tours (no reservations needed), though it's a good idea to check ahead for private events.

Visit the Museum of Natural and Cultural History: Okay, I'm a proud University of Washington alum (so technically a rival to the University of Oregon), but I have to admit—this museum is incredible. It tells Oregon's story in a fascinating, immersive way, from towering fossils of prehistoric animals to archaeological finds, such as the world's oldest known shoes (yep, ten thousand years old!). It was wild to be shadowed by the seven-foot-tall Harlan's ground sloth from the Ice Age!

Lunch at the Saturday Market: Join this local tradition, in which more than two hundred vendors bring tie-dye, ceramics, art prints, and more to life, all with live music in the background. Once you've shopped up an appetite, head to the International Food Court for a variety of cuisines. You just might find the best mac and cheese or taco salad you've ever had.

OAKRIDGE

Explore Oakridge

- **Hike to Salt Creek Falls:** It's pretty amazing that all it takes is a sense of adventure and a couple of footsteps to see the second-highest single-drop waterfall in the state! You'll find it in the Willamette National Forest.
- **Ride mountain bikes:** Oakridge is practically synonymous with mountain biking, so if you're up for some thrills, hit the trails! Alpine Trail is one of the most iconic and is an easy shuttle. Rentals are available at Oakridge Bike Shop.
- **Admire the historic covered bridges:** I wasn't expecting to come across so many charming, picturesque covered bridges near Oakridge. Two I highly recommend are the Office Covered Bridge (the longest in Oregon) and Lowell Covered Bridge (the widest in Oregon).

Dinner at Stewart's 58 Drive-In: Before heading back to Eugene, grab a casual, feel-good meal at this roadside gem. The crispy onion rings, Tillamook ice cream milkshakes, and hot burgers are the perfect way to wrap up the day.

OFFICE COVERED BRIDGE

DAY 3

Breakfast at Jazzy Ladies Café: A weekend in Eugene isn't complete without breakfast enchiladas—yes, seriously. Every dish here is packed with flavor, and the coffee comes with fun, musically inspired latte art that's one of a kind.

Explore the Mount Pisgah Arboretum: For one last dose of Eugene's natural beauty, wander the trails at this two-hundred-acre nature preserve. Stroll along the river, meander through an oak savanna, or climb to the summit for one final scenic view before heading home.

The Takeaway: If you or someone you know is hooked on mountain biking, the Eugene–Oakridge duo is a must-explore adventure. Eugene bursts with personality—from a dreamy romantic fantasy bookstore to a vibrant Latin fusion happy hour and scenic overlook trails that steal your breath. For day trip escapes, Oakridge serves as the Northwest's mountain biking mecca, where thrilling trails meet charming historic covered bridges and stunning waterfalls. Eugene offers the perfect launching pad for exploring everything from Cascade peaks to coastal day trips, all while maintaining that authentic, welcoming spirit that makes you want to return again and again.

SEAWALL PARK

37

LANGLEY

Introduction

Whidbey Island was the first island I ever fell in love with—not because it's the largest in the Pacific Northwest, but because it's the place where I feel most like myself. It's hard to explain, but the moment I'm standing on the outer ferry deck, watching the island grow closer, something shifts. My shoulders relax, my breathing slows, and I catch myself smiling—just because.

Surprisingly, even though Langley is the closest of Whidbey's more touristy towns to Seattle, it was the last part of the island I explored. I've always been drawn to the rugged beauty of Deception Pass State Park and the charm of Anacortes, so most of my time was spent on North and Central Whidbey. But one day, with a few extra minutes before our ferry home, we decided to swing through Langley—and I was instantly hooked.

The town was bustling, alive with the hum of conversation, the scent of fresh coffee, and the sight of people ducking in and out of boutiques and galleries. I could tell immediately that this place, known as the Village by the Sea, had a special energy. It made a strong first impression—and every visit since has only reinforced that feeling.

Langley is a haven for artists and nature lovers, a town that wears its love for the environment (and whales!) on its sleeve. It's walkable, welcoming, and packed with incredible views of the water and mountains beyond. The combination of creative

GLASS ART

MUKILTEO-CLINTON FERRY

spirit, environmental consciousness, and stunning Pacific Northwest scenery creates experiences that feel both sophisticated and authentically island-relaxed. If you're looking for a place that captures the magic of island life, you've found it. I can't wait for you to experience it for yourself.

At a Glance

Location: South Whidbey Island, Washington
Best Season to Visit: May through September
Suggested Duration: Two nights

Getting There

Seattle to Langley: 35.8 miles, ~1 hour 10 minutes

- Includes the Mukilteo–Clinton ferry (~20 minutes)

Portland to Langley: 209 miles, ~3 hours 50 minutes

- Includes the Mukilteo–Clinton ferry (~20 minutes)

Where to Stay

Inn at Langley: Nestled along Saratoga Passage, this serene retreat is perfect for a romantic getaway or special occasion. The best part? Every room boasts a stunning water view—some even have lanais! It's dog friendly, but note that children under twelve aren't allowed, making it an ideal spot for a peaceful escape.

Saratoga Inn: If you're dreaming of a cozy, elegant bed-and-breakfast experience, this charming inn is the place to be. With fireplaces in every room and a home-cooked vegetarian breakfast served daily, it's a warm and inviting stay just steps away from all the town's attractions. Bonus: dogs are welcome!

SARATOGA INN

WHALE SCULPTURE AT SEAWALL PARK

Vacation rentals: Whether you're looking for a waterfront cabin, a forest retreat, or a stylish apartment in town, Whidbey Island has plenty of beautiful vacation rentals to fit every budget and travel style.

Itinerary Outline

DAY 1

Walk at Double Bluff Beach: If you love dogs, you'll love this beach. The first time we visited, we had no idea it was an off-leash area—until we stepped onto the sand and saw dogs zooming around, having the time of their lives. It was adorable! This is the perfect spot to stretch your legs after the ferry ride, soak up the salty air, and, on a clear day, take in incredible views of Mount Rainier.

Visit Bayview Garden & Flower House Café: One look at the golden Laburnum Arbor archway, and I knew I'd stumbled upon a hidden gem on Whidbey Island. Part garden center, part cozy café, this place is as charming as it gets. (Plan your visit between late May and early June to catch the arbor in full bloom!) It's the perfect spot to sip a latte, browse for quirky treasures, such as whale-shaped planters, and pick up a living souvenir—or a cozy Whidbey crewneck to remember it by.

Dinner at Taproom@Bayview Corner: End the day with a relaxed meal at this local favorite taproom, which serves up Pacific Northwest-brewed beers and ciders, hearty sandwiches, and some seriously good tots. If you're a seafood fan, don't miss the Penn Cove Mussels, sourced fresh from Coupeville, which is just up the island.

FRANK D. ROBINSON BEACH COUNTY PARK

DAY 2

Breakfast at The Braeburn restaurant: This bright, laid-back café serves up some of the best food on the island. If you've got a sweet tooth, go for the apple crisp or stuffed French toast. If you're craving something savory, the *shakshouka* or The Braeburn (buttermilk waffles with fried chicken) will not disappoint.

Explore the town of Langley

- **Langley Whale Center:** Dive into the fascinating world of whales and learn about the endangered Southern Resident orcas. The interactive exhibits and friendly volunteers make this a must-visit. Plus, the whale-themed gift shop is full of fun finds!
- **Seawall Park:** Go whale watching from the shore, and if you spot one, ring the brass bell!
- **Sweet Mona's:** Adorable animal-shaped truffles that taste just as good as they look? Yes please! My favorite is the dark chocolate kitty truffle, but the hazelnut hedgehog and milk chocolate pup are equally delightful. It's the kind of treat that makes you smile before you even take a bite.
- **Alma:** This sustainably minded boutique—run by a conscious mother-daughter duo—is the kind of place that makes you want to slow down and browse every corner. You'll find thoughtfully selected clothing, home goods, and some seriously good vintage. (I'm still dreaming about that perfectly worn-in denim rack that looks like it belongs on a Pinterest board.)

Lunch at Langley Kitchen: On a sunny summer day, there's truly no better spot to grab lunch than the patio at this community gem. Everything here radiates good vibes—from the ever-changing daily specials (we loved the enchiladas), to the cinnamon roll latte, to the buttery, can't-miss pastries.

Hike in Saratoga Woods: Walk through this hundred-acre forest known for its towering trees and quiet trails. There's no grand viewpoint at the end, but the beauty is in the details—mushrooms tucked into the moss, birdsong in the canopy, and the massive glacial erratic hidden among the trees. Download the trail maps ahead of time!

Wine tasting at Spoiled Dog Winery: What's better than sipping pinot noir in a vineyard? Doing it with your pup by your side! This dog-friendly winery is the perfect place to unwind and taste some award-winning organic wines.

Dinner at Ikaika Grill: Island life calls for island flavors, and this Hawaiian food truck delivers. From kalua pork to garlic shrimp and, of course, Spam musubi, it's an authentic taste of Polynesia right here on Whidbey. We need more places like this!

IKAIKA GRILL

Catch the sunset at Frank D. Robinson Beach County Park: End the day barefoot in the sand as the sun dips behind the Olympic Mountains, painting the sky in soft pinks and golds. From this peaceful stretch along Mutiny Bay, you're gazing out toward the largely undeveloped forested shoreline—a view that feels raw, quiet, and beautifully wild.

DAY 3

Breakfast at Whidbey Island Bagel Factory: If I've had a bagel sandwich more times than I can count, you know it's good. The rosemary chive sea salt bagel is perfect, and paired with a latte, it's the ideal ferry ride snack. Trust me—it's a whole vibe.

Explore Possession Beach Waterfront Park: Not ready to say goodbye to island time just yet? Make one last stop at this rocky pocket beach, just a short drive from the ferry terminal. It's the perfect place to soak up the water views before heading home.

The Takeaway: Whidbey Island has a way of getting under your skin—in the best possible way. From Langley's creative spirit to quiet beach moments and forest trails that invite you to reconnect with nature, this island weekend offers the kind of reset that we all need more of. It'll be tough to say goodbye as the ferry pulls away, but isn't that how you know it was a good trip? The town's combination of artistic energy, environmental consciousness, and stunning natural beauty creates memories that linger long after you've returned to mainland life—and ensures you'll be planning your return before you've even left the dock.

TRILLIUM LAKE

38

MOUNT HOOD

Introduction

You probably know that Oregon's tallest mountain is the iconic, pointy peak of Mount Hood. But did you know it's also home to some of the most refreshing waterfalls and vibrant sunrises? And that's just the beginning. This mountain, along with the surrounding Mount Hood National Forest, offers a year-round nature escape that's surprisingly easy to reach. (If you're from Portland, I'm probably preaching to the choir.)

Come summertime, Mount Hood embodies the perfect outdoor adventure—think racing down mountain biking trails, cooling off with an afternoon swim, and ending each day as the mountain glows pink against the evening sky. When Kyle and I visited, it felt like every moment was memorable, partly because we spent nearly every minute outside, from sunrise to sunset. With endless outdoor recreation and charming small mountain towns to explore, there's no shortage of things to do on a weekend getaway here.

One practical lesson we learned? Pack snacks—depending on where you stay, restaurants can be few and far between.

At a Glance

Location: East of Portland, Oregon
Best Season to Visit: June through September
Suggested Duration: Two nights

Getting There

Seattle to Government Camp: 222 miles, ~3 hours 40 minutes
Portland to Government Camp: 56.4 miles, ~1 hour 15 minutes

JONSRUD VIEWPOINT

Bestie Tip: Government Camp sits at 3,500 feet—pack layers even in summer as temperatures drop significantly at elevation, and the weather can change quickly.

Where to Stay

Mt. Hood Oregon Resort: For a cozy getaway with your furry friends, this resort at the foot of the mountain has your back. The forest grounds are beautiful and include a twenty-seven-hole golf course, outdoor pool, and tennis courts. Walk-in showers and a spa make for a relaxing stay.

Best Western Mt. Hood Inn: If you want to stay closer to the mountain, this standard hotel is a solid choice, complete with an indoor hot tub and complimentary breakfast.

Vacation rentals: For the ultimate woodsy retreat, book a cabin. Plenty are available between Brightwood and Rhododendron. If you're traveling with a group, this could be a fun (and more spacious) way to stay!

Itinerary Outline

DAY 1

Mount Hood Cultural Center & Museum: This little gem has a bit of everything—vintage ski collections, information about the mountain's geology, and pioneer history. Don't skip the gift shop! It's packed with local-interest books and art from skilled regional artists.

Dinner at Thai Home Restaurant: Every time my family is in the area, we have to stop here for a meal on the patio. Don't let the small building fool you—this place delivers big flavors. Need more heat? The homemade spices on every table will do the trick.

Catch the sunset at Jonsrud Viewpoint: Stop by this overlook for picture-perfect views of Mount Hood towering over the Sandy River Valley. It's beautiful anytime, but especially at sunset when the mountain glows pink just before the sun dips below the horizon.

DAY 2

Catch the sunrise at Trillium Lake: For a magical morning, wake up early and head to this popular spot for photographers. Whether you hike around the lake or paddle out onto the glassy waters, you won't regret the early start. I remember my sunrise visit like it was yesterday—we weren't alone, but there was something special about sharing the moment with a group of strangers equally in awe of the view.

Breakfast at Zigzag Mountain Café: This cozy log cabin serves up bear-shaped pancakes, buttery homemade biscuits, and other homestyle favorites. Try to grab a seat by the window for a peaceful view of Bear Creek.

RAMONA FALLS

MOUNT HOOD

Explore Mount Hood

- **Timberline Highway:** Drive all the way to the top for sweeping views of Oregon's highest peak. I personally love this drive in early summer, before too much snow has melted.
- **Magic Mile Sky Ride:** Want to get even closer to the mountain without hiking? Ride a chairlift up to seven thousand feet!
- **Timberline Bike Park:** Whether you're a beginner or a pro, this spot has freeride and technical trails to test your skills. Ride the lift up, then cruise down on two wheels! Rentals are available, and booking online usually saves you a few bucks. First-time mountain biker? Sign up for a lesson!
- **Mt. Hood Adventure Park at Ski Bowl:** If you've got kids (or just want some carefree fun), try the alpine slide! This half-mile ride through meadows is pure joy. Other activities include go-karts and disc golf.

Lunch at Wrapitude Gourmet Wraps, Burgers & Beers: The name says it all! Whether you go for a wrap, burger, or taco, you can't go wrong. And the fries are dangerously good. Besides beer, wonderful kombucha and cider are also available.

Hike to Ramona Falls: I swear—there's something magical about this waterfall. I've hiked to more waterfalls than I can count, but Ramona Falls took me by surprise. The delicate, cascading streams cover a wide area, creating a fairy-tale-like atmosphere. Plan for an eight-mile round trip with about one thousand feet of elevation gain. There's a river crossing that can be tricky—you'll need to either wade through a shallow section or carefully cross fallen logs.

Dinner at Koya Kitchen: After a day of adventure, fill up on *yakisoba*, sushi, and ramen. On a warm night, grab a seat outside under the glowing lanterns—or even lounge in one of the hammocks! The vibes here are immaculate.

DAY 3

Breakfast at Mt. Hood Roasters: This cozy café, tucked among the trees, serves up some of the area's best coffee. If you fall in love with the brews, you're in luck—you can buy a bag of freshly roasted beans to take home! While coffee is the specialty, you'll also find tasty pastries on the menu, such as scones and muffins.

Explore the Wildwood Recreation Site: Wrap up your trip with a peaceful nature walk at this verdant preserve. Stroll along wooden boardwalks through wetlands, stopping to read the interpretive signs along the way. If the weather's warm, cool off with a quick dip in the river. For a bigger adventure, tackle the longer and steeper Boulder Ridge Trail to get off the beaten path.

The Takeaway: If the mountains are calling your name, a weekend escape to Mount Hood is sure to answer with experiences that capture the essence of Pacific Northwest adventure. Ramona Falls, with its veil of delicate streams cascading down the rock face, is mesmerizing enough to bring me back again and again—a testament to nature's ability to create art that never gets old. Add in glassy lakes perfect for a swim and cozy mountain details—like bear-shaped pancakes that taste even better after a morning hike—and you've got yourself a getaway worth repeating. Whether you're racing down mountain bike trails with adrenaline pumping, floating peacefully on Trillium Lake as the first light hits Mount Hood's summit, or discovering that perfect waterfall viewpoint where cascading water creates its own ethereal soundtrack, this corner of the Cascades proves that some of the most accessible mountain adventures also happen to be the most memorable. It's a place where Portland's urban energy gives way to alpine tranquility in just over an hour, reminding you that the best outdoor escapes are often closer than you think.

39 SAN JUAN ISLAND

Introduction

The most-visited of the San Juan Islands, this is a must-visit destination that I hope you get to experience at least once. Many people come for the chance to spot whales from the stunning shores—one of the best summertime activities. While I can't say I've seen a whale from here, I have seen foxes, alpacas, and some absolutely killer sunsets that make every visit memorable.

In true island fashion, many businesses close or have limited hours in the offseason, so for the full experience, summer is your best bet. That said, summer also means peak ferry traffic, so planning ahead for both directions of travel is key. And another island quirk? Don't expect reliable cell phone service. We learned this the hard way on our first visit—it wasn't impossible to navigate without it, but it was inconvenient for checking restaurant hours and menus. Another reason to plan ahead!

Something I didn't expect was how peaceful it is to stay outside of Friday Harbor, though the town itself is full of charm. During one visit, we booked a lodge room at Lakedale Resort without knowing much about the property, and we were instantly smitten. The moment we turned off the main road and drove by Fish Hook Lake—one of three lakes on the property—we knew we'd picked a special spot. During our stay, I loved sitting on the rocking chairs outside our room, listening to birds chirp in the morning, and cozying up by the fireplace (in our room and in the lodge). We also spent time wandering the onsite trails, and I think it'd be an incredible place to camp! And don't even get me started on breakfast—the made-to-order hot breakfasts were omelets during our visit, and they were exceptional.

San Juan Island offers the perfect blend of natural beauty, fascinating history, and island tranquility that makes Pacific Northwest island-hopping so addictive. Whether you're drawn by world-class whale-watching opportunities, intriguing stories of international boundary disputes, or simply the chance to slow down to island time, this destination rewards visitors who take time to fully immerse themselves in its unique character.

At a Glance

Location: San Juan Islands, Washington
Best Season to Visit: May through September
Suggested Duration: Two or three nights

Bestie Tip: Don't make the mistake of squeezing San Juan Island into a quick day trip. During our stay at Lakedale Resort, the general manager, Karl, told us it's impossible to see the whole island in such a short window. And after exploring it myself, I couldn't agree more. If you've already made the journey out here, you might as well settle in and soak it all up.

SAN JUAN ISLANDS FERRY

SAN JUAN ISLANDS FERRY

Getting There

Seattle to San Juan Island: 107 miles, ~3 hours 30 minutes

- Includes the Anacortes–San Juan Island ferry (~1 hour)

Portland to San Juan Island: 280 miles, ~6 hours

- Includes the Anacortes–San Juan Island ferry (~1 hour)

LAKEDALE RESORT

Bestie Tip: If you're visiting in spring or summer, in addition to buying ferry tickets, be sure to book a free vehicle reservation both ways. Ferries fill up fast during peak season, and securing a spot in advance will save you stress later. While the reservation is free, there is a $19 no-show fee if you don't use it. On the day of your sailing, aim to arrive sixty minutes early to check in (thirty minutes is the absolute latest your spot will be held for you).

Where to Stay

Friday Harbor House: If you want to be right where the ferry drops you off, this scenic hotel is the perfect stay. Every room comes with a fireplace, jetted tub, and comfy bathrobes. Celebrating something special? Upgrade to a room with a patio overlooking the harbor—you deserve it!

Lakedale Resort: Miss those nostalgic summer-camp vibes? Book a stay here. Choose from cozy log cabins, charming yurts, and glamping tents that'll take you right back to childhood adventures—or go classic with a lodge room. Budget-friendly campsites for tents and RVs keep things simple. Tucked among the trees with birdsong in the background, this peaceful place made a big impression on me, and I'd come back in a heartbeat.

LAKEDALE RESORT

Roche Harbor Resort: If you've stayed in Friday Harbor before and want to explore a different part of the island, try Roche Harbor. The historic Hotel de Haro offers rooms with en suites or access to private shared bathrooms—you can even stay in President Theodore Roosevelt's room! Traveling with a group? There are also spacious condos and village homes available.

Itinerary Outline

DAY 1

Explore San Juan Island National Historical Park—American Camp: Start your adventure at one of the most interesting parks on all the San Juan Islands. With access not only to beaches but also to native prairies and forested hills, keep a lookout for sea life in addition to foxes, deer, and rabbits. (Reminder: enjoy watching, but don't feed or interact with them!)

- **American Camp Visitor Center:** Stop by to learn about the 1859 Pig War standoff that happened on the island and to get a map of trails (also available online).
- **Granny's Cove:** Go tide pooling at low tide to see sea anemones and crabs.
- **South Beach:** With lots of pebbly beach to explore (and lots of driftwood), this is a fun place to feel the wind in your hair.
- **Jakle's Lagoon and Mount Finlayson trails:** For views of the Cascade Mountains, wander these forested and meadow trails. With about 380 feet of elevation gain, this hike is pretty beginner friendly (and worth every step).

Dinner at Downriggers: This was the first place we ate after we stepped off the ferry, which was very convenient since it's right on the waterfront. Be sure to make a reservation if visiting during the summer. With excellent clam chowder, salmon burgers, and blackened halibut fish tacos, I wouldn't be surprised if you wind up back here before your trip ends!

DOWNRIGGERS

DAY 2

Breakfast at The Restaurant at Friday Harbor House: For breakfast with a view, reserve an outdoor table at this elevated brunch spot. The Canadian bacon eggs Benedict and bananas foster French toast make for a tough decision, but you really can't go wrong.

Stroll through Friday Harbor: Whether staying in Friday Harbor or elsewhere on the island, carve out time for wandering through the charming shops.

- **The Whale Museum:** Even if you don't see whales on your trip, this conservation-focused museum will satisfy your curiosity. Listen to orcas communicating, step inside a whale ribcage, and learn about the Southern Resident pods' family trees.
- **Griffin Bay Bookstore & Café:** Pick up a book about the Pig War, orcas, or books by local authors. It's a perfect spot for coffee and literary island discoveries.
- **Joe Friday's Shirt Co.:** Find your perfect souvenir T-shirt or hat at this shop. If

ENGLISH CAMP

you've ever been to Hawaii, it reminds me of Crazy Shirts!

- **Kings Marine:** If you forgot your hiking boots or a windbreaker, this is the place to go for outdoor gear and maritime supplies.

Lunch at Lime Kiln Café: This casual spot is known for its Alaska cod fish and chips, and we loved them! Since we weren't staying in Roche Harbor, it was fun to check out the little village while we were there.

Explore San Juan Island National Historical Park—English Camp: Head to the English Camp section of the San Juan Island National Historical Park, on the other side of the island, for a day full of adventure.

- **Parade Grounds:** Walk down the hill to a lovely garden-like labyrinth and what remains of old military buildings. I was surprised at how lovely this is—the perfect place for a picnic!
- **Hike Young Hill:** This is the truest hike we did on the island, quite manageable at around 2.2 miles and six hundred feet of elevation gain. Other than the solitude that comes from walking through the forest, the reward is an expansive view of other islands and sparkling blue water. On your way down, stop by the cemetery, which reveals some tragic tales but also gives a better understanding of what life was like here in the 1860s. You can start the trail from either the visitor center (like we did) or the small parking lot off of San Juan Valley Road.

Visit The Farm at Krystal Acres: One animal you might not expect to see on the island is an alpaca! But sure enough, you can meet and feed them at this warm, family-run farm. Also, the store has super soft blankets, beanies, and socks—crafted with alpaca fibers, of course. This is a souvenir that will fill you with joy whenever you remember where you got it.

Dinner at San Juan Island Brewing Co.: Enjoy a flight of locally brewed beer on your last night. There is also a mouthwatering food menu, such as wood stone pizzas (The Pig War being a popular pick), sandwiches, and salads. Chocolate lovers, save room for the amazing chocolate lava cake—I have to order it every time!

LIME KILN POINT STATE PARK

Catch the sunset at Lime Kiln Point State Park: Known as the best spot in the world for onshore whale watching, this small shoreline park is worth at least one visit during your vacation. The historic lighthouse is especially magical in the golden light. Don't forget your binoculars!

Bestie Tip: Given Lime Kiln's popularity, it's smart to arrive about an hour before sunset—or linger after for the dreamy glow of blue hour like we did. If the parking lot is full, head just six minutes north to San Juan County Park. The views are just as stunning, with Lime Kiln offering a sea-level perspective and the county park giving you a bluff-top vantage point. Both have advantages!

DAY 3

Breakfast at Salty Fox Coffee: For a quick bite before hopping on the ferry, come here for the great breakfast sandwiches, burritos (available all day), acai bowls, and rice bowls. Best of all, the porch has an easy view of the ferry, so you can keep a close eye on it! It also features local artists—I had to leave with a trinket or two!

Fairweather Park: Have a few minutes to spare? Walk over to this pocket park along the marina. It includes a beautiful piece of Coast Salish art titled "Interaction."

Spring Street Landing Aquarium: Walk over to the next block and out onto the dock (look for the one with a small building on it). Inside, there is a fun surprise: a mini four-hundred-gallon aquarium with rotating local sea creatures. Free to visit.

The Takeaway: From the moment you watch Friday Harbor grow closer from the ferry deck to those final blue-hour moments at Lime Kiln Point, San Juan Island offers experiences that capture the essence of Pacific Northwest island magic. Settle into a rustic lodge that feels straight out of summer camp, such as my favorite childhood movie *Camp Rock*—think crackling fires, wood-paneled charm, and that slow, sweet pace of island life. Cross paths with orcas, red foxes, and alpacas as you explore land and sea. The combination of fascinating history, world-class wildlife viewing, and that indefinable island atmosphere creates memories that linger long after you've returned to mainland life. Make your summer weekend count with a getaway to San Juan Island, where the island dream is very much alive.

MIDDLE FORK
SNOQUALMIE RIVER

40 NORTH BEND

Introduction

Nestled at the base of the Cascades, North Bend is Seattle's closest mountain town and an outdoor paradise. It's the perfect base camp for exploring the hiking trails that line I-90 near Snoqualmie Pass, and it's home to some of the most iconic landmarks in the region—Mount Si, Little Si, and Rattlesnake Ledge, to name a few. But really, North Bend is more than just a base camp. It's a place where the adventure starts right in town.

Beyond the breathtaking mountain views, North Bend has a tight-knit, friendly community, including a herd of over four hundred elk that call the area home! You can often spot them at Meadowbrook Farm Preserve, a local favorite for walking and wildlife watching, no matter the season.

And for those who love discovering hidden gems, the Big Cedar tree—over five hundred years old—stands quietly in the forest, overshadowed by more famous trails but well worth a visit.

I've explored North Bend in every season, and while it shines year-round, late summer is truly special. By then, the winter snowmelt has made higher-elevation trails fully accessible, and the long, golden evenings are perfect for unwinding at one of the area's scenic wineries. One of my favorites offers outdoor tastings in a stunning, peaceful setting where you can truly appreciate the craft and care poured into every bottle. Whether you're a wine connoisseur or just looking for a relaxing afternoon, it's the best way to end a day of exploring.

At a Glance

Location: King County, Washington
Best Season to Visit: August through September
Suggested Duration: Two nights

ROOSEVELT ELK

Getting There

Seattle to North Bend: 30 miles, ~30 minutes
Portland to North Bend: 183 miles, ~3 hours

Where to Stay

Vacation rentals: Cozy up in a woodsy-chic cabin along a river or with breathtaking views of Mount Si. Many are dog friendly, making them a great option if your four-legged friend loves exploring trails as much as you do!

Tolt MacDonald Park: This county park in nearby Carnation offers a mix of RV sites, traditional campsites, and even a few yurts for those who want a little extra comfort while still sleeping under the stars.

Middle Fork Campground: Tucked deep in the lush Taylor River valley within the Mount Baker-Snoqualmie National Forest, this minimalist campground offers a peaceful retreat with easy access to hiking trails, just thirty minutes outside of town.

Itinerary Outline

DAY 1

Look for Roosevelt elk: Can you spot the large herd of North Bend's four hundred resident elk? You'll find them at Elk Fields within Meadowbrook Farm Preserve. There are a few different gravel parking lots where you can stop to take photos. Keep a respectful distance and keep your pups on a leash, as these elk are wild animals. If you time it right, you might catch the elk at sunset, when the lighting is prime for photographs and the elk are more active. Bring binoculars for a closer look at these majestic creatures in their natural habitat.

Dinner at Twede's Café: This retro, homey café made its claim to fame as part of the *Twin Peaks* TV show, a crime drama filmed in the Snoqualmie Valley in 1989. Today, it's a friendly, no-fuss spot for burgers (the menu options are endless), and the classic milkshakes are another must-try that you can pair perfectly with a slice of the café's legendary cherry pie.

Hike to Snow Lake: From North Bend, your hiking options are endless. One of my favorite summer hikes here is Snow Lake, tucked into the stunning Alpine Lakes Wilderness. It's a moderately hard trek. The trail shifts beautifully as you go, moving from dense forest to open valley views, then finally down to the sparkling lake itself. On a hot summer day, jumping in for a swim is pure bliss! Along the way, you might spot wild huckleberries (if you're lucky and they're in season), remnants of an old stone cabin, and even wildlife—once, we saw a black bear scrambling over the rocks above the lake. All told, it's about a 6.5-mile round trip with roughly 1,684 feet of elevation gain.

DAY 2

Breakfast at Arête Coffee Bar: This hidden gem is tucked inside a ski and outdoor shop, serving up excellent coffee and breakfast sandwiches. My go-to is The Spicy Pig—a bagel sandwich with house-made sriracha aioli and Mama Lil's peppers. So good! If you forgot any of your outdoor gear at home, this is the place to get it. You can also browse through high-quality outdoor apparel and pick up trail maps before heading out on your next adventure.

Bestie Tip: If Snow Lake feels a little ambitious or you just want an easier option that still provides the opportunity to swim, check out Rattlesnake Lake. It's super accessible—just a short, flat walk from the parking lot to the water's edge. You can also stretch your legs on the Rattlesnake Lake Trail, which is an easygoing loop of just under half a mile. This well-loved trailhead (especially for hikers destined up to Rattlesnake Ledge) definitely fills up on weekends, so arriving as early as possible is recommended.

CHÂTEAU NOELLE

Wine tasting at Château NoElle: This hidden gem boutique winery will charm you with its garden-like setting, friendly service from owners Lorrie and Tom, and local Washington wine. While the Bordeaux blends have made a name for themselves, it's the "Grace" sparkling viognier 2022—pet nat that came home with me. Be sure to call ahead and make a reservation. The outdoor seating area is the perfect place to wind down after a day of hiking.

CHÂTEAU NOELLE

Dinner at South Fork Restaurant: Besides North Bend's coffee shops, the restaurant that I am most obsessed with here is this community gathering space. Tucked in a forested area a few miles from downtown, this expansive eatery has its own coffee shop, food truck, and dog-friendly beer garden. It serves up delicious dishes all day long, but the BBQ brisket sandwich with sidewinder fries is the star of the show. Pair it with a signature cocktail, local brew, or glass of wine, and you're set for a memorable evening.

DAY 3

Breakfast at Huxdotter Coffee: This modern, grounded coffee shop has some of the best coffee shop views you can find in the Pacific Northwest. While enjoying the views of Mount Si looming overhead, sip locally roasted coffee and snack on one of the breakfast sandwiches or burritos. This is the only place I order energy drinks, and I am obsessed, especially with the pink cactus drink, made with desert pear, guava, and rose.

Hike to Twin Falls: No North Bend weekend is complete without chasing at least one waterfall, and Twin Falls is a great choice. This short-but-steep trail winds through lush old-growth forest and hugs the river, making the journey just as beautiful as the destination. You'll log about a 2.4-mile round trip with 940 feet of elevation gain, and after hiking it a few times, I'd call it moderately challenging—but I've seen plenty of kids powering through like it's nothing!

Bestie Tip: Be sure to make it to the third viewpoint, Upper Falls, where you'll be treated to sweeping views of the valley—it's totally worth the extra steps.

The Takeaway: In North Bend, outdoor adventure is only half the story. Between hikes, you'll find yourself lingering over a glass of local wine with Mount Si in full view or pausing to watch a herd of elk grazing at sunset. It's a place where nature and community intertwine—and where every moment feels a little more down-to-earth. Whether you're conquering the challenging switchbacks to Snow Lake's alpine beauty, discovering that perfect wine varietal while surrounded by Cascade peaks, or simply watching the way morning light transforms Mount Si's face from your coffee shop window, North Bend proves that some of the best mountain experiences happen when serious outdoor adventure meets genuine community warmth. This is Pacific Northwest mountain living at its most accessible and authentic—close enough for spontaneous escapes, wild enough to remind you why the mountains call, and welcoming enough to make you feel like a local from the moment you arrive.

TWIN FALLS

FALL
GETAWAYS

ASTORIA-MEGLER BRIDGE

41

ASTORIA

Introduction

While there are plenty of fall destinations I love for their foliage, Astoria is one of my favorites, mostly for its vibe. Tucked in the far northwest corner of Oregon, between the Columbia River and the Pacific Ocean, this historic Victorian town may surprise you—it holds the title of the oldest American settlement this side of the Rockies. Fall often brings moody weather, which, as I quickly learned, only adds to its charm. Plus, there's the perfect balance of scenic outdoor adventures and cozy indoor escapes.

My brother and I visited in October for Oktoberfest, hosted by Buoy Brewing Company. It was both of our first times in the "Little San Francisco of the Pacific Northwest," and we were instantly won over by its walkable downtown, eclectic boutiques, and unique piers—not to mention the sound of sea lions barking in the distance.

Over the course of a weekend in Astoria, you can see a real shipwreck on the beach, watch elk roam through Warrenton, and dive into as many museums as your heart desires. Whether you're intrigued by World War II military history, the perils of navigating this stretch of the Columbia, or what life was like during the Victorian era, there's a museum (or two, or three) just for you!

At a Glance

Location: Northwestern corner of Oregon
Best Season to Visit: October through November
Suggested Duration: Two nights

Getting There

Seattle to Astoria: 181 miles, ~3 hours
Portland to Astoria: 97.6 miles, ~1 hour 50 minutes

Where to Stay

Cannery Pier Hotel & Spa: For scenic stays right on top of the Columbia River, this hotel is hard to beat. With massive windows flooding the suites with natural light, it's perfect for ship watching and admiring the Astoria–Megler Bridge. Complimentary breakfast is included.

Bowline Hotel: When in Astoria, why not stay somewhere that makes the most of its riverfront location? This hotel offers incredible views, plus the chance to warm up in a cedar barrel sauna. Bonus: it's in a super walkable spot.

Holiday Inn Express & Suites: For a more budget-friendly riverfront stay, this place checks all the boxes. Enjoy a complimentary breakfast, take a dip in the indoor pool, and, if you're feeling fancy, upgrade to a room with a fireplace.

> **Bestie Tip:** Looking for the most affordable stays? Check out Fort Stevens State Park. We've camped here during almost every season, and it's been wonderful every time. In addition to hundreds of campsites, there are also a handful of cabins and yurts.

Itinerary Outline

DAY 1

Explore Fort Stevens State Park: Located in neighboring Warrenton, this park is an absolute gem. Camping trips here were my first introduction to the area, and between the massive bull elk and the eerie shipwreck, it was unforgettable, and it kept me coming back. With 4,300 acres to explore, we had the best time biking around.

- **Historic Area:** Wander through spooky bunkers and gun batteries, keep an eye out for elk, and check out the small but informative visitor center. Disc golf fans will love the twenty-three-hole course (discs available for purchase at the visitor center).
- **The *Peter Iredale* shipwreck:** Seeing a shipwreck in person always felt so far-fetched—until I came here. This British-built ship ran ashore in 1906, and you can still walk right up to it today (depending on the tide).
- **Columbia River Beach Access:** While the park has no shortage of ocean access, one of my favorite spots is actually along the river. It's an excellent place for bird-watching, though—fair warning—it can get pretty windy!

ROOSEVELT ELK AT FORT STEVENS STATE PARK

Dinner at Bridgewater Bistro: For a bright, lively dinner, this is the spot. Start with the crispy Thai brussels sprouts, pick your entrée, and top it all off with an Oregon berry cobbler. Depending on the night, you might even catch live piano music! Reservations are recommended.

DAY 2

Breakfast at Astoria Coffee Girl: This cozy café in a historic fish cannery might just become your new favorite PNW coffee spot. It serves up scrumptious fresh pastries, panini, and adorable latte art—it's hard to visit just once!

ASTORIA COFFEE GIRL

ASTORIA STEPS

Bestie Tip: Don't skip the Hanthorn Cannery Museum next door. While the coffee and views are unbeatable, this free museum (donations appreciated!) was a highlight for me. Not every coffee run serves brews with a backstory.

Columbia River Maritime Museum: This is one of the most captivating museums I've ever visited. It covers a lot—shipwrecks, Coast Guard rescues, and more. For an immersive experience, don't miss the 3D movie theater or the Lightship Columbia, a floating lighthouse you can actually step inside.

Lunch at Bowpickers Fish & Chips: For casual but seriously delicious meals, head to this boat turned kitchen. It's a well-loved spot, so go for an early lunch before the line gets too long.

Stroll Downtown Astoria

- **Finn Ware:** Browse unique Nordic gifts.
- **Sea Gypsy Gifts:** Pick up sweet ocean-themed artworks.
- **Reclamation Marketplace:** Find antique and artisan treasures.
- **Godfather's Books:** Discover a book you didn't know you needed.

Explore Youngs River Falls: Located along the Lewis and Clark National Historical Trail, this popular swimming hole is just ten miles from town. From the parking lot, it's a short scramble down to the water.

Dinner at Mo's Seafood & Chowder: Honestly, I'll take any excuse to go to Mo's. They're an Oregon Coast staple, and I'll say it again—the Cannonball bowl of clam chowder is a must-try!

Catch the sunset at The Astoria Column: For a bird's-eye view of Astoria, head to this 126-foot column perched on a hill. Wrapped in a mural depicting Oregon's history, it's a sight to see—and you can even climb to the top! A 164-step spiral staircase leads to a panoramic viewing platform with breathtaking views.

DAY 3

Breakfast at Broder Strand: Start your day Scandinavian-style. This cheery café serves up incredible Danish pancakes and savory scrambles. And don't skip the coffee—it's fantastic.

MOUNT SHUKSAN

Visit the Flavel House Museum: Round out your museum-filled weekend with a visit to this elegant Queen Anne home, built in the late nineteenth century. Your adventure starts at the carriage house with a short film about the Flavel family, then continues through the beautifully preserved mansion and gardens. Photos don't do it justice—you really have to see it for yourself!

The Takeaway: Autumn in Astoria feels like stepping into a storybook with its beautiful Victorian homes, its breezy spot right on the Columbia River, and that signature moody Pacific Northwest vibe. There's something spellbinding about wandering the piers while sea lions bark nearby or exploring the eerie shipwreck that's been stranded on the beach for over a century. Don't miss the chance to peek inside the Flavel House, where history whispers from every corner, or to climb the Astoria Column for views that stretch from the river mouth to the Pacific horizon. This town perfectly balances cozy charm with a touch of mystery, making it one of my favorite fall escapes.

42 BELLINGHAM

Introduction

Where the Cascade Range meets the Salish Sea, you'll find the outdoorsy retreat of Bellingham. I'd argue that it's tough to find a friendlier town anywhere in the Pacific Northwest—not to mention a more scenic one. Gosh, Bellingham Bay has my whole heart! Just twenty miles south of the Canadian border, this welcoming community (historically four separate towns that merged) offers not one, but two walkable downtowns—Bellingham and Fairhaven—each brimming with boutique shops, cozy coffee spots, and exceptional eats, including some of the best breweries in the region.

While you could easily spend a weekend exploring these charming districts, you'd be missing out if you didn't venture beyond to the nearby parks and mountain areas.

The highlight of fall trips? Hands down, it's witnessing the fall foliage at Mount Baker. Whether you're taking the scenic drive or lacing up your hiking boots, the views are nothing short of phenomenal. One of my all-time favorite hikes, the Chain Lakes Loop, is here. The question isn't what you can see on this trail but rather what you can't see. Every step had me in awe—entire hillsides painted in vibrant yellows, oranges, and reds! The bright red huckleberry bushes against the glacier-capped mountains—honestly, my first thought was, *It looks like Christmas!*

Beyond Mount Baker, make time for Bellingham's local gems, such as Whatcom Falls, Sehome Arboretum, and Lake Samish—each offering unbelievably scenic views. And whatever you do, don't skip the Chuckanut Drive Scenic Byway. Especially if you're coming from the south, this drive is a must. We always make a point to take it either on the way in or out—those sweeping views of Bellingham Bay are absolutely breathtaking and never get old.

Fall is the perfect time to visit Bellingham, when every sense is delighted, from your eyes feasting on vibrant landscapes to your taste buds savoring some of the best food around. The combination of peak autumn colors, comfortable hiking weather, and cozy indoor experiences creates the ideal Pacific Northwest fall getaway.

At a Glance

Location: Whatcom County, Washington
Best Season to Visit: September through October
Suggested Duration: Two or three nights

Getting There

- **Seattle to Bellingham:** 89 miles, ~1 hour 25 minutes
- **Portland to Bellingham:** 262 miles, ~3 hours 50 minutes

Where to Stay

The Chrysalis Inn & Spa: How does a cozy room with a view sound? At this 3-star hotel, you can curl up in a reading nook by the fireplace and soak in water views to your heart's content. If you're a light sleeper, be aware that the train tracks run right next door.

Larrabee State Park: For a more budget-friendly stay in a similar bayfront setting, this forested campground is a great option. If you're tent camping, be prepared—the railroad noise takes some getting used to (earplugs help!).

Vacation rentals: One of the best things about Bellingham is that there's so much more to explore beyond downtown: lakes, rivers, and mountains. Whether you're looking for a city-center stay or a peaceful nature retreat, you'll find plenty of home-away-from-home options to match your mood.

Itinerary Outline

DAY 1

Explore downtown Bellingham

- **SPARK Museum of Electrical Invention:** Be entertained at this fun, electrifying experience for science lovers of all ages.
- **Backcountry Essentials:** Head to the second level for great deals on second-hand outdoor gear.
- **Third Planet Boutique:** Discover a treasure trove of unique gifts, handcrafted jewelry, and beautiful crystals.
- **NEKO Cat Café:** Snuggle up with more than twenty adoptable rescue cats while sipping your favorite drink. You can even sign up for cat yoga!

CHAIN LAKES LOOP

Visit Bellewood Farms & Distillery: If you've never been to an apple orchard, here's your opportunity! This family-owned farm in Lynden was the first one Kyle and I ever visited, and it's the largest in Western Washington. We had an absolute blast picking our own (massive) Honeycrisp apples. Beyond the orchards, the farm shop is a must-stop for its fresh apple cider and homemade caramel—seriously, don't leave without them. Plus, it's a two-for-one fall adventure since the orchard also has a pumpkin patch and a corn maze. Perfect for making the most of the season!

Dinner at Black Sheep: Settle into town with mouthwatering tacos and top-notch drinks. We love the dog-friendly patio. The veggie options are excellent too!

DAY 2

Breakfast at Avenue Bread: With a handful of locations in Bellingham, this cozy café is the perfect place to begin your day. The Eggenue breakfast sandwiches always hit the spot. Order lunch sandwiches, such as the Avenue Club, to go as there aren't a ton of dining options at Mount Baker.

Explore Mount Baker: Fall in the Pacific Northwest is another type of beautiful, and nowhere is that truer than in the mountains. Mount Baker, Washington's northernmost volcano, is a stunner—especially when paired with its neighbor, the breathtaking Mount Shuksan.

- **Scenic drive:** Wind through charming rural areas before ascending into one of the most scenic drives in the Pacific Northwest. Must-visit viewpoints include Picture Lake, Heather Meadows, and Artist Point.
- **Hike Chain Lakes Loop:** It's 100 percent worth going for a hike, and my favorite is a 7.6-mile loop trail that will have your jaw on the ground the entire way. This trail winds by four alpine lakes and consistently offers scenic views of Mounts Shuksan and Baker. I recommend hiking counterclockwise from Artist Point. In total, expect to gain around 1,872 feet of elevation.
- **Nooksack Falls:** On the way back, take a quick roadside stop to see this stunning waterfall. It's just a few steps from the parking area and is safely fenced for viewing.

CHUCKANUT DRIVE

Dinner at the Filling Station: Full of vintage vibes, delicious milkshakes, and seriously good sandwiches, this is one of my favorite places to grab dinner in Bellingham. My go-to? The BSA sandwich with fried chicken, bacon, and avocado. Big enough to share!

Catch the sunset at Boulevard Park: I can't tell you how many times we've soaked up every golden moment of sunset here, walking the boardwalk with Lilo. It's a lively place to overlook the bay, train watch, and see the Canadian mountains in the distance. It's not uncommon to see people swimming either—though taking the plunge is still on my bucket list!

Evening entertainment at the Mount Baker Theatre: Whether you're in the mood for live music, stand-up comedy, or a Broadway-style production, this hundred-year-old venue is a treat all on its own. The historic space sweeps you into another era, with ornate moldings, plush red velvet seats, and a stunning gilded dome that steals the show before the curtain even rises.

DAY 3

Breakfast at Mount Bakery Café: Bellingham has no shortage of amazing breakfast spots, but this laid-back hole-in-the-wall café is always a winner. It's known for fresh-baked pastries, eggs Benedict, and crepes—plus great espresso!

Visit Village Books and Paper Dreams: Trust me—you'll want to carve out some time to get lost in this beloved local bookstore. With a wide selection of new reads, secondhand gems, a cozy café, and a whimsical gift shop, you never know what treasures you'll stumble upon. If you have a little extra time, be sure to wander through the rest of downtown Fairhaven—it's full of charm and perfect for a leisurely stroll.

Scenic Drive on Chuckanut Drive: As you wave goodbye to Bellingham, prepare for one more adventure by taking Chuckanut Drive—one of the most breathtaking roads in Washington. This forest-lined, winding highway hugs the coastline where the Cascade

CUTTHROAT PASS

Mountains meet the ocean (the only place in Washington where this happens!). There are a few roadside pull-offs that are great places to snap pictures. If you're looking for a place to get out and stretch your legs, then hit one of the many trails or the beachfront at Larrabee State Park.

The Takeaway: I dare you to find a place that feels more "Upper Left USA" than Bellingham. From sea level at the edge of the Salish Sea to the 10,786-foot summit of Mount Baker, this region is packed with adventure at every elevation. Whether you're strolling a scenic boardwalk at sunset while Canadian mountains glow in the distance, lacing up your boots for high alpine hikes where autumn transforms entire mountainsides into living paintings, or discovering that perfect used book in Fairhaven's historic brick buildings, Bellingham wraps you in its charm and lingers like the last page of a book, begging for a reread.

43 NORTH CASCADES NATIONAL PARK

Introduction

What's it like to hike through a deep green forest, only to suddenly step into a luminous golden one? There's no better place to find out than North Cascades National Park. This mountainous wonderland, tucked near the Canadian border, is somehow the least-visited national park in the Pacific Northwest—a designation that feels almost impossible given its spectacular beauty.

As a local, I wouldn't necessarily call it a hidden gem; after all, the Gatorade-blue waters of Diablo Lake and the brilliant fall foliage do draw in a fair share of visitors. If you go on peak weekends, it certainly feels popular. But compared to other national parks in Washington, it still flies under the radar for many residents and out-of-state travelers alike. I didn't visit it myself until my twenties, and my parents, who grew up in the state, still haven't been. With over 90 percent of the park designated as wilderness, there's something undeniably special about being in a place like this. It's one of the last of its kind.

Most of the year, the park's remote location makes it feel peaceful. I've been here just as winter was setting in—when the jagged peaks and forests were completely covered in fresh snow, and I had the trails nearly to myself. And then there's the magic of Larch Madness, the nickname for the phenomenon of these high-elevation pine trees turning bright yellow in early fall. The very first time I came to witness it, we were caught in the first snowfall of the season. It was surreal: light flakes gently fell as we stood at 6,800 feet, surrounded by golden trees, in absolute silence. It was definitely a pinch-me moment!

If you're seeking that kind of experience, I recommend visiting on a weekday. During peak larch season, trailheads fill up fast on weekends, and the solitude that makes this place so special is harder to find. Generally, larches reach peak color in late September and hold their golden needles until early October, but timing varies each year. Early snowfall can also affect trail access, so the best way to stay updated is by checking recent trip reports on the Washington Trails Association website.

Because this area is so remote, dining options are limited. If you're staying in Winthrop (east of the park), you'll find a handful of restaurants (see pages 146–148 for recommendations). Otherwise, if you're on the western side, I'd suggest booking a vacation rental with a full kitchen so you can cook meals. After a long day of hiking, nothing beats a cozy night in with a warm meal and a view of the mountains.

At a Glance

Location: Northwestern Washington
Best Season to Visit: September through October
Suggested Duration: Two nights

Getting There

Seattle to North Cascades National Park: 116 miles, ~2 hours 30 minutes
Portland to North Cascades National Park: 290 miles, ~5 hours

Bestie Tip: Start keeping tabs on the weather about a week before your trip and check the WSDOT website for pass reports and live cams a few days out—it's the best way to stay ahead of changing road conditions. For trail updates, I always turn to recent reports on Washington Trails Association and AllTrails to get the latest on downed trees, wildlife sightings, and more.

Packing Tip: During this in-between season when fall can quickly turn to winter in the North Cascades, I recommend packing a few key emergency supplies, just in case the weather takes a snowy turn. Bring microspikes for traction, extra layers (including a warm hat and gloves), a waterproof shell, and an emergency blanket. It's also smart to carry a headlamp, a power bank, a first-aid kit, high-calorie snacks, and a map or offline navigation app—you never know when early snow might make a hike slower or more challenging than expected.

Where to Stay

Vacation rentals east of the park: If you want to be as close as possible to the larch hikes, Mazama and Winthrop are the perfect home bases. These charming mountain

CUTTHROAT PASS

towns offer cozy cabins, riverside lodges, and convenient access to restaurants, coffee shops, and small-town general stores—ideal for grabbing last-minute hiking snacks or winding down after a long day on the trails.

Vacation rentals west of the park: For a shorter drive on Day 1, consider staying in one of the quiet, rustic communities west of the park, such as Marblemount, Sauk, or Concrete. Tucked into the foothills, these small towns offer a true cabin-in-the-woods experience while keeping you within easy reach of the North Cascades Highway.

Itinerary Outline

DAY 1

Visit the Park and Forest Information Center in Sedro-Woolley: By October, the visitor centers inside the park have closed for the season, but if you want to pick up a souvenir or get your National Park Passport stamped, this joint National Park Service and US Forest Service center is your best bet. This is also where you can grab any necessary passes or permits before heading into the mountains.

Ladder Creek Falls: Shortly after turning onto the North Cascades Highway, make a stop in Newhalem for a short (but slightly steep) walk to a hidden waterfall. The trail takes you across a scenic suspension bridge, past a historic powerhouse, and through a mossy forest before revealing a cascading, crystal-clear creek. It's a great spot to stretch your legs.

Explore Diablo Lake: You've probably never seen a lake quite as turquoise as this one. Thanks to glacial runoff, Diablo Lake practically glows—especially on sunny days. You can admire it from above at the iconic Diablo Lake Vista Point, rent a kayak or paddleboard for a peaceful float (best in late summer or early fall), or hit the trails for a different perspective. My personal favorite? The Thunder Knob Trail—a relatively easy 3.6-mile out-and-back hike that gains 635 feet in elevation. It's the perfect warm-up hike, leading to an incredible panoramic view of the lake and surrounding peaks. Heads up: In fall, expect a creek crossing early on, as seasonal bridges are removed before winter.

DAY 2

Hike Cutthroat Pass Trail: While most fall hikers flock to the famous Maple Pass Loop, I recommend Cutthroat Pass for a slightly longer but less crowded experience. This eleven-mile round-trip hike gains 2,300 feet of elevation—but thanks to the steady, gradual incline, it feels much more approachable than you might expect. Maybe it's the impression that the name gives, but I don't think I've ever seen larch views in an area that felt quite as rugged as this.

The highlight? Spotting my first golden larch, a tiny baby tree along the trail, and then making my way up and over the ridge, where the world seemed to open up all at once. Below me, Cutthroat Lake shimmered in the distance, framed by rugged peaks dotted in gold. It was one of those moments where nature makes you feel small in the best possible way.

Alternative hike—Cutthroat Lake Trail: Looking for a shorter, family-friendly larch hike that still delivers stunning fall colors? Try the Cutthroat Lake Trail. At just under four miles round trip with only four hundred feet of elevation gain, this mellow walk through the forest leads to a glassy lake, with golden trees clinging to the mountainsides above. It's also a favorite among mountain bikers!

> **Bestie Tip:** One of my favorite ways to photograph larch trees is to use them as a natural frame for your subject—the more golden needles in the shot, the better! Shooting from a higher angle, like we did here, can also help you avoid including the sky if it's a moodier day or if you're going for a more forest-focused feel.

WASHINGTON PASS OVERLOOK

BLUE LAKE

Catch the sunset at Washington Pass Overlook: After an epic day on the trails (and roughly one thousand photos later), make one final stop at Washington Pass Overlook. Here, you'll be treated to jaw-dropping views of Liberty Bell Peak, a striking set of spire-like mountains that tower over the winding highway below. If an early snowfall has closed the road, you can still make the easy trek in—it only adds to the adventure and makes you wonder how they ever managed to build a road here in the first place!

DAY 3

Hike Blue Lake Trail: I know, your legs might be feeling a bit tired from yesterday's miles—but if you're up for it, there's one more bucket-list-worthy hike waiting. Blue Lake Trail is a moderate 4.4-mile round-trip hike with 1,050 feet of elevation gain, leading to a breathtaking alpine lake. The real postcard-worthy view? The reflections on the water, which on a calm day create a near-perfect mirror image of the golden landscape above, are mesmerizing.

> **The Takeaway:** For hikers, a few fall days spent in the North Cascades is *the* trip—one that will paint your memories a glorious golden. Between the glowing larches, glacier-carved peaks, and alpine lakes that shimmer like glass, it's the kind of place that feeds your soul long after you've left. Whether you're chasing fall color, savoring the silence of a snow-dusted trail, or catching the sunset from a mountain pass, this wilderness wonderland offers a little slice of heaven. One that humbles, quiets, and completely captivates.

OTIS PERKINS

44 LOPEZ ISLAND

Introduction

Seeking a salty getaway? I mean a true getaway, where you can step back from being glued to your phone, sitting in traffic with the never-ending pings of your inbox? I know just the spot where you can clear your mind, spend your days strolling laid-back nature trails, and catch breathtaking sunsets.

Lopez Island is an underrated gem, often overshadowed by its neighbors, particularly San Juan Island and Orcas Island. It's less touristy than the other two, but it still offers plenty of endearing amenities—restaurants, coffee shops, and even a delightful little bookstore. While I love all the San Juan Islands, I have to say that Lopez embodies the truest island vibe. Life moves at a slower pace here, and it's the kind of place where drivers wave to each other—yes, really! Be sure to return the friendly wave. Welcome to the Friendly Isle.

WATMOUGH BAY PRESERVE

The best time to visit? Summer, late spring, or early fall, when most businesses are open. Personally, I love a fall trip—Lopez, nestled in the Olympic Rain Shadow, gets a dreamy mix of lingering summer sunshine and crisp autumn air. Life slows down a little, and Lopez's laid-back spirit is the perfect match.

This itinerary is all about embracing the island's natural beauty, with peaceful parks, easygoing coastal hikes, and a few treasured local businesses, such as Lopez Island Creamery, home to some of the best small-batch ice cream around. If you ask me, you and a weekend on Lopez Island were meant to be.

At a Glance

Location: San Juan Islands, Washington
Best Season to Visit: September through November
Suggested Duration: Two or three nights

Getting There

Seattle to Lopez Island: 102 miles, ~3 hours

- **Includes the Anacortes—** San Juan Island ferry (~40 minutes)

Portland to Lopez Island: 276 miles, ~5 hours 20 minutes

- **Includes the Anacortes—**San Juan Island ferry (~40 minutes)

Where to Stay

Vacation rentals: Whether you're planning to cook your own meals or traveling with a larger group, renting a home is a fantastic way to experience Lopez. I especially recommend this option if you're staying longer than two nights—dining options can be limited in the offseason.

Lopez Farm Cottages: If you're bringing your four-legged friends along, this delightfully simple stay will bring a smile to your face (and give them something to wag their tails about). Choose between a private cottage with shared hot tub access or a glamping tent—a spacious, furnished tent with a queen bed and a cozy porch.

Spencer Spit State Park: To fully embrace the serenity of the island, consider camping at this peaceful park. You'll find campsites tucked into the forest and even a few right by the shore! Just note that there are no showers here, but you can find public ones at Lopez Village Park.

Itinerary Outline

DAY 1

Explore the Lopez Island Historical Society & Museum: If you thought a small island meant a small museum, think again! This community-centered gem blends outdoor and indoor exhibits for a memorable experience. Learn about the Straits Salish, the island's original inhabitants, and the evolution of Lopez's local economies, and even explore inspiring native gardens.

Shop at Lopez Village Market: Stock up on snacks, drinks, and groceries at this family-owned market. We loved trying local goodies, such as ice cream from Lopez Island Creamery, chips and salsa from San Juan Salsa Co., and San Juan Seltzer—I always reach for the Rainier Cherry flavor!

Dinner at Setsunai Noodle Bar: Cozy up with a bowl of ramen made with responsibly sourced ingredients, many of which are grown locally. The dog-friendly outdoor patio is the place to be. Reservations are always a good idea.

SPENCER SPIT

Catch the sunset at Otis Perkins Day Park: With plenty of beachfront to wander, this quickly became our favorite spot to watch the sun go down. Expansive views of San Juan Island stretch across the channel, and if you're lucky, you'll spot seaplanes coming and going.

DAY 2

Breakfast at Holly B's Bakery: It's practically a tradition to grab a cinnamon roll at least once while visiting Lopez Island, and this is the best place to do so. Freshly baked every morning, these pastries have been a community favorite for over forty years, along with almond butterhorns and other delicious treats.

Visit Lopez Bookshop: This independent bookstore is a treasure trove of new and used books. I was so excited to pick up *Quigley Lopez*, a heartwarming children's book about a golden retriever who lives on the island.

Explore the south side: island hiking adventures

- **Iceberg Point:** Start at Agate County Park and walk respectfully through a residential area (staying on the marked trail) before reaching the forest. From there, the trail opens into a rocky meadow with sweeping ocean views. It felt like standing on top of the world. Depending on how many side trails you explore, expect to log between three and four miles.
- **Watmough Bay Preserve:** Park in the forest and follow the short trail to one of the most stunning beaches in the Pacific Northwest. Nestled between dramatic cliffs, the water here is remarkably calm.
- **Shark Reef Sanctuary:** This scenic spot offers a short but rewarding one-mile walk. I loved gazing across the water at Cattle Point Lighthouse on San Juan Island—and I spotted quite a few harbor seals swimming by!

ICEBERG POINT

Lunch at Vortex Café & Juice Bar: After working up an appetite, head to this café for fresh burritos, bowls, and wraps made with seasonal, locally sourced ingredients. Pair your meal with a fresh juice or smoothie and enjoy it at a picnic table outside.

Explore Spencer Spit State Park: Go beachcombing at this fascinating park, where a lagoon, sailboats, and Frost Island create a postcard-perfect scene. At low tide, you can walk out on the narrow spit—it almost feels like you could reach out and touch the island! If you visit in the summer or early fall, you can rent a kayak from the Outdoor Adventure Center. Keep an eye out for this park on your ferry ride in—it's an easily recognizable landmark.

Dinner at Islander Bar & Grill: This down-to-earth restaurant is known for its wonderful waterfront views of Fisherman Bay. Expect seafood staples, burgers, and a relaxed atmosphere.

Dessert at Lopez Island Creamery: Treat yourself to handmade ice cream in a fresh waffle cone. I'm obsessed with the Latte Chip—if you're a coffee lover like me, you need to try it!

DAY 3

Breakfast at Isabel's Espresso: The best coffee on the island is found at this homey espresso bar. The lattes are made with organic milk, and the latte art is some of the best I've seen. Don't miss out on the locally made pastries!

ISABEL'S ESPRESSO

Explore Odlin County Park: Before catching the ferry home, sink your toes into the sandy shores of this peaceful park, just over a mile from the ferry terminal. Fair warning: stopping here will make it even harder to leave Lopez—but, still, you have to do it.

> **The Takeaway:** Island time is good for the soul, and I think you'll agree after visiting the lesser-known Lopez Island. There's no sweeter place to reconnect with nature, with yourself, and with what really matters. From madrona forests and windswept bluffs to cinnamon rolls and friendly waves from strangers, Lopez has a way of easing you into a slower pace of life—something I know I can use more of. Lopez doesn't demand your attention with dramatic peaks or bustling attractions. Instead, it quietly invites you to rediscover the simple pleasure of being present, making it the perfect antidote to our increasingly connected but often disconnected world.

45 SNOQUALMIE VALLEY

Introduction

With roaring waterfalls, maple leaves the size of your head, and historic downtowns, the Snoqualmie Valley is one of those places that is likely to become a favorite escape if you live in the greater Seattle area. It certainly has for me. Kyle and I have been hiking here for over a decade, ever since our senior year of high school. We've stood atop Rattlesnake Ledge in just about every season, sometimes crunching through snow, other times basking in the summer heat. We've watched Snoqualmie Falls nearly freeze solid in the dead of winter and slow to a trickle in the peak of summer. Along the way, we've discovered some incredible post-adventure eats.

But there's something extra special about the valley in autumn. With a mix of towering evergreens and brilliant deciduous trees, the whole landscape turns into a patchwork of fiery reds, oranges, and golds. You don't have to go far to see the colors—even popular spots, such as Snoqualmie Falls, get a seasonal glow-up. So, if you're craving a weekend full of crisp autumn air and small-town charm, all within an easy drive from Seattle or Tacoma, this is the place to be.

To make it even more magical, stay in a one-of-a-kind treehouse—just be sure to book ahead because this fairy-tale forest fantasy books up fast. The Snoqualmie Valley represents the perfect accessible fall destination where you can experience spectacular autumn colors, world-class outdoor recreation, and unique accommodations without venturing far from urban conveniences.

At a Glance

Location: King County, Washington
Best Season to Visit: September through November
Suggested Duration: Two nights

Getting There

Seattle to Snoqualmie: 28.5 miles, ~30 minutes
Portland to Snoqualmie: 182 miles, ~2 hours 50 minutes

TREEHOUSE POINT

SNOQUALMIE VALLEY

Where to Stay

Treehouse Point: If you've ever dreamed of sleeping among the trees, this magical hideaway will spark your imagination. With seven uniquely designed treehouses perched above the Raging River, it's a sweet stay—perfect for celebrating special occasions. Plus, the delicious breakfast and warm hospitality make it even more special!

Salish Lodge & Spa: Have you ever stayed at a resort perched atop a 268-foot waterfall? These modern yet cozy rooms feature fireplaces, soaking tubs, and spacious showers, plus dreamy river views. With an onsite spa and two excellent restaurants, it's the ultimate spot for a relaxing getaway.

Vacation rentals: If you're looking for a more budget-friendly option, there are plenty of charming guesthouses and cabins in the area, many offering stunning views of the surrounding rivers and forests!

Itinerary Outline

DAY 1

Grab afternoon coffee from Aroma Coffee Co.: Kick off your trip with a stop at this small-town coffee shop that will totally steal your heart. If you visit around Halloween, you're in for a treat—each year, this historic house turned café gets a festive makeover. In recent years, I've seen it transformed into Barbie's Dreamhouse and Hogwarts! The pumpkin pie latte? I'm obsessed.

AROMA COFFEE CO.

SNOQUALMIE FALLS

Explore the Tokul Creek Trestle: Hit the Snoqualmie Valley Trail from the Tokul Road trailhead and follow this former railroad route through the forest. Your reward? A breathtaking view of a hundred-year-old trestle bridge spanning a deep canyon. It's a hidden gem you'd never stumble upon unless you were looking for it! If you're bringing bikes, this is a great place to ride.

Catch the sunset at Rattlesnake Lake: Set at the base of one of the most popular hiking trails near Seattle, this peaceful lake is a go-to for sunset lovers. Whether you want to picnic, paddle, or just soak in the views, it's a perfect way to wrap up your first evening.

Dinner at South Fork Restaurant: After a full day of exploring, settle in at this cozy, locally loved spot. With a roomy beer garden (that's dog friendly!) and a menu full of comfort food, you can't go wrong. The Brisket Mac and Cheese and BBQ Brisket Sando are crowd favorites!

DAY 2

Breakfast at The Restaurant & Terrace Bar at the Salish Lodge & Spa: For a memorable brunch with a hard-to-top view, grab a window table overlooking Snoqualmie Falls. The fall-favorite chai-spiced French toast (or strawberry rhubarb come summertime) and eggs Benedict are must-tries, but the real showstopper is the Honey From Heaven ritual, where your server drizzles local honey over fresh biscuits in a waterfall-like fashion to honor the sacred falls. It's a sweet experience in every way!

Walk to the base of Snoqualmie Falls: While the upper viewpoint offers epic photo opportunities (and a refreshing mist!), I highly recommend taking the short trail down to the lower viewpoint. The walk is easy and takes you past historic hydropower buildings along the Raging River. In fall, the foliage here is straight out of a storybook. If it's crowded, be kind and offer to snap a photo for the group in front of you—they'll appreciate it and likely return the favor!

Mountain biking at Duthie Hill: Swing by Ride Bicycles to rent bikes, and the friendly staff will help you find the perfect route to explore. If you're in the mood for a casual ride, the East Lake Sammamish Trail is a great choice. But if you're feeling adventurous, head to Duthie Hill Mountain Bike Park—an ideal spot for beginners and experienced riders alike.

Lunch at The Well and Table: Savor a farm-to-table feast that truly celebrates fall's flavors in a warm, cozy setting. My top pick? The seasonal butternut squash lasagna is comfort food at its finest. And whatever you do, save room for dessert—the warm apple cobbler is worth a try.

Explore downtown Snoqualmie:

- **Snoqualmie Trading Co.:** This fully stocked gift shop has all the PNW souvenirs you could need—from Christmas ornaments to graphic hoodies.

> **Bestie Tip:** I always stock up on the sweet-smelling body scrubs made by local Carnation Soap Co. These make for great holiday gifts!

- **Snoqualmie Ice Cream:** Experience fall in a cup with a scoop of their seasonal flavor (my favorite is German Chocolate Cake)! This local Washington dairy brand makes small-batch, big-yum ice cream.
- **Ride the Snoqualmie Valley Railroad:** Hop aboard a historic train for a scenic tour-house tour through the valley, stopping at the Railway History Campus for you to explore a museum. In the fall, they even hand churn apple cider, and it's delicious!

Dinner at Snoqualmie Falls Brewery: After just one meal here, you'll have a hard time driving through town without stopping again! It's known for locally named beers and homemade root beer. The burgers and sandwiches are fantastic, and the lively outdoor patio is pup friendly!

DAY 3

Breakfast at Arête Coffee Bar: This hidden gem is tucked inside a ski and outdoor shop, serving up excellent coffee and breakfast sandwiches. My go-to is The Spicy Pig—a bagel sandwich with house-made sriracha aioli and Mama Lil's peppers. So good!

Hike Little Si Trail: Since there's no shortage of hiking trails in this beautiful area, it's worth swinging by one more before heading home. I recommend the Little Si, which is a moderate hike that provides a bird's-eye view of North Bend and the occasional mountain goat sighting.

> **The Takeaway:** Fall in Snoqualmie isn't just a season; it's a feeling—a refreshing escape where nature's colors blaze brilliantly and every moment feels inspired. From discovering hidden railroad trestles where century-old engineering meets nature's artistry to mountain biking through forests painted in every shade of gold and red, the Snoqualmie Valley offers adventures that satisfy both thrill-seekers and those simply seeking peaceful moments in nature's cathedral. So go ahead, book that once-in-a-lifetime treehouse stay, let waterfall mist refresh your spirit, and satisfy your soul with incredible seasonally inspired meals that taste like autumn itself.

LITTLE SI

BALD EAGLE

46

COUPEVILLE

Introduction

What could make a walk on the beach even more magical? How about seals gliding through the water, bald eagles soaring overhead, and the breathtaking Deception Pass Bridge towering beside you? I've lost track of how many times I've visited this iconic place, yet every time, it still steals my breath. I don't think photos do justice to the mesmerizing swirl of the currents, the wind whipping through your hair as you stand atop the bridge, or the shared sense of wonder among visitors from near and far. Welcome to Deception Pass State Park—Washington's most-visited state park, and for good reason. Just a half hour from Coupeville, it's an unparalleled paradise teeming with natural beauty and wildlife.

If you're exploring the central and northern reaches of Whidbey Island, consider staying in Coupeville, a charming waterfront town along Penn Cove. Here, beautifully preserved Victorian architecture meets vibrant storefronts filled with local treasures. Stroll through small businesses, such as Kingfisher Bookstore (don't miss the lower level!) and Lavender Wind, a delightful shop rooted right here on the island.

Just minutes from Coupeville, you'll find Fort Casey and Fort Ebey State Parks, where military history meets jaw-dropping coastal views. Like all the PNW's temperate islands, Whidbey is worth visiting year-round. But early fall? That's the sweet spot. The trails are dry, the air is crisp, and the summer crowds have thinned. The combination of accessible outdoor recreation, rich maritime history, and authentic island character makes Coupeville the perfect base for exploring Whidbey's most spectacular natural areas.

By the time you leave, I wouldn't be surprised if you're just as obsessed with Whidbey Island as I am! There's something about the way golden autumn light hits the historic waterfront, the way morning mist rises from Penn Cove, and the way every trail seems to lead to another breathtaking vista that makes this place feel truly magical.

At a Glance

Location: Whidbey Island, Washington
Best Season to Visit: September through November
Suggested Duration: Two nights

Getting There

Seattle to Coupeville: 57.5 miles, ~1 hour 45 minutes

- **Includes the Mukilteo:** Clinton ferry (~20 minutes)

Portland to Coupeville: 231 miles, ~4 hours 30 minutes

- **Includes the Mukilteo:** Clinton ferry (~20 minutes)

Where to Stay

Deception Pass State Park: After camping in countless places across the Pacific Northwest, I can confidently say this is one of the most breathtaking campgrounds out there. Whether you pick a site tucked into the forest or steps from a calm bay, you really can't go wrong. With hundreds of campsites (though some loops close after October 1), this spot is a must for nature lovers.

Vacation rentals: For a cozy stay in the heart of Coupeville, renting a quaint cottage is the way to go. Some even offer phenomenal water views and beach access! We did this for Kyle's birthday, and honestly, it made us want to move here!

Best Western Plus Oak Harbor Hotel & Conference Center: If you're looking for a classic hotel stay, this dog-friendly 3-star hotel has everything you need, including a complimentary breakfast.

DECEPTION PASS BRIDGE

Itinerary Outline

DAY 1

Hike to Rosario Head: I can't think of a better place to kick off your trip than Bowman Bay. This quiet cove with calm waters is the perfect starting point for a short but scenic hike to Rosario Head (1.5 miles round trip, two hundred feet elevation gain). The trail climbs up a bluff and follows the water to an expansive view of the sea—it's especially surreal at sunset! If you want a shorter option, you can start directly from the Rosario Head trailhead.

Dinner at Phad Thai: Set inside a charming blue-and-pink Victorian home, this Thai restaurant serves up all the classics—think fried rice, curry, and noodles. I've grabbed takeout here a few times, but the cozy indoor seating looks just as inviting. If you're dining with a big group, it's best to call ahead.

EBEY'S LANDING

DAY 2

Breakfast at Sunshine Drip: Kick off your morning at one of the best cafés in the Pacific Northwest. Its Greek avocado toast, banana bread, and smoothies are *chef's kiss*. Kyle and I like to share the biggest size of its peanut butter smoothie—it's that yummy! And if you're traveling with a pup, they can join you on the outdoor patio.

Hike Ebey's Landing: If you love long walks on beaches, this trail is a dream come true. The loop starts with a climb up the bluff, follows the coastline above a lagoon, and then descends to the rocky beach. It's one of those hikes that reminds me why I love islands so much—and, honestly, it might be my favorite trail ever. Plan for around four miles and 335 feet of elevation gain.

Explore Fort Casey Historical State Park: There's a little something for everyone here—fly a kite, tour the 1903 lighthouse, or wander through historic military batteries. On a clear day, you can even spot Mount Rainier on the horizon! She's nearly fooled me a few times, when I almost mistook her for clouds.

Lunch at Front Street Grill: Treat yourself to a waterfront meal featuring famous Penn Cove mussels, which I've heard are so fresh you can taste the local waters they came from. The fish and chips, burgers, and Mediterranean gnocchi are also solid choices.

ADMIRALTY HEAD LIGHTHOUSE

COUPEVILLE WHARF

Explore downtown Coupeville

- **Island County Historical Museum:** Learn about the island's history, from Native Peoples to early settlers, and even see the remains of a Columbian mammoth!
- **Kingfisher Bookstore:** Pick up a book written by a Whidbey author or one about Northwest wildlife and fauna.
- **Penn Cove Gallery:** Stock up on island-crafted art treasures, from ceramics to paintings to jewelry.

Explore Deception Pass State Park: With over four thousand acres to roam, this is Washington's most-visited state park for a reason. Fall is the perfect time to visit when the crowds thin out, leaving you with peaceful beaches, calm waters for paddling at Cranberry Lake, and sweeping views from the top of Goose Rock Summit. It's impossible not to be awed by its unrivaled, rugged beauty.

Dinner at Oystercatcher: Settle in for a meal to remember with the chef's five-course tasting menu. Each beautifully plated dish rotates with the seasons so that you can try something new every visit. Owners Sophia and Ben are known for thoughtfully sourcing ingredients and minimizing food waste, making every bite as intentional as it is delicious.

Catch the sunset at Fort Ebey State Park: Arrive well before sunset to explore the old bunkers before making your way to the beach. Walk out to the bluff (brace yourself for the wind!) for jaw-dropping views of the water and the Olympic Mountains. It's the kind of sunset that makes you stop in your tracks. Then, head down to the shore, where the waves will lap at your feet as you bask in golden light.

DAY 3

Breakfast at Sunshine Drip (again!): If you're anything like me and love revisiting your favorite coffee spots, head back for one last breakfast. If you're in the mood for something heartier, Island Café is another great option.

Explore Price Sculpture Forest: Don't leave Whidbey without strolling through this beautiful blend of art and nature. You'll

FORT EBEY

find it surprisingly close to town and full of surprises. It's an outdoor art gallery, not just set in the forest but embedded into it, making it a truly unique experience!

The Takeaway: From the moment you first glimpse Deception Pass Bridge rising from swirling waters to those final sunset moments at Fort Ebey, where the Olympic peaks paint the horizon, Coupeville and central Whidbey Island offer experiences that capture the essence of Pacific Northwest island magic. This corner of Washington offers both adventure and tranquility in equal measure. It's a place where military pastimes meet wild coastal beauty, where every trail seems to lead to another breathtaking vista, and where the simple act of watching sunset from a windswept bluff can remind you why falling in love with islands is so easy and so life-changing.

47 WILSONVILLE

Introduction

If you're like me and totally thrive in fall, then listen up. Whether you don't have time for a long vacation or just aren't in the mood to travel far, I know the perfect spot where you can soak up all the best parts of the season without venturing too far from the city. Nestled just south of Portland and conveniently located along I-5, Wilsonville is an underrated weekend getaway destination. Known for its family-friendly atmosphere, this charming town sits near some of the region's most scenic natural spaces, perfect for a crisp autumn escape. My personal favorite? Champoeg State Heritage Area. This historic site, once a pioneer ghost town, now offers a peaceful retreat along the Willamette River. Beyond its fascinating history, I was struck by how serene it felt, wandering through oak groves, marveling at old-growth trees, and spotting wildlife along the trails. We even got lucky with a beaver sighting!

WILLAMETTE RIVER FROM CHAMPOEG STATE PARK

But Wilsonville isn't just about fall foliage—it's a hidden gem for food lovers too. One of my most-visited Oregon coffee spots is tucked away in the Charbonneau neighborhood. From the moment I spotted the bubblegum-pink telephone booth outside, I knew Lux Sucre Bakery + Café was something special. Step inside, and you're greeted with a vibrant, welcoming space filled with beautifully crafted pastries, picture-perfect latte art, and a buzzing sense of community. It's the kind of place that makes you want to linger—and trust me, you'll want to return again and again.

At a Glance

Location: Clackamas County, Oregon
Best Season to Visit: September through October
Suggested Duration: Two nights

Getting There

Seattle to Wilsonville: 190 miles, ~3 hours
Portland to Wilsonville: 17.4 miles, ~20 minutes

Where to Stay

Hilton Garden Inn: Our room here felt more like a chic, spacious studio apartment than a hotel. The mini walk-in closet, bright bathroom, and modern workspace made an excellent first impression. To top it off, the restaurant downstairs served up delicious meals with warm hospitality. We'd stay here again in a heartbeat!

Vacation rentals: For a cozy stay in one of Wilsonville's welcoming neighborhoods, check out the charming rental homes. If you're craving a relaxing getaway, staying outside the city center can offer a refreshing change of pace.

Champoeg State Heritage Area: Just seven miles out of town lies a pioneer ghost town turned state park that's full of surprises! Once a thriving settlement, Champoeg was washed away by the Willamette River flooding, but it remains a historic gem. This is where Oregon pioneers cast their votes to form the region's first provisional government. Stay the night in budget-friendly campsites, cabins, or yurts, and enjoy more time exploring this hidden treasure.

FERN

COFFEE LAKE WETLANDS

Itinerary Outline

DAY 1

Explore the Tualatin River National Wildlife Refuge: Grab your binoculars and comfy walking shoes for an afternoon of wildlife watching at this urban refuge. The visitor center offers insight into the park's resident animals. If you visit before the end of September, you'll have access to four miles of trails (though the Wetland Trail closes in winter to protect migrating birds). Keep an eye out for great blue herons, bald eagles, and frogs!

Catch the sunset at Coffee Lake Wetlands: Ease into your trip with this underrated natural area—once home to Ice Age megafauna, including mammoths!

> **Bestie Tip:** Don't follow Google Maps' pin for this spot. Instead, park at the small lot at Southwest Villebois Drive North and Southwest Coffee Lake Drive. Take the short trail and soak in the neighborhood charm.

Dinner at Vanguard Brewing: Cozy up in this craft brewery, just minutes from the wetlands. The wood-fired pizzas are a must, and the drinks are even better. We loved the WiggleButt IPA and couldn't resist the beer dazzle—yes, glitter in our glass! It also serves fantastic local ciders. Bonus: the beer garden is pup friendly!

DAY 2

Breakfast at Pearl Bakery: For next-level croissant breakfast sandwiches and fresh cinnamon rolls, head to this bakery tucked into an unassuming industrial center.

VANGUARD BREWING

Explore Champoeg State Heritage Area: Hands down, this is my favorite park near Wilsonville—serene, vast, and steeped in history. It's a place to slow down and savor.

- **Champoeg Visitor Center:** Start with an intro film, browse a small museum, and pick up a local read to dive into the area's history.
- **Take the Townsite Trail:** Best explored on foot or bike, this paved 3.5-mile trail begins at the visitor center and winds through history.
- **Pioneer Memorial Building:** Stand where pioneers voted to establish the Oregon Territorial Government in 1843. Don't miss the impressive, towering old-growth trees, which blew my mind!
- **Play disc golf:** For a fun group activity, bring your discs and let them fly at this twenty-three-hole course that is relatively flat and located in an oak grove.

Explore Graham Oaks Nature Park: Walk an easy, breezy three-mile loop path at this 250-acre park brimming with native plants. You might spot deer, coyotes, or a variety of birds as you cross wetlands and oak woodlands. The mix of paved and gravel paths makes for an easy, enjoyable walk. Time your visit around sunset for a dreamy shot of the Elder Oak tree!

Lunch at Thai Village: For a flavorful lunch in a warm setting, try this lovely spot for delicious Thai cuisine. Swing by on a weekday to take advantage of the lunch specials!

Explore the Aurora Colony National Historic District: Known as the first designated National Historic District in Oregon, this quaint town is well loved for its over twenty charming stroll-worthy shops. I love the handful of antique shops, which can easily keep you entertained as you search for treasures to bring home with you. The Old Aurora Colony Museum is also an interesting stop, which tells the story of communal living in the mid-nineteenth century.

Dinner at Parkway Grille: Tucked inside the Hilton Garden Inn, this spot delivers both on flavor and ambiance. The funky-fresh decor and variety of seating make it a great choice for a girls' night or a cozy date. The menu highlights seasonal ingredients—our favorite fall dish? The soul-warming, creamy Autumn Ravioli.

MEMORIAL PARK

DAY 3

Breakfast at Lux Sucre Bakery + Café: I might sound like a broken record, but this pink, Instagrammable café is one of the best coffee shops in the PNW. After my first visit, I don't think I've ever passed through Wilsonville without stopping! From stunning latte art to a picture-perfect pastry selection (like the pumpkin roll below), this café is a 10/10!

LUX SUCRE

Explore Memorial Park: Wrap up your Wilsonville adventure with a peaceful walk on the Memorial Park Forest Trail. Follow the path toward the Willamette River, where a small dock offers one last scenic moment before heading home.

The Takeaway: Whether you live in Portland or are simply looking for an easy-to-get-to Oregon spot with complete amenities, Wilsonville is a town that I think will surprise you. It's one of those places that reminds us that if you're curious, you never know what you'll find! Between the golden oak groves at Champoeg, glittery IPAs at the local brewery, and pumpkin rolls at Lux Sucre, fall in Wilsonville is full of cozy comforts. It's a destination where you can spot bald eagles in urban wildlife refuges, explore antique treasures in America's first National Historic District, and end each day knowing you've found another reason to love the Pacific Northwest's ability to surprise and delight. Whether you're escaping Portland for a weekend or making Wilsonville a base for exploring the greater Willamette Valley, this charming town proves that sometimes the most memorable adventures happen in the places we might otherwise drive right past—all the more reason to take the time to stop and look a little closer.

48 STEVENS PASS

Introduction

As the air turns crisp and the days grow shorter, there's one place that always calls me back. No matter how many times I go, I find myself drawn to the winding stretch of Highway 2 that cuts through Stevens Pass, where towering evergreens meet misty mountain peaks, and the rivers run cold and clear. Over the years, Kyle and I have taken countless day trips here, lacing up our boots for hikes that have become as familiar as old friends. If you're an avid hiker in western Washington, you probably have too. But here's the thing: there's just something about this place that makes it so much more than a quick in-and-out adventure. The rugged remoteness, the sheer number of trails, and the way the scenery transforms with the seasons make it worthy of a dedicated weekend getaway.

Funny enough, the first time I ever booked an Airbnb was in Index, a tiny town tucked along the North Fork Skykomish River. It was a snug, tiny home, just big enough for two, and I still remember how the golden leaves practically glowed against the misty hillsides. I don't think I've ever seen so many shades of amber, crimson, and yellow in one place. It felt like stepping into a painting.

Another time, I planned a trip for my parents. It was my first time ever taking them on vacation, and it felt like a full-circle moment after all the adventures they took me on growing up. We stayed in Skykomish, and it poured rain the entire time. But somehow, that only made the trip feel more fitting for the Pacific Northwest. We embraced the drizzle, taking slow walks through moss-draped forests, listening to the steady rush of the river, and watching mist weave through the peaks. In the evenings, we cozied up in our rental, cooking dinner together and settling in for movie nights, the sound of rain pattering on the roof.

Whether you're looking for misty morning hikes, the magic of fall colors, or a quiet retreat where you can sip your coffee while watching the fog roll over the mountains, this stretch of Highway 2 is the kind of place that sticks with you. And if you haven't yet turned a day trip into a weekend getaway, let this be your sign—it's worth every second.

At a Glance

Location: King and Chelan Counties, Washington
Best Season to Visit: September through November
Suggested Duration: Two nights

Getting There

Seattle to Stevens Pass: 82.3 miles, ~1 hour 30 minutes
Portland to Stevens Pass: 250 miles, ~4 hours 15 minutes

> **Bestie Tip:** Start keeping tabs on the weather about a week before your trip and check the WSDOT website (wsdot.wa.gov) for pass reports and live cams a few days out. It's the best way to stay ahead of changing road conditions. For trail updates, I always turn to recent reports on Washington Trails Association and AllTrails to get the latest on snow levels, closures, and more.

Where to Stay

Vacation rentals: Depending on where you want to set up your base camp, vacation rentals offer the most flexibility. Whether you're after a cozy cabin tucked in the

STEVENS PASS

woods or a riverside retreat, there are plenty of charming stays to choose from. I especially love having a kitchen out here—it's a game changer when restaurants are few and far between, plus there's something special about making your morning coffee while surrounded by towering evergreens. My favorite is SkyCabin in Skykomish (it's dog friendly).

Bush House Inn: If historic charm speaks to you, then a stay at Bush House Inn is a must. This beautifully restored hotel has been welcoming guests for over a century, and its warm, inviting atmosphere makes it feel like stepping back in time. Be sure to book a room with a full view of Mount Index—you'll want to wake up to that dreamy sight. Bonus: the onsite restaurant serves up some seriously good food!

Best Western Sky Valley Inn: If you're traveling with a pup or looking for a budget-friendly stay, the Best Western in Monroe checks both boxes. It's conveniently located near grocery stores, restaurants, and other amenities, making it a great option for those who want easy access to town. Plus, a complimentary breakfast means you can fuel up before hitting the trails.

Itinerary Outline

DAY 1

Hike Heybrook Ridge: While Heybrook Lookout often steals the spotlight, Heybrook Ridge Trail deserves just as much love. This quiet alternative offers stunning views of Mount Index without as many crowds. We took the Leovy Trail with Lilo, and the panoramic scenery at the top left us in awe. If you look closely, you can even spot a waterfall cascading down the rock face—that's Bridal Veil Falls, which you'll be hiking to tomorrow! Expect to log about 3.5 miles round trip with a moderate 775 feet elevation gain.

> **Bestie Tip:** Fuel up with build-your-own smoothies and sandwiches from Vinaccio Coffee. Eat an early dinner there or pack it for your hike to enjoy with a scenic view!

DAY 2

Coffee at Sky River Coffee: A big part of small-town charm comes from local coffee shops, and this one is not to be missed. If you have a kid in tow who loves trains, then this is the perfect place for you—you can watch them roll by from the cozy interior while sipping your latte.

Breakfast at LouSkis Deli: A small-town staple, this is the place to go for a satisfying breakfast before a full day of exploring. The build-your-own breakfast sandwiches hit the spot, and the laid-back, welcoming atmosphere makes you want to linger just a little longer.

Hike to Bridal Veil Falls: One of the most breathtaking waterfalls in the state, Bridal Veil Falls is a must-see. The trail winds through a forest before bringing you right up to the base of the falls, offering a rare, up-close perspective. It's about a four-mile round trip with a steady one thousand feet

HEYBROOK RIDGE

BRIDAL VEIL FALLS

elevation gain, making for a solid workout. If you're feeling ambitious, continue onward to Lake Serene for even more jaw-dropping scenery.

Lunch at 59er Diner: After all that hiking, it's time to reward yourself. Hop in the car and take a scenic drive over Stevens Pass to 59er Diner, a retro-inspired spot that serves up nostalgic American classics. And let's be real—you've earned an old-fashioned chocolate malt.

Explore Lake Wenatchee State Park: Arguably one of the most stunning state parks in Washington, Lake Wenatchee is a downright extraordinary destination. This time of year, the lake takes on a serene beauty. Towering mountains surround the crystal-clear water, and there's even a sandy beach. It reminds me a little of Glacier National Park in Montana!

Bestie Tip: If you time your visit right, you can see golden larch trees! I've spotted them in the campground loops around mid-October. Usually, you have to hike into the mountains to see them, so this is an easy-access spot that doesn't require breaking a sweat.

DAY 3

Coffee from Espresso Chalet: This social-media-famous roadside coffee shop is known for its fun Sasquatch theme and excellent views of Mount Index. I brought my parents here on a drizzly fall day, and we had a fun time snapping selfies and eating cookies shaped like Sasquatch's feet—tastes better than it sounds, I promise!

Explore Wallace Falls State Park: You're not done adventuring just yet! Wallace Falls State Park in Gold Bar boasts some of the best hiking in the area. The trail to the falls is a fan favorite, leading you past three tiers of cascading water. Along the way, you'll meander through a mossy, fairy-tale-like forest with peekaboo views of the North Fork Wallace River. The full hike is about 5.8 miles

LAKE WENATCHEE

round trip with 1,300 feet of elevation gain, but you can always turn back at the lower or middle falls if you're short on time.

The Takeaway: Hot cocoa season calls for waterfall hikes and mountain drives, and Stevens Pass is the ideal place for both. While it's not on the coast, it still gives that moody vibe—like vampires or werewolves might be watching you . . . or maybe just Sasquatch! Either way, it's the perfect spot to unplug, pull on your oversized flannel, and bring along your favorite book for nostalgic rereads while autumn embraces you in its misty, magical arms. It's a destination where every waterfall tells a story, every trail offers a different perspective on the same magnificent mountains, and every visit reminds you why turning day trips into weekend getaways creates space for the kind of memories that last long after the last autumn leaf has fallen.

49 BANDON

Introduction

Let's be honest: transitioning between seasons can be tough, especially from summer to fall. The shorter, gloomier days can take a toll on mood and energy levels, and as much as I love fall, I often find myself missing the sunshine. If you can relate and are looking for a weekend getaway where summer seems to linger just a little longer, these next two Oregon destinations are for you!

First up is Bandon, a charming town on the Southern Oregon Coast. Known as the "Cranberry Capital of Oregon," Bandon enjoys mild weather and relatively few rainy days in early fall. While it may not be your typical fall foliage destination, it offers the perfect chance to soak up those last golden days of summer. Sunny beach days boost my spirits, and the joy they bring lasts long after I leave.

With plenty of public sandy beaches, you likely won't be able to walk the entire stretch of shoreline in one visit—but, hey, that's just an excuse to come back! One of my favorite spots is Face Rock Scenic Viewpoint, a place I could return to a hundred times and still discover something new. Trust me, it's a phenomenal sunset spot.

Beyond its coastal charm, Bandon is also close to some of the best mountain biking on the Oregon Coast. The Whiskey Run Trail System, an ever-expanding network set to span over thirty miles, gives riders a chance to zoom through a variety of landscapes. You'll find yourself in open recently logged

FACE ROCK

zones with young trees, dense dark forest where you feel like you are riding through a tunnel, and mature forest with lush green understory growth that is a trademark of the coastal forests of Oregon. As a fun touch, the trails have drinking-themed names such as Hangover, Bottoms Up, and Speakeasy, leaning into the Whiskey Run theme.

At a Glance

Location: Southern Oregon Coast
Best Season to Visit: September through October
Suggested Duration: Two nights

Getting There

Seattle to Bandon: 419 miles, ~6 hours 55 minutes
Portland to Bandon: 246 miles, ~4 hours 30 minutes

Where to Stay

Table Rock Motel: The newly built north building is home to modern suites with ocean views. Some even come with patios, electric fireplaces, and kitchenettes. Kick back and relax in the beautifully designed suites.

Vacation rentals: For a private, one-of-a-kind stay, Bandon has a great selection of homes, apartments, and cabins. The one that swept me off my feet was the Bandon Beach Shack—a colorful, cutesy A-frame just steps from the sand.

Bullards Beach State Park: If you're looking for a budget-friendly stay, it doesn't get better than this forested campground just two miles north of town. Opt for a yurt, tent site, or full-hookup RV site.

THE LOFT RESTAURANT AND BAR

Itinerary Outline

DAY 1

Visit the Charleston Marine Life Center: On your way into town, stop at this underwater discovery center to meet some of the creatures that live underwater—some who even call the deep sea home. Stand next to towering whale skeletons to get a sense of their size, say hello to starfish and anemones in the touch tanks, and watch fishermen unloading their catch at the harbor.

Explore Cape Arago and Shore Acres State Parks: Side by side, these two parks showcase the rugged beauty of the Oregon Coast. Start with the short-but-steep Cape Arago South Cove Trail, leading to a protected sandy beach with calm waters. It's a small beach, but it leaves a big impression! Next, stop by Simpson Reef Overlook to count how many sea lions are lounging on Shell Island and Simpson Reef. Finally, swing by the stunning Shore Acres Japanese Garden. Coastal gardens like this are rare, making it a refreshing stop.

Dinner at Bandon Brewing: Whether you're in the mood for wood-fired pizza or sharing a few rounds of classic brewery appetizers, this is a great spot to settle in on your first night. I'm obsessed with the Mediterranean pizza—loaded with veggies, homemade pesto, and feta. Wash it down with one of the handcrafted drinks, such as the Mint Hibiscus Hop Tea, Cold Brew Coffee Stout, or One-Eyed Jack IPA.

DAY 2

Breakfast at The Loft Restaurant and Bar: Perched above the Coquille River, this delightful spot is known for its incredible eggs Benedict—the smoked salmon version is my go-to! The flavors and presentation are impeccable, and drinking coffee on the outdoor deck is the perfect way to start the day.

Explore Old Town Bandon

- **Face Rock Creamery:** Delight in delicious cheeses and Umpqua ice cream. Since you're in the cranberry capital of Oregon, you need to sample the Cranberry Cheesecake flavor. We love it, along with Chocolate Brownie Thunder.
- **Art by the Sea Gallery:** Peruse fused glass, ceramics, and paintings created locally on the Oregon Coast.
- **Big Wheel General Store:** Wander through a driftwood museum, a fudge factory, and an endless selection of coastal souvenirs. You never know what you'll find.
- **Explore Cape Blanco Lighthouse:** Known as Oregon's westernmost point, this historic lighthouse is worth the forty-minute drive south of Bandon. A short quarter-mile walk takes you inside the beautiful brick-lined tower.

FACE ROCK

Lunch at Tony's Crab Shack: This is where you'll find some of the freshest seafood around—think crab cakes, oysters, and lobster rolls. My favorite? The fish tacos, topped with *pico de gallo* and a house-made spicy aioli that's a match made in heaven!

Mountain biking at Whiskey Run: Enjoy a ride in the largest mountain biking trail system on the Oregon Coast. This space has a wide variety of trails ranging in difficulty from beginner to expert. Fall is the tail end of the ideal riding season, so make the most of it!

Dinner at Foley's Irish Pub: Head here for a fun mix of foods you've never tried before, such as Scotch eggs, as well as comforting traditional dishes, such as shepherd's pie, Irish meatloaf, and fish and chips. I enjoyed the clam chowder, which comes with delicious garlic bread.

Catch the sunset at Face Rock State Scenic Viewpoint: Plan to arrive early so you have time to explore the beach. This was our very first stop in Bandon, and it immediately won us over! The dramatic rock formations—such as Wizard Hat and The Castle—along with sea caves and tide pools make for an unforgettable experience. Watching the sunset here sealed our love for this magical stretch of coastline.

DAY 3

Breakfast at Bandon Coffee Café: Before heading home, grab a hot cup of coffee and a breakfast bagel sandwich or fresh pastries. Or, if you sleep in and are in the mood for brunch, take advantage of the lunch menu! The café has comforting rotating soups and fluffy quiche.

Explore the Bandon Marsh National Wildlife Refuge: If you love bird-watching, don't skip this quiet nature preserve. Walk along the short boardwalk trail to spot migrating birds in the mudflats during low tide. Then, meander the half- to one-mile Myrtlewood Grove Nature Trail, which loops through a mix of forest and meadow. It's an easy, peaceful way to wrap up your trip—you never know what wildlife might make an appearance!

The Takeaway: If you want to chase after the last golden days of sunshine before winter sets in, Bandon is just the place. From tide pool treasures and candy-colored sunsets at Face Rock to cozy brunches and cranberry sweets, this stretch of the Southern Oregon Coast feels like a warm hug during that bittersweet in-between season. Whether you're biking through forest tunnels at Whiskey Run or beachcombing beneath dramatic sea stacks, Bandon offers that perfect blend of adventure and serenity. It's not your typical fall getaway—but that's exactly what makes it feel like your own little secret.

50 BEND

Introduction

In addition to Bandon, another Oregon town I highly recommend visiting in the fall for a sunshine-fueled dopamine boost is Bend. Perched at 3,625 feet, this outdoorsy mountain town shines in September and October when temperatures hover in the upper sixties to seventies, and you could count the number of rainy days on one hand. After Kyle and I first visited in

SPARKS LAKE

January, we brought my family back later that same year in early October. It was the sweet spot—cool nights, warm days. While it was a tad early for peak fall foliage, especially the cottonwoods, the trip was exactly the vitamin-D-filled getaway we needed. And since Bend is famously dog friendly, we brought our pup Lilo along too!

One of the best perks of visiting in early fall is that no snow has fallen yet, meaning hiking trails, scenic drives, and mountain biking routes are all easily accessible. Given Bend's high elevation, many roads and trails require snowshoes or microspikes later in the year. So, if you're planning an autumn visit, I recommend taking advantage of the great weather to explore the stunning landscapes nearby—think lava fields, brilliant night skies, and cascading waterfalls. Trust me, after a fall trip to Bend, you might just find yourself daydreaming about moving here—I've been there myself!

At a Glance

Location: Central Oregon
Best Season to Visit: September through October
Suggested Duration: Two nights

Getting There

Seattle to Bend: 328 miles, ~5 hours 40 minutes
Portland to Bend: 163 miles, ~3 hours 10 minutes

Where to Stay

The Oxford Bend: This hotel will spoil you with gelato, coffee, and the Deschutes River just steps from your posh room. Make your stay unforgettable with vinyl albums and a pillow menu to customize your experience to perfection.

LOGE Bend: If you took the spirit of Bend's outdoorsy culture and turned it into a hotel, it would be this. With hammocks hanging from the ceilings, bike racks by the front door, and proximity to Mount Bachelor, it's the perfect blend of comfort and adventure. We stayed here on our first visit to Bend.

Campfire Hotel: In this town of year-round adventure, it's no surprise that this hotel boasts an outdoor saltwater pool that is so refreshing—I am obsessed! The central location is a plus, and the onsite Canteen serves up drinks and tapas, so really, you have everything you need.

PILOT BUTTE

Itinerary Outline

DAY 1

Explore Tumalo Falls: This breathtaking ninety-seven-foot waterfall is an icon of Central Oregon and is easily accessible before winter sets in. In early fall, you can drive up the gravel road and park at the Tumalo Falls Day Use Area. From there, it's a quick quarter-mile stroll to spectacular views of the falls! If you have time, I recommend continuing on the trail to visit additional waterfalls (though the first one is the most dramatic).

Dinner at Fire on the Mountain Buffalo Wings: Have you ever tried veggie wings? You can here! Known for its award-winning sauces, this is the place to go for a fun, flavorful meal. I love the lime cilantro sauce—it's a staple. And if I'm in the mood for a challenge, the extra-hot sauce definitely does the trick! The sandwiches are great too.

Catch the sunset at Pilot Butte: You can't convince me there's a better place to end your day in Bend. This time of year, you can drive up to the top (arrive early to snag a parking spot) and watch the prominent peaks of the Cascades put on a show.

DAY 2

Breakfast at Burrito Sunrise: Home to the best burritos in Bend, this bright yellow food truck is sure to add some sunshine to your morning. Conveniently parked outside the Campfire Hotel, it's a must-visit if you're staying there. The plain burrito is my go-to, but don't let the name fool you—it's packed with hash browns, pico de gallo, and grilled peppers.

Explore Deschutes National Forest: Take a scenic drive through Bend's backyard, a landscape unlike your typical forest. Expect hiking trails, roadside mountain views, glistening lakes, and even a volcanic area filled with lava rocks! Pack a picnic lunch and explore:

- **Newberry National Volcanic Monument:** Experience Lava Lands by walking along the one-mile Trail of Molten Land up to a great viewpoint of Lava Butte. You can usually drive to the top until mid-October—you can get free permits to drive up from the Lava Lands Welcome Station.

- **Sparks Lake Day Use Area:** Nestled in the shadow of South Sister and Broken Top, this is a popular spot for a picnic, paddleboard, or kayak. The gravel road can be rough, so a high-clearance vehicle is recommended.

- **Mount Bachelor:** If you time your visit in September or the first week of October, you can see all the fun that this mountain (known as the youngest of the Cascade volcanoes) has in store. You can go ziplining, soak up great views on a chairlift ride, or spend your time at the bike park.

Dinner at Sunriver Brewing Pub: Spend the evening a short drive south of Bend in Sunriver. Start with a cozy meal and craft brews at this family-friendly spot. With options such as sesame chili noodles, turkey dip sandwiches, and a Mediterranean sampler, choosing just one dish is tough. My favorite drink? The Cocoa Cow Chocolate Milk Stout—I've never found another beer quite like it!

Stargaze at the Sunriver Nature Center & Observatory: Trust me, there's something so special about gazing up at the night sky here. Not only is Sunriver a designated International Dark Sky Place (Oregon's first!), but the educational program you can participate in here will help you build a closer connection to the stars. During the ninety-minute experience, you'll get to climb up and squint your eyes to look through telescopes at fascinating features, such as planets, star clusters, and nebulae. Also, you'll get to partake in a lecture about the night and ask any burning questions you have. This place will change the way you think of the night—a time that holds treasures for those who go looking!

DAY 3

Breakfast at The Sparrow Bakery Northwest: A visit to Bend isn't complete without trying the Ocean Roll, a pastry swirled with vanilla and cardamom. It also offers a range of delicious bread, sandwiches, and French toast sticks. Good luck choosing just one!

Mountain biking at Phil's Trail: Whether you're an experienced rider or just starting out, Phil's Trail offers fun, flowy routes through a ponderosa pine forest. No bike? No problem. Rent one from Pine Mountain Sports, where you can ride straight to the trailhead (no transportation needed).

Soak at the McMenamins Old St. Francis School: You won't believe your eyes the instant you step into this beautifully adorned Turkish pool, complete with vibrant tilework, stained glass, and an elegant central fountain. Are you still in the Pacific Northwest? Somehow, yes. Soak in the 105-degree water while staying connected to the natural world—thanks to the open ceiling that lets in fresh air, soft light, and the occasional snowflake.

McMENAMINS OLD ST. FRANCIS SCHOOL

The Takeaway: Frolicking around Bend in the fall fills your cup in every way—sunshine warming your face, lava rocks crunching under your boots, and mountain air filling your lungs. Whether you're pedaling through pine forests, watching the sky turn pink from a volcanic butte, or soaking in a European-style soaking pool, there are countless moments that just make you pause and smile. And when night falls, stargazing under Central Oregon's dark skies reminds you that even after the sun sets, the magic keeps going.

McMENAMINS OLD ST. FRANCIS SCHOOL

ICICLE CREEK AT SLEEPING LADY MOUNTAIN RESORT

51 LEAVENWORTH

Introduction

Most people don't realize there's a small window of time between Leavenworth's bustling summer season and its festive holiday rush—a time when the valley is painted in every shade of fall foliage. It's the perfect last chance to hit the trails before winter sets in and to experience the charm of Washington's Bavarian Alps at a slower pace, without the crowds. I'm talking about fall—specifically, November. October is undeniably beautiful, but with Oktoberfest in full swing, it can still be pretty busy. If you're craving a peaceful getaway where you can see the village in a whole new light, plan your trip for November. For the best fall colors, aim for early in the month.

When we visited during the first week of November, we were thrilled by how vibrant the foliage was, especially since we thought we might have missed it! As soon as we checked in at the woodsy Sleeping Lady Mountain Resort, we were greeted by golden larches at their peak. The irony? Just days before, we'd tackled a tough hike specifically to see these trees, and here they were in all their glory—easy peasy!

Throughout our trip, we spotted plenty of trees still dressed in their autumn best. Some leaves had fallen, but the scenery was still breathtaking. And I wasn't the only one soaking it all in—locals I chatted with were just as excited to enjoy the rare peace and beauty of November in this special corner of the Cascade Mountains. (Although when I asked one barista what her favorite season in Leavenworth was, she ran me through the benefits of each, concluding that it would be impossible to choose!)

My family's favorite place to stay in Leavenworth is Sleeping Lady Mountain Resort—I only wish we'd discovered it sooner! I've never stayed somewhere that feels so wild and tucked away when it's just minutes from one of Washington's most popular mountain towns. It's the little things that make it so special: stargazing from the

SLEEPING LADY MOUNTAIN RESORT

hot tub, spotting a herd of deer while walking Lilo, and saying hi to the resident cats, Kiska and Reuben.

In this itinerary, we'll balance wellness, creativity, and outdoor adventure for a fall vacation in one of the Pacific Northwest's top-rated destinations.

At a Glance

Location: Central Cascades of Washington
Best Season to Visit: November
Suggested Duration: Two nights

Getting There

Seattle to Leavenworth: 117 miles, ~2 hours 10 minutes
Portland to Leavenworth: 288 miles, ~4 hours 30 minutes

Where to Stay

Posthotel: If you've browsed social media for places to stay in Leavenworth, chances are you've come across this

DEER AT SLEEPING LADY MOUNTAIN RESORT

boutique, wellness-centered hotel. Just steps from the village, it's an adults-only retreat (eighteen-plus), perfect for a serene getaway.

The Sleeping Lady Mountain Resort: For a true nature escape, stay a couple of miles out of town at this historic, environmentally mindful retreat. It's my kind of place—relaxing, eco-conscious, and dedicated to the community, with 100 percent of net profits supporting local arts, the environment, and the history of North Central Washington. Plus, it's pet friendly!

Howard Johnson by Wyndham: This affordable spot offers a fair price and is just a few blocks from the heart of town. It provides great bang for your buck.

Itinerary Outline

DAY 1

Dinner at Rhein Haus: No visit to Leavenworth is complete without dining at a biergarten, and Rhein Haus is my go-to spot. The second-story patio offers the best view of town, making it a must for outdoor dining. The German food is fantastic—we loved the Hungarian beef goulash (a special), giant pretzels, and bratwurst. And, of course, sampling local beers is a highlight for many!

BLACKBIRD ISLAND

Explore Blackbird Island: For far too many years, I had no idea this hidden gem existed. Tucked right next to town, Blackbird Island is the perfect spot for an easygoing yet scenic stroll. Situated along the Wenatchee River, this cottonwood-filled paradise is ideal for dog walks, peaceful nature breaks, and catching the sunset. You can access the trails via Waterfront Park or Enchantment Park—either way, you're in for a quiet escape just steps from the village's lively streets.

DAY 2

Brunch at Bear Bear: Kick off your morning at this charming café, where the outdoor patio is buzzing, and the cold brew is strong. Start with a basket of the famous cinnamon rolls, then dig into something heartier. The salmon latkes and ricotta frittatas are beautifully crafted and taste even better than they look.

Soak at The Springs: You're on vacation, so why not start the day with some self-care? The Springs is Leavenworth's newest hydrotherapy retreat, complete with cozy soaking pools, cold plunges, and steamy saunas. The setting is just as dreamy as the experience itself, surrounded by mountain views and fresh alpine air. Honestly, I could spend all day here!

Create at Leavenworth Art Haus: Now that your body is relaxed, unwind your mind with a little creativity. This welcoming art studio offers ceramics and canvas painting, and the best part? You can take your masterpiece home the same day! Prefer to create in your own space? There are also take-home art kits so you can get crafty at your leisure.

Lunch at Leavenworth Cider House: Treat yourself to a pretzel—or two! This cozy cider house is known for its creative spins on the classic Bavarian snack. My personal favorite? The Honey Hot Habanero Pretzel—sweet, spicy, and perfectly paired with a cider flight. And if you've got a sweet tooth like me, don't skip the dessert pretzels!

Hike the Icicle Ridge Trail: Leavenworth is stunning from the ground, but trust me—it's even more breathtaking from above. This six-mile round-trip trail (with 1,800 feet of elevation gain) rewards hikers with sweeping views of the surrounding mountains, winding rivers, and the charming Bavarian village below. If you visit in fall, expect a mesmerizing mosaic of golden leaves and evergreens—pure magic!

Dinner at the Kingfisher Restaurant & Wine Bar: Even if you're not staying at the Sleeping Lady Mountain Resort (which you really should—it's near and dear to my heart), this hidden gem is worth a visit for a memorable dining experience. The

SLEEPING LADY MOUNTAIN

menu changes with the seasons and local ingredient availability, but if you can, try the roast Alaska salmon. It's perfectly crafted with chardonnay beurre blanc, lemon, potlatch seasoning, and dill. Pair it with butter-whipped potatoes and the seasonal vegetable—you won't be disappointed!

DAY 3

Breakfast at Bavarian Bagel Co.: If you love bagels (and honestly, who doesn't?), this little spot is a must. The breakfast and lunch sandwiches are downright delicious—so good, in fact, that I wish I lived closer so I could visit every week!

Explore the Leavenworth Fish Hatchery: Before heading out, take some time to explore this fascinating hatchery. Start at the visitor center, where free educational exhibits explain the incredible journey of salmon. If you arrive knowing nothing about these resilient fish, you'll leave with a whole new appreciation. The salmon born here travel five hundred miles to the Pacific Ocean, navigating seven dams, only to return when it's time to spawn. Now that's an adventure worth learning about!

The Takeaway: November is Leavenworth's secret season—quiet, golden, and wonderfully uncrowded. The trails are still open, the larches still glowing, and the village slows to a peaceful hum. Cozy up with roasted salmon at the homey Kingfisher Restaurant, stroll riverside paths under cottonwoods, and soak in every last moment of calm before the holiday season arrives. It's a softer, slower side of Leavenworth that reveals itself only to those who venture beyond the busy seasons—and one well worth discovering. From watching deer graze in resort meadows while resident kitties weave between your legs to hiking above the valley for panoramic views of fall's final flourish, November in Leavenworth offers experiences that feel both intimate and spectacular. Soak in every last moment of calm before the holiday bustle begins, because this peaceful interlude is exactly what makes November visits so restorative.

NACHES PEAK LOOP

52

BUCKLEY, BONNEY LAKE & SUMNER

Introduction

Have you ever planned an entire trip around one hike? I know I have—and more than once! While summer may be the busiest season at Mount Rainier, fall offers a fleeting but spectacular display of color, as the landscape transforms into vibrant reds, oranges, and golds. October is prime time for foliage, but it's also when many roads and facilities—especially in the Sunrise Corridor—begin to shut down for the season, making it tricky to figure out where to go. That's why this fall weekend getaway focuses on the charming small towns in Pierce County that sit in the mountain's shadow. Not only do they offer easy access to one of my all-time favorite hikes, Naches Peak Loop, but they also set the stage for a cozy autumn retreat.

Whether you're hiking with kids, new to hiking, or simply looking for an adventure with a major payoff, this trail delivers. Plan your visit after the summer crowds have faded but before Chinook Pass closes for the winter, and if you're lucky, you'll catch a warm, sunny day to soak in the stunning scenery.

Beyond the trail, this itinerary is all about embracing the fall season from a local's point of view. Visit a beloved pumpkin patch, witness the wonder of salmon making their journey upstream, and browse independent bookstores to stock up on reads for cozy evenings ahead. It's the perfect mix of adventure and relaxation to savor autumn's magic!

At a Glance

Location: Pierce County, Washington
Best Season to Visit: October
Suggested Duration: Two nights

Getting There

Seattle to Buckley: 46 miles, ~55 minutes
Portland to Buckley: 161 miles, ~2 hours 35 minutes

Where to Stay

Vacation rentals: Take your pick of rustic chic apartments in Buckley, charming cottages in neighboring Enumclaw, or even spacious mountain cabins near Greenwater. These vacation rentals can fit a range of budgets and styles, whether you'd rather be within walking distance of town or far out in nature.

Crystal Mountain Campground: If you're looking for the most budget-friendly option, pack your tent or RV and head to Crystal Mountain. Not only is it an affordable stay, but you'll also be right next to one of the best scenic gondolas in Washington, with sweeping views of Mount Rainier.

Itinerary Outline

DAY 1

Walk or bike the Foothills Trail: Start your trip by stretching your legs on this paved, multiuse trail that was once a railroad. It winds twenty-two miles through Pierce County communities, but my favorite stretch is the section near South Prairie. In the fall, the foliage around Veterans Park is gorgeous, especially along the creek. If you brought a bike, you can head toward Buckley and back, a roughly ten-mile round-trip ride. Prefer to take it easy? Walk as far as you feel like and keep an eye out for spawning salmon in the water!

Explore Maris Farms: Nothing says autumn quite like a pumpkin patch, and this small-town getaway is the perfect chance to embrace the season. Nestled between Buckley and Bonney Lake, Maris Farms is a local favorite, with amazing Mount Rainier views. But this isn't just a place to grab a pumpkin. You can weave your way through a corn maze, take a ride down the fun slide, or even launch apples at targets with a cannon. If you love a good scare, stick around for the Haunted Woods experience, where actors keep you on edge as you navigate a spooky cornfield and forest.

Dinner at Sumalee's Thai Cuisine: After a day of adventuring, cozy up at this family-owned restaurant for a delicious meal. The *pad see ew* and spicy basil chicken are top tier, and the cute star-shaped carrots are a fun touch. If you're in the mood for something comforting, the pineapple fried rice is also a must-try!

DAY 2

Breakfast at Anchor House Coffee Roasters: The best vacation days start with a great cup of joe, and Anchor House delivers with its organic, fair-trade brews, roasted right in its historic building. The rustic-meets-elegant vibe makes this place feel extra posh, and the sandwiches are just as good as the coffee. The turkey sandwich with sliced apple on sourdough? Absolute perfection.

Hike Naches Peak Loop Trail: If you already have a favorite hiking trail, get ready to reconsider. The Naches Peak Loop Trail might just steal your heart. This easy, 3.5-mile loop with six hundred feet of elevation gain along Chinook Pass is pure magic, with alpine lakes, sprawling meadows, and unbeatable views of Mount Rainier. Fall is an especially incredible time to visit, with vibrant red huckleberry bushes adding bursts of color to the landscape. Take your time, soak in the views, and pack a lunch to enjoy along the way. My uncle Joey and I have had the best time returning here over the last couple of years.

Bestie Tip: If you see huckleberries, feel free to snack—but remember to stick to the main trail! The meadows here are fragile, and it's important to leave no trace so future hikers can enjoy them just as much. I've lost track of how many times I've repeated this trail because it is simply stunning around every turn.

Catch the sunset at Sun Top Lookout: Did you know there's a fire lookout in Washington that you can drive to? Sun Top is the one, and the gravel road leading up to it is usually pretty manageable. Even if the gate is closed for the season, the hike up is only about half a mile. Once you reach the top at 5,721 feet, you'll be rewarded with panoramic views, and Mount Rainier feels almost close enough to touch. If you time it right, watching the sun dip behind the mountains from here is an experience you won't forget.

Dinner at Wally's Drive-In: After a day well-spent outside, treat yourself with a classic diner meal. Wally's Drive-In is all about retro vibes and comfort food. Whether you go for a burger, sandwich, or the famous fish and chips (which are all-you-can-eat when you dine in at certain times), you can't go wrong. The thick-cut fries and soft-serve milkshakes seal the deal. And if you're a Dole Whip fan? This is the place to get it!

DAY 3

Breakfast at Electric Coffee House: Before heading home, make a pit stop in Sumner—a.k.a. the "Rhubarb Pie Capital of the World." Start your morning at Electric Coffee House, a bright, plant-filled café that serves up some of the best latte art in Pierce County. The vibes are a 10/10, and the menu is just as fun, with options such as breakfast tacos, toasts, and crispy tofu. Trust me, this place is a hidden gem!

ELECTRIC COFFEE

Explore downtown Sumner: Take some time to wander Sumner's charming downtown and check out a few local favorites:

- **A Good Book:** Pick up a new (or used) read to keep you company on the short winter days ahead.
- **Five12 Apparel:** Shop sustainable athletic wear made of recycled materials—yes, even coffee grounds!
- **Inta Vintage and Sparrow & Nightingale's:** Hunt for a secondhand treasure—maybe even the perfect holiday gift for a friend!
- **Hometown Charm Café:** You can't leave Sumner without trying a slice of rhubarb pie made with the town's famous locally grown rhubarb.

The Takeaway: Some hikes are so beautiful, they become the reason for the trip, and Naches Peak Loop is exactly that. But what makes this weekend so special isn't just the jaw-dropping mountain views or crimson huckleberry bushes—it's everything wrapped around it. A slow morning at a plant-filled coffee shop, pumpkin picking with a view of Rainier, and comfort food that hits just right after a day on the trail. Buckley, Bonney Lake, and Sumner may sometimes fly under the radar, but in fall, they offer the perfect outdoor access and small-town charm that will leave you with a camera roll of reasons to return.

NACHES PEAK LOOP

CONCLUSION

As the seasons change, so do the adventures that await us here in the Pacific Northwest. From golden mountainsides dotted with larch trees in the fall to volcanic-formed lakes that become winter wonderlands—their deep, piercing blue framed by sparkling white snow—each time of year brings something magical. In summer, the meadows below the most glaciated peak in the lower forty-eight—yep, that mountain in my backyard—become a wildflower wonderland, bursting with color and life. And in spring, the salty air of the islands mixes with the creative buzz of small-town art galleries and cafés, reminding us that warmth can come from more than just the sun.

If there's one thing I hope you carry with you from these pages, it's that *every* season is worth exploring. Not just summer—though she's a gem—but the quieter months, too, when the crowds thin and the landscape feels more personal. Some of my most unforgettable moments have happened in the so-called off-season: sipping a pumpkin spice latte in a coffee shop decked out like Hogwarts for Halloween, waking up to a mystical fog drifting through the forest at a beachside campsite, or having an entire trail to myself as the first snowflakes of the season gently fell. When you travel with an open mind—and a rain jacket—the Pacific Northwest has a way of showing up for you.

Throughout this book, you've wandered with me through small towns where the best local coffee shops serve more than just great lattes; they offer connection and community. We've browsed indie bookstores that still smell like paper and ink and feel like treasure troves waiting to be explored. We've found charming dog-friendly stays where memories are made.

But here's the secret: adventure doesn't always require a plane ticket or packed itinerary. It can start with a walk in a state park, a visit to the coffee shop around the corner, or a spontaneous road trip to a nearby town you've always meant to check out. Some of the best getaways are just that—a getaway from your usual routine, even if it's just for an afternoon.

Whether you're flipping through this book from the passenger seat on a weekend road trip or pulling it from your tote bag on a cloudy afternoon for inspiration, I hope it helps you dream up your next escape. This beautiful corner of the world is full of surprises, no matter the season. All you have to do is go.

So cheers to your next Pacific Northwest adventure, wherever and whenever that may be. I'll see you out there.

— Kara, a.k.a. Your Northwestie Bestie

ACKNOWLEDGMENTS

It feels surreal to be writing this. You mean to tell me the ideas that once lived in my head—then in Google Docs—are now printed in a real-life book that you're holding in your hands?! No way.

For as long as I can remember, I've dreamed of becoming an author. I never quite knew what shape or form that dream would take, but I've always followed my passions. From blogging in college to travel content creation in my twenties, I've learned that it doesn't have to make sense to anyone else—the journey is yours to chart.

As much as I love to dream, I don't think this book would've become a reality without the unwavering support of my dear friends, Megan and Emi. Thank you for letting me bounce every big idea off you—and never once telling me they were *too* big.

A huge thank you to my partner, Kyle. You've stood by my side for nearly all fifty-two destinations in this book, and thinking back on those memories fills me with so much joy. Thank you for saying "yes" to adventure—whether it was last minute or totally jam-packed. And of course, thank you for letting me be a passenger princess.

To my family—especially my parents, May and Denise, and my brother, Alec—thank you. Our camping trips helped plant the seeds of my love for the outdoors, and I'm so grateful we still get to share those kinds of moments together today.

And to my Grandpa Joe, thank you for showing me how to stay present and find joy in the little things. I wish you could read this. I hope you'd be proud.

And to my Uncle Joey for always being in my corner and cheering me on every step of the way.

I'm also very grateful to my editor, Avalon, for believing in me. I couldn't have asked for a better person to help shape this book and guide me through the process. Your insight was always clear, grounded, and refreshing.

Thank you as well to everyone at Sasquatch Books—especially my publisher Jill and designer Tony—who helped bring this book to life behind the scenes.

And finally, big thanks to every person who has followed along on my blog and Instagram, @YourNorthwestieBestie. This book is possible because of you—and I am forever grateful for your presence in my life. Happy adventuring!

INDEX

A

B

V

W

Printed in China

SASQUATCH BOOKS with colophon is a registered trademark of Blue Star Press, LLC

9 8 7 6 5 4 3 2 1

The authorized representative in the EU for product safety and compliance is Authorised Rep Compliance Ltd., Ground Floor, 71 Lower Baggot Street, Dublin D02 P593, Ireland.
www.arccompliance.com

Editor: Avalon Radys
Production editor: Peggy Gannon
Designer: Tony Ong

ISBN: 978-1-63217-593-9

Sasquatch Books
1325 Fourth Avenue, Suite 1025
Seattle, WA 98101
SasquatchBooks.com